Counselling – The Deaf Challenge

of related interest

Deafness and Mental Health
John C Denmark
ISBN 1 85302 212 8

Counselling Adult Survivors of Child Sexual Abuse
2nd edition
Christiane Sanderson
ISBN 1 85302 252 7

Structuring the Therapeutic Process
Compromise with Chaos:
The Therapist's Response to the Individual and the Group
Murray Cox
ISBN 1 85302 029 X

Shakespeare as Prompter
The Amending Imagination and the Therapeutic Process
Murray Cox and Alice Theilgaard
ISBN 1 85302 159 8

Counselling –
The Deaf Challenge

Mairian Corker

Jessica Kingsley Publishers
London and Bristol, Pennsylvania

The right of Mairian Corker to be identified as author of this work has been asserted by her in accordance with the Copyright, Designs and Patents Act 1988.

First published in the United Kingdom in 1994 by
Jessica Kingsley Publishers Ltd
116 Pentonville Road
London N1 9JB, England
and
1900 Frost Road, Suite 101
Bristol, PA 19007, U S A

Library of Congress Cataloging in Publication Data
A CIP catalogue record for this book is available from the Library of Congress

British Library Cataloguing in Publication Data
Mairian Corker
Counselling – The Deaf Challenge
I. Title
362.4

ISBN 1-85302-223-3

Printed and Bound in Great Britain by
Biddles Ltd., Guildford and King's Lynn

For Janet –
Who makes me happy to be alive and deaf

Acknowledgements

There are always a multitude of people who become involved when one writes a book, some whose involvement is significant, and others who may not know that they have become involved at all.

This book began as a module on *Counselling and Emotional Support of Deaf Young People* for the MEd distance learning programme for teachers of the deaf at Manchester University. I would like to thank the University for their permission to use extracts from this module for *Counselling – The Deaf Challenge*.

I must also thank in particular Jan Walmsley at the Open University's Institute of Health, Welfare and Community Education, who motivated me to begin writing on this subject; Sue Gregory of the Open University's faculty of Social Science and Warren Nickerson of ECSTRA, who have been an enormous professional influence and inspiration in the area of deaf issues; Lyn Atkinson, Julia Botsford, Maureen Cooper, Joanna Katz, Liz Shaw, and Sue Sowerbutts, who believed in me; Pat Rigg, who relieved me of some of the typing; Paul Redfern, who was patient with me and influenced me more than he realises; Laraine Callow, Margaret Kennedy, Jane McIntosh, Ruth Wood, Sharon Ridgeway and Rachel Wood for joining with me in meeting *The Deaf Challenge*, and helping me to feel less alone; Sara Head, Head of the Primary Section at Derby School for Deaf Children, who did the cartoons for Chapter 3; Julia Caprara for her 'woven feelings' and Joanna Atkinson, for teaching me so much about the artistic expression of deaf people; Jessica Kingsley for having the courage to publish my work, and, lastly, my children, Oliver, Ruth and Daniel, who have endlessly put up with 'their grumpy old Mum' (the frustrated writer).

CONTENTS

Section 2: Deaf Experiences of Counselling Process and Counselling Training

PREFACE

I am not blind
But you can't see I am not deaf
But your ears are
A million times more closed
Than mine. I am not dumb
But you speak nothing
Intelligible. I am not epileptic
But you have fits
At the mere thought of
Disability. I am not paralysed
But you are more unfeeling
Than a stone. I cannot walk
But you are more unmoving
Than a mountain. I am weak
But my willpower is even
Stronger
Than your fixed determination
To give me degradation
And worse treatment
Than baggage.

(Ellen Wilkie, 1989)

A Personal Odyssey

This book is the product of many years of study and learning, largely through silent observation, in a world which often overlooks the role of the observer, demeans the role of the theoretician and the thinker, and which fears silence and views it as the voice of complicity. This is the world of hearing and speech in which I was born and to which I now no longer wish to return. To me, this world is of direct relevance to the process and practice of counselling as it forms what is often the deepest level of the counsellor's skill and an integral part of the counsellor's search for their client's meaning. And yet, it seems, the deaf world and the world of the counsellor are locked in a strange kind of mutual embargo where, for all their mutuality, neither can easily acknowledge the existence or value of the other. As both a deaf person and a counsellor, I have been able to experience this embargo directly in my inner landscape and in my relationships with others, and this has persuaded me to challenge what I see, through the pages of this book. It is therefore important to say something about who I am and where I am writing from, for, as Michel Foucault says:

> 'Someone who is a writer is not simply doing his work in books, in what he publishes...his major work is, in the end, himself in the process of writing his books...the work includes the whole life as well as the text. The work is more than the work; the subject who is writing is part of the work.'

(Foucault, 1986, p. 184)

This will be familiar to counsellors who stress, as I do, the importance of knowing ourselves; but immediately that is said, the divergence begins. I know myself only too well and am continuing to discover things about myself,

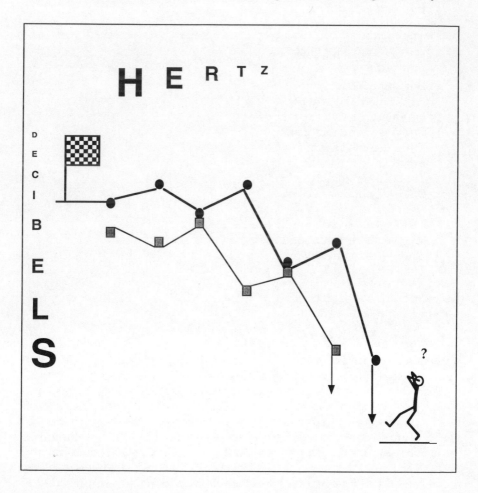

Figure P.1 'The Precipice'

some of which delight and some of which disturb me. This is the natural outcome of personal growth. Although, from time to time, I can see myself behaving in ways which shock or disturb others, I am learning to recognise why this happens and that by behaving in this or any other way, surely I am not so very different from the majority of my fellow human beings? However, I have made a startling observation in recent years. Apparently, I *am* vastly different from this majority and my behaviour, whatever form it takes, is, in the eyes of that majority, a negative 'symptom' of my difference. If I were then to believe what I see, I would conclude that I am not *me*, but some kind of construct of other people's perceptions of *a small part of me*. Thus, I am conscious that I have spent a large part of my life isolating myself from the de-humanising, blinkered vision of the majority out of a sense of self-preservation, a need to understand why these perceptions existed, and a strong conviction in my right to be human.

Arriving at an understanding has not been easy – recognising our own reality and how it merges or conflicts with the reality of others is never easy and takes a great deal of time and patience. Within the confines of the deaf – hearing dichotomy, however, feelings can become very confused from whichever perspective they are viewed. Even my early life was characterised by the growing recognition that the path of self-exploration and the achievement of self-realisation could be steep, rocky and strewn with obstacles and challenges which needed to be cleared or explained before the journey could proceed.

The choice of the illustration opposite is no accident. Those of you who have any connection at all with deaf people will recognise the pure tone audiogram. This is one of a battery of tests which is conducted on a deaf child or adult when deafness is first suspected. It has become the symbol of obstacles for me because, as a child, I used to imagine standing at the bottom of the precipice, awed by its height and wondering how I would be able to climb to the top without the help of ropes or spiked shoes and with a very great fear of hurting myself on the cruel barbs. I realised, much later, that I came to be at the bottom of the precipice in the first place because this was the way I had been taught to view myself. As a deaf child I was objectified as 'impaired' and not 'normal'. This became central to my self-esteem under the wealth of external reinforcements, from the abuse of psychological testing to 'does she take sugar?' attitudes.[1]

I subsequently retreated into and gained solace from a fantasy world peopled by characters who were more companionable than those who occupied the real world. In this world, it did not matter what I lacked because that could always be imagined and allowed to assume its proper place in the identity that was attempting to shape itself in spite of the wiles of the adult majority. Being deaf could be transformed into something beautiful and colourful, something good. I can remember feeling greatly confused, even angered by the dichotomy between the messages of the verbal and the more subtle communication of bodily language and facial expression, by the depth

---

1   This refers to the situation where a person is seen to be incapable of
     communicating directly or making decisions for themselves. Questions are
     therefore directed at a third party who is expected to answer on behalf of that
     person, often as if that person were not in the room.

of a glance that could warm or freeze. Even in those early days, I suppose I was given to philosophical musings, because I wondered how the doleful eyes of my dog could convey the same depth of expression and the same feelings; and yet there were no words. I looked at flocks of birds in the sky, flying in formation, great shadows sweeping across the fields, perfectly ordered and perfectly harmonised, and the patterns within patterns of trees and oceans, and saw communication; and yet there were no words. I felt the rippling, velvet muscles of horses and sensed the language of excitement at the imminent taste of freedom in the world outside the stable-box; and yet there were no words. But the words, by themselves, conveyed little; they became a cacophony of noise, and feelings became jarred by the distortion. Finally, there were no words for me, only 'a mouthful of air' (W.B.Yeats, quoted in Burgess, 1992) and a jumble of lip patterns which, in their defiance of the laws of nature, could not create order out of chaos. So deficient were the spoken dialogues of the real world that it was not long before the desire to bring to life my inner landscape translated itself into the dance of words before my eyes.

As my isolation continued, I began to put names to vague feelings. The process of learning was given more profundity by the time available for reflection and for searching deeper for understanding by opening myself to the truths of others. Again, perhaps, we feel echoes of the counsellor's trade for, like many counsellors, I read anything and everything to broaden my horizons and I write and re-write my journey through life and my relationships with others. But, for a long time, my reading was another manifestation of my fantasy world, a substitute for the world I had lost. As I searched deeper, I came upon the work of practitioners and theorists as diverse as Carl Rogers, Abraham Maslow, Michel Foucault, Alice Miller, Sheldon Kopp, C.G. Jung, Virginia Satir, Liz Greene and Dorothy Rowe. Their words communicated and continue to communicate to me a penetrating sense of meaning which assists me in understanding what I do and who I am and enables me to go one step deeper in my search for truth. They also granted me words when I had none, have opened doors when the majority closed them, and have given me life when I might have been condemned to the half-life of a construct who could be re-built and moulded on the whim of the majority.

As I sought my own way of building my self, my 'real' education continued. To stand a chance of furthering myself I was told that I had to be prepared to climb the precipice, suffer the cuts and bruises to my sense of humanity in silence and cope with my broken ears. Only then could I attain the prize awaiting me at the top. I dutifully climbed, feeling hollow inside, and *was* hurt. When I reached the top, I discovered that the prize was a life in the hearing world, under the guise of a hearing identity – whereupon I suffered an acute attack of vertigo because I realised that I was being offered the stick without the ice-cream 'for my own good' (Miller, 1987a, 1987b). The precipice became a different kind of symbol. It meant that I *became* my broken ears and that there was nothing in between. The chasm which had opened up between who I thought I was and who I actually was was of such enormity that my roots had become shrouded in the mists of the past. I had, in effect, lost my self. Correspondingly, as the hearing world moved the goalposts further and further away, I lost faith in my ability to achieve and lost touch with both my own feelings and the feelings of others. It was at this point in my life that I had, in the 1970s, my initial contacts with the counselling community, first as a client and later through an introduction to counselling skills and experiential encounter groups. It was as if I needed to establish a bridge between the client and the counsellor part of myself, as if I wanted to find my own wise counsel because I had been so often betrayed by the counsel of others. I was finally found, and 'held', enabled to feel safe, and empowered to rebuild my life and to find love through counselling. But my story is not yet over, for there are elements of it which remain in a half-light, hidden behind the explicit messages it carries. It is the deeper meaning of my story that constitutes *The Deaf Challenge*.

HEARING AND LISTENING – THE TOOLS OF THE COUNSELLOR'S TRADE

The counselling community is no different from many other professional communities in some respects. It contains a large variety of individuals who practice their trade with varying degrees of skill and varying levels of awareness or perceptions of what counselling is, what it hopes to achieve and how it hopes to achieve it. In some ways this has blurred the boundaries between the use of counselling skills and the task of counselling, to the extent where the British Association of Counselling (BAC) has needed to clarify and restate these boundaries within its various codes of practice. From the client's perspective, the distinction is an important one. The use of counselling skills may well patch up 'problems' on a temporary basis and enable the client to feel professionally supported, but rarely achieves lasting change in the client's fundamental patterns of behaviour in dealing with 'problems'. Counselling, on the other hand, is a more rigorous task and requires a much higher level of commitment from the professional involved to both their own growth and that of their clients, in addition to a more advanced level of skill. The counselling profession also has its inbuilt hierarchies where accredited counsellors and courses are implicitly endowed with seniority and counselling as a 'talking through' of problem situations and a verbal exploration of the depths of the psyche is given precedence over counselling methodologies or philosophies which focus on different kinds or levels of communication. The task of counselling is generally to work within the whole infrastructure of the client's communicated messages, whether explicit or implicit, whereas the use of counselling skills may confine the counsellor to the explicit, or the information content of the client's spoken messages. This is the difference between basic and advanced empathy. However, *as 90 per cent of communication occurs in a non-verbal way*, it is likely that focus on the explicit will not reveal the client's whole truth and will deny many of the client's thoughts and feelings which are expressed non-verbally. As a test of this statement, think for a moment about the letters we receive from friends or acquaintances. How difficult or easy is it to read between the lines, and gauge what the person is really thinking or feeling? How do we know whether or not the words have been written in the way they are written because the writer believes we have some expectation of them? If we get as far as reaching a conclusion, what are the realistic chances of our conclusion being an accurate one and can we actually determine the accuracy anyway by asking the person what they were feeling when they wrote that letter? Feelings are of the moment, and the special quality of feelings is often lost if we focus on the information content of what people say. But feelings are the 'stuff' of counselling, whether they are the counsellor's 'stuff' or the client's, and the expression of feelings weaves the counselling relationship, however those feelings are expressed, provided that the counsellor and the client have developed a common language. Inexperienced counsellors or informal helpers may fail to listen accurately and misunderstand what is being said by and in response to their clients because they have not developed the counsellor's skill of knowing their client's personal language or of knowing themself. But if the client does not use words, if the client cannot understand words, even experienced counsellors can feel out of their depth because the power of the non-verbal becomes that much more immediate. It may reveal professional and human inadequacies because it demands a deeper level of response which transcends words.

We must assume from the outset that the vast majority of those who read this book will be working with deaf people in various professional roles or they will be involved, at different levels, in counselling. Thus we arrive at the outward manifestation of the dichotomy referred to earlier. On the one hand, we have a readership which knows very little about counselling, and on the other, we have a readership which knows very little about deaf people. What these two groups will have in common, however, is that both will be aware of the importance of language and communication, albeit from different perspectives, and both are dominated by hearing people. It is probable, moreover, that spoken language is so central to their existence, that the sense of 'hearing' is ever-dominant. Because of the information they lack, it may become over-dominant. 'Listening', for example, is certainly high on the counselling agenda, and rightfully so in a world where listening is so often relegated to the waste bin, but 'hearing' or understanding deaf people may be difficult because this seems to be accompanied by the notion that in order to participate fully in the counselling process, counsellor and, by implication, client must be able to 'hear'. Those working with deaf people have agendas which are dominated by how they can communicate with deaf people, and, if we are to believe the wealth of published material, how deaf people can become proficient in spoken language in order that they can communicate with hearing people and have access to the fabric of a hearing society.[2] From this perspective, the energy which is poured into the how of communication, and the expressive parts of language, may encourage working within a restricted definition of listening. To begin to resolve this dichotomy, it is important to understand how deep the hearing veins run, and on a practical level, we need look no further than some of the most widely used and

2   Deaf education, for example, hinges on the debate between oral/aural teaching, which focuses on the development of speech using 'residual hearing' and amplification through hearing aids, and bilingual or total communication approaches to communication, which attempt to tap a deaf child's natural tendency to make more efficient use of their visual sense by introducing sign language in various forms. Currently, the majority of schools use oral/aural approaches to communication, and bilingual and/or bicultural education remains a rarity in practical terms.

well-known texts on counselling to see the beginnings of what, for many deaf people, has become a wicked alliance:

> 'I make a distinction between hearing and listening. Hearing involves the capacity to be aware of and receive sound. Listening involves not only receiving sounds but, as much as possible, accurately understanding their meaning. As such it entails hearing words, being sensitive to vocal cues, observing movements and taking into account the context of communications.... *At its most basic level, good listening involves the capacity to hear and remember accurately what has been said*...choosing to listen well entails choosing to discipline your hearing. Put another way, you need to be able to hear the client accurately prior to choosing whether to respond from either their frame of reference or your own.'

(Nelson-Jones, 1988, pp. 13, 23–24, italics added)

Why is 'hearing' seen to be so essential to the counselling process that it becomes the foundation of 'good listening'? Does the spoken word always convey the client's truth? Whereas I would not want to suggest that the expressed view is necessarily the intended view, perhaps it is because of the notion that 'self' is to be found not inside people, but *in their talk* (Honess, 1992) that encourages counsellors to make the unbreakable links between hearing and listening. In the counsellor's world, it is recognised that some difficulties in personal relationships occur because people are unable to use and/or learn certain types of language, and the therapy lies in learning how to use a new language. Dryden (1986) for example says that 'since good education depends upon effective communication, it is important that the therapist uses words that the client can understand'. To achieve this, a counsellor undoubtedly needs to draw from a large inventory of different ways of 'talking', verbally and non-verbally, but surely this is not the same as asking that a client 'talk' in the counsellor's language when there is a linguistic divide to be crossed?

It is a predisposition of the hearing world to believe that language is confined to spoken language and therefore that 'hearing' is inseparable from language and communication. Thus, from the counsellor's perspective, it could be said that the possibility of not hearing or of not speaking becomes synonymous with a loss of infinite proportions in experiential, psychological and socio-emotional terms; this runs the risk of being displaced onto clients who harbour the deepest of feelings but may not have the words or the language to 'talk' them through. The prospect of blocked or damaged communication within the counselling relationship can therefore become associated with professional failure. For those that do not know themselves in the counsellor's way, the risk of displacement is even greater. American psychologist and linguist, Harlan Lane, well known as a chronicler of the lives and history of deaf people, has referred to the fear of losing speech and hearing as 'existential dread' which originates from an 'extrapolative leap' or 'egocentric error' made by hearing society which is based on a stereotypical view of the state of deafness. He says:

'To imagine what deafness is like, I imagine my world without sound – a terrifying prospect, and one that conforms quite well with the stereotype we project onto members of the deaf community. I would be isolated, disorientated, uncommunicative, and unreceptive to communication. My ties to other people would be ruptured. I remember my parents censoring me with silence; it was bearable for four hours, and then I implored their forgiveness. I recall the "silent treatment" of offenders in the army. The Tunisian novelist Albert Memmi, author of several sociological studies of oppression, observes in his book on dependency: "The person who refuses to communicate severs the psychological ties that connect him to the other person. In so doing, he isolates the other person and can drive him to despair." A world without sound would be a world without meaning. What could be more fundamental to my sense of myself than my sensory milieu – unless it be my spoken language?'

(Lane, 1992, pp. 10–11)

While deaf people search for a meaningful existence, they are faced with the knowledge that existential dread has eaten its way into the core of the counselling profession and the minds of even the most eminent of psychotherapists:

'Most recently, I have been into something so serious, comprehensive and preoccupying, that I have chosen to discuss it with all of my patients, in groups and individually. The problem was physical, but had many overwhelming feelings related to it.

About three years ago, I suffered a sudden and profound hearing loss in my left ear. It was diagnosed correctly as irreversible nerve deafness but was mistakenly attributed to an exotic, highly selective virus. Hearing aids were of no use, and *after a brief period of panic (lest I lose the hearing in my other ear)*, I adjusted with counter phobic insistence that other people recognise my limitation; sorry they had to contend with it, but after all I give a good deal, and there was no reason why they couldn't help out by speaking up.'

(Kopp, 1971, pp. 159–60, italics added)

The goal of a common language is a seductive one, for language is the means by which human beings live together and the medium of their cultural and experiential expression. The presence of an 'alien' language strikes fear into the soul of the outsider, because it has no meaning relative to the experience or culture of that outsider. Thus, as Lane says, the prospect of losing the means of living causes deafness to become a hurricane sweeping across the inner landscape and demolishing everything in its path. Whose fear is this and from whence came the hurricane? And why is that fear etched in the inner landscapes of so many deaf people, who, even if they are successful in reaching the top of the contrived precipice, arrive with open wounds and emotional scars which serve as a constant reminder of their deaf selves? Deafness and hearingness are the two ends of a vast and complex continuum which tends to be regarded as a divided community; but it is the legacy of the hearing majority that the two ends of the continuum came to be perceived as two distinct groups in the first place. They are psychologically, like strength and weakness, but two sides of the same coin, and, in being so, are inseparable. It may be that the emphasis on the positive aspects of being deaf or on 'coping' with deafness is linked to a widespread and very human tendency to shy away from the 'problems' of others to the point of outright dismissal guided by the old philosophy 'laugh and the world laughs with you, weep and you weep alone'. In counselling terms, we need to be careful with the attribution of value; admiration or respect for one side of the coin should not result in the oppression of the other, for all clients deserve the opportunity to feel safe and to grow from the sanctuary of the counsellor's core values and not from the precariousness of the counsellor's deepest fears. Counsellors who remain unaware of these fears are at risk from perceiving their deaf clients' 'problems' to be the result of an anomaly, with a 'solution' which resides in the belief that accepting a narrow interpretation of the 'norm' will somehow resolve a deaf person's internal struggles. Against such a background, the 'solution' will be incomplete and temporary, and possibly lead to a situation where the client becomes dependent on the counsellor or, at worst, is irreparably damaged by the misconceived values underlying counselling process.

THE DEAFNESS OF COUNSELLING

It has long been my belief that, in essence, counselling is 'all about loving' and that counsellors reject 'the pursuit of authority or control over others' in order to 'seek to share power' (Mearns and Thorne, 1988). I find it hard to grapple with the evidence that counsellors, in being human, are not infallible to the abuse of power or to the forces of prevailing attitudes and assumptions about deaf people, though it is not difficult to see how this has happened. Counsellors will have very little information about deaf people, unless they have lived or worked with number of them. They could be forgiven for general assumptions such as all deaf people can learn to speak, all deaf people use sign language, all deaf people feel bad about being deaf, all deaf people want to be hearing again, BSL is the natural or preferred language of all deaf people, because these are examples of general statements which are made time and time again in denial or in ignorance of the diversity of Britain's deaf community. Moreover, these statements say nothing about Black deaf people, deaf women, deaf gays and lesbians, older deaf people, deaf children and so on because the focus is on deafness and not the individual deaf person. But this does not explain away the ample evidence that the existence of deaf people has been widely ignored within the counselling profession, which can be seen in the absence of reference to deaf people in highly respected counselling texts and on most training courses. Existing trends suggest further that the counselling profession runs the risk of taking the same route as other professions in formulating its understanding of deafness. History repeats itself, as deaf people are once more being marginalised to fringe activities and are being prevented from gaining valuable insight into counselling process or contributing to it, because they are being viewed within the context of an 'infirmity' or 'medical' model of disability.[3][4] Within the counselling profession, I find the use of this model, and the assumptions that underpin it, difficult to reconcile, because it seems to work against acceptance and non-judgemental-ism and to deny the role of societal attitudes and assumptions in shaping the individual identity. This is particularly important because this book is neces-sarily about *people*, about their inner worlds of feelings, thoughts and intui-tions, about their own experiential landscapes and their relationships to those of other people, and, in particular, about their need to harbour a strong and real sense of themselves. Deaf people, whatever the reasons for their deafness, or their linguistic or cultural affiliations are capable of leading the counsellor into unexplored territories. If influential members of the profession can experience, even temporarily, existential dread, what hope is there for the deaf client who, on seeking help, realises that he or she personifies something of which the counsellor is very afraid? Such a polarisation may well exist within many deaf–hearing counselling relationships, and possibly, as we shall see, within deaf–deaf counselling relationships also. But this polarisation seems to belie the fabric of communication of which we are *all* a part, despite our different experiences. Rather than learning how to deal with fear and preju-dice, or the perceived threat of professional inadequacy by viewing *The Deaf Challenge* as an opportunity for further growth and understanding, the paro-chial view of the hearing majority within the counselling profession mitigates against a truly integrated approach to counselling capable of responding to all manifestations of deaf clients' problem situations and contexts, and has worked against access of some deaf people to the therapeutic milieu:

> 'This propensity to stereotype deaf people as difficult and high-risk candidates for (counselling), as is done with the poor, disadvantaged, disabled, old, and nonverbal populations serves only to thwart their opportunity for emotional growth and psychological enhancement.'

> (Sussman, 1988, p.5)

Counsellors may yet be ignorant of the knowledge held by those who work with deaf people. This is that medical and infirmity models of disability have their origins in a history of oppression which has ensured that deaf people are part of a dependency culture who are 'cared for' by the hearing majority. It is this image of deaf people which has been perpetrated by those who, contrary to the counsellor's creed, do not wish to share power nor accept deafness as

---

3   The 'infirmity' or 'medical' model of disability or deafness is based on the assumption that disability or deafness is an illness, and the consequences are ultimately the responsibility of the person who 'suffers from' the illness. Such models deny the possibility that a person who is disabled or deaf, as part of the intricate network of society, can be disabled by society which as a whole has come to view deafness or disability in terms of disabling models and stereotypes and therefore contributes to the way in which disability or deafness manifests itself in the individual.

4   In the 1993 edition of the *Handbook of Counselling in Britain* (edited by Dryden, Charles-Edwards and Woolfe), there is one chapter devoted to 'Counselling people with disabilities/chronic illnesses' which states as one of its five principles: 'People with disabilities and handicaps should be offered counselling which is as near "normal" as possible'. It does not mention deaf people.

a different kind of 'norm'. It can be anticipated that if the counselling profession were to respond to *The Deaf Challenge* by remaining true to its core values, and working towards the empowerment of deaf people, it will cause a great deal of trouble for those who use these models as frameworks for their work with deaf people:

> 'When we accept and value our own self we cease to be afraid of other people. We no longer have superiors and inferiors, but only equals with whom we can co-operate and share while we take responsibility for ourselves. We no longer feel deprived and envious, so we can abandon revenge and greed. We have learnt the wisdom of Lao Tsu: "He who knows that enough is enough always have enough." Because we value ourselves, we value others, now and to come, and the planet on which we all live. We reject those who seek to dominate and manipulate us, and who, in elevating greed, revenge and pride to virtues, place our lives and our planet in jeopardy. Obviously, if we all decided to accept and value ourselves, we would cause those who have power over us a great deal of trouble.'

> (Dorothy Rowe, in Masson, 1989, pp. 22–23)

I *am* deaf, and in being deaf I, like many other deaf people, present a challenge to the communicative foundations, the norms and the values of a hearing world. I am also a counsellor, and in being a counsellor, my task in life is often to challenge my clients' negative perceptions of themselves in journeying with them towards personal growth and change. As a deaf person, I have been so demoralised and sickened by what these norms and values mean to deaf people that I have wished I could change the hearing world. I have dreamed of a power-sharing union and of equality, and, in trying to be an agent for change I have wasted energy, sacrificed my sense of self, and lived in a state of constant anger to the point where I was torn to pieces. As a counsellor, and through counselling, I have learnt that the only real change that can be achieved is within ourselves, through the liberation of the unconscious and the acceptance of who we are. Against this, all other change is temporary and transparent. The counsellor's way of self-exploration and self-acceptance has pointed me in the direction of the light from the mire of my darkest hours, but in looking outwards, I have seen that deaf consciousness, in its many different forms, is often prevented from making these discoveries and from learning to value or accept itself. It has become submerged in hearing people's fear of the other side of hearingness, and this has prevented an attraction of opposites which, our learned scholars tell us, is the spice of life and even the bedrock of evolutionary change. Many 'counsellors' working with deaf people have become caricatures of the counsellors I have grown to respect, in their belief that deaf people are 'faulty' and the key to growth therefore lies in conforming to the hearing way. Genuine counsellors do not have the information with which faulty perceptions can be challenged. And so, paradoxically, *The Deaf Challenge* and the counselling challenge, instead of complementing each other, have arrived at this state of embargo.

IDENTIFYING THE DEAF CHALLENGE

I feel that this embargo is a reflection of the vastly different ways in which counsellors interpret the term 'challenge' and the particular quality of *The Deaf Challenge*. Most practising counsellors acknowledge that helping clients to identify and challenge self-defeating perspectives on their problem situations is an activity which often occurs in the first stage of any counselling relationship. Self-defeating behaviours are those comfortable but outmoded frames of reference which keep us fettered to patterns of thinking and behaving which may feel safe but which can deny our reality and our creativity. The initial response to challenge and confrontation is often a defensive one, the level of defence being related to the strength of the challenge or confrontation and the degree of safety experienced by the client in their present scenario, and so the skill of challenging carries an aura of risk. The first stage of the counselling relationship can be prolonged if the client is resistant to moving beyond their initial subjective understanding of what is happening to them, and indeed, if the resistance is strong, the client may never move to a position where they can sow the seeds for growth and change, unless the counsellor is prepared and able to take that risk. This is helped by the fact that there is a preponderance of counsellors who are 'first stage specialists' (Egan, 1990).

For the counselling profession, *The Deaf Challenge* is a stern one, because it asks that difficult issues are made explicit and may carry with it a hint that the values of the profession are being undermined. Further, because the challenge comes from a sphere of existence which is largely unknown, it is quite difficult to present it in a way which is not threatening or confrontational, for, in the end it is an expression of deaf people's anger and despair at the harm that has been done to them by the so-called 'helping' professions, with their 'mask of benevolence' (Lane, 1992).

The Deaf Challenge is on two levels. The first is to do with the access of deaf people to counselling and the second is related to the professional contribution that deaf people might make to the development of advanced counselling skills and the understanding of non-verbal communication. It invites the profession to:

- move beyond the idea of counselling as a 'talking through' of clients' problem situations
- modify stereotyped perceptions and behaviours in respect of deaf people and the concept of deafness
- modify theoretical and practical approaches to counselling
- modify the language of counselling
- own their fear of deafness
- develop new perceptions of deafness and deaf people which would allow them to face their own challenges from a position of strength
- accept their flawed interpretation of critical experiences, behaviours and feelings on the part of deaf people
- cease evading and distorting deaf people's real issues

- identify and understand the consequences of their behaviour towards deaf people
- abandon resistance to deaf people's uniqueness and recognise its relevance to the counselling profession as a whole.

When faced with the challenge of painful truths, it is sometimes difficult to look beyond the dark storm clouds and see the glimpse of a rosy dawn, because, as counsellors know, few welcome change unconditionally and with open arms, and, as it is part of the counsellor's work to assist clients in finding the inner resources to meet change, it is part of the profession's task to inform itself and to grow. The counselling profession, in common with other helping professions, is slowly beginning to adjust to the reality of our diverse and multi-cultural society, and time is therefore increasingly ripe for introducing new ideas and concepts. But this does not remove the possibility that such ideas and concepts will be challenging, even threatening, because they pose searching questions about counselling process.

BOOK AND READER – THE MAKING OF A RELATIONSHIP

My energy finally came to be harboured in using the deaf experience to stimulate the potential for further growth within the counselling community, and to unite deaf people and counsellors in their search for an easier truth and a more valued existence. In this, I hope that *The Deaf Challenge* will appeal to strengths rather than weaknesses. A counselling relationship necessarily begins with both client and counsellor unconsciously, and sometimes consciously addressing their hopes and fears in respect of each other, contained within a confidential, safe environment. The understanding and acceptance of these hopes and fears generates trust, genuineness and empathy, on which all counselling relationships thrive. It follows from this that it is entirely appropriate to begin our journey by developing a deeper understanding of our hopes and fears as counsellors and as deaf people, in order to acknowledge the existence of deaf experience and attempt to understand what this means for deaf people. From my own deaf experience, I am convinced that the hearing way is only one way of being in the world. The 'problem' that deaf people present to the dominance of hearing people is not so much a result of ignorance of this fact, but more to do with the realisation that the deaf way comes from a different 'centre'. I use the term 'centre' here to mean the soul or identity, or the point from which something grows.[5] Deaf people's centre, and the possible source of their unity, at the most fundamental level, comes from their unique experience and their potential to love and express themselves, in different ways, as a response to or through the visual, spatial world. When realised, this potential belies the concept of silence, for the deaf world is not and need not be a silent world made only of fear and prejudice. It can relate to and inform that part of the hearing experience which is implicit and hidden. In our deaf world, we see things and people in ways which hearing

---

5   This term has also been used in a slightly different sense by Padden and
     Humphries (1988) to describe cultural differences between deaf and hearing
     people, which will be discussed in Chapter 1.

people are often at a loss to understand, and we have given these 'seeing skills' expression in ways which can be transferred. That is, in part, what this book aims to do, but it has presented me with a personal challenge as I float the possibility of relationships. How can I show the experiential divide between deaf and hearing people, and the multiple realities of the deaf community in such a way that empathy can grow? How can I find new options and generate new potential instead of eliminating them? How can I make counselling a more usable, visual experience for deaf people? How can I develop a common language? No matter how clear and straightforward the written words, the concepts explored in this book may have limited meaning for some people because they are presented in a language which can only partially express the deaf experience, and the concepts themselves may be alien to hearing people. I have explored many ways of resolving this problem, and, in the end, I always came back to the words of this book made visual by pictures or images, sometimes serious and sometimes humorous. It is part of my hope that this dual approach will facilitate a joining. Like many deaf people, I am just a small cog in a massive wheel of history and tradition and am searching for truth and justice for the inhabitants of our planet. That I began with my own truth, which, on the surface, may be of little relevance for others, is not something that removes the challenge of the search, nor my belief in the existence of a greater truth and a common humanity, however deeply they are disguised or hidden. I am also, like many counsellors who are still, and perhaps always will be learning from the wisdom of their teachers and their clients, cautious and humble in my expression and driven only to share it in the best way I know how.

The 'sailing image' has become an important part of my inner landscape, and I will use it in many different forms throughout this book. In part, I am sure that this is to do with my strong roots in nature, and my love of the symbolism and mystery of natural objects which harbour the clues in my hunt for answers. But it is also because I see the process of counselling as a journey to the island of growth over seas which can be calm, motionless and crystal clear by the light of a guiding moon, or wrecked by tidal waves thrown up by vast storms and the darker side of the moon. As deaf people and counsellors embark from their own communities in their search for the island, they know that they must learn how to sail alongside each other and navigate the waters together. Each boat carries different seeds for learning and for nurture and growth of the other. The deaf world has a beauty, a richness and a vibrancy which is at least equal to that of the hearing world, and certainly complementary to it. Ours is a silence laden with the sound of visual observation, awareness of space, texture, taste, touch and smell. For us, these grant and define our existence in their capacity to inform us of our environment and where we stand in relation to it. Yet our world, which could so easily be a haven of peace, is a world which is constantly under threat from the plague of sound and the flood of denial, and ravaged by the poverty of ignorance. The potential for peace becomes both a *Deaf Challenge* to the dominance of hearing experience, and a reason for denial as it is twisted by labels such as 'impairment', 'handicap' and experiential 'impoverishment'.

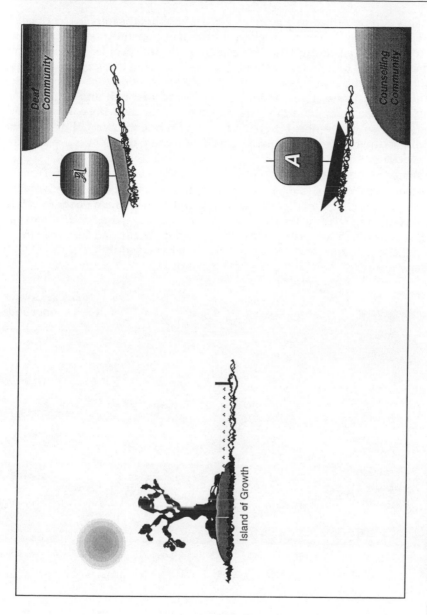

Figure P.2 'The Journey Begins'

This book is aimed primarily at those who think they know deaf people better than they know themselves, but it will hopefully be of interest to anyone, deaf or hearing who has contact with deaf people. It is not about clinical settings or patients or about deaf*ness*, but about two *people* in a unique *relationship* – the counsellor and the deaf client, striving for mutual under-standing and deaf empowerment. For the task of this book, and therefore the task of the reader, is a quest for empowerment of the deaf consciousness, and a recognition of the phoenix rising from the ashes, the symbol of *The Deaf Challenge* and of deaf humanity. In the act of writing this book, I am inviting the reader to experience the essence of that consciousness in the space created by these pages. It is entirely appropriate, in the realms of feeling, that the words of this book should be conveyed in this way. It is a way which is symbolic of both the quality of my silence and of the human need for safety, both yours and mine, when the going gets tough. The words of this book are not easy words to accept or perhaps even to understand, and they may incite the kind of 'trouble' that Dorothy Rowe refers to, but they do not carry a hollow message.

Mairian Corker,
London, October 1993

SECTION 1

IDENTIFYING THE DEAF CHALLENGE

The aim of the first section is to explore some of the underlying themes which either mitigate against or enhance effective counselling with deaf clients. Chapter 1 begins with a look at the status quo of counselling provision for deaf people in Britain as compared to that in other countries, and the wider influences on the counselling process which can prevent deaf people accessing and benefiting from counselling. These include societal influences which lead to predispositions to view deaf clients in a particular way and emphasise divisions within the deaf community, and institutional contexts and environments which encourage destructive counsellor behaviours. The chapter introduces three issues which are of crucial importance for working with deaf people in the counselling role: power, identity, and need, and proposes frameworks for addressing these issues which are relevant for the counselling context. The importance of distinguishing counselling from counselling skills and seeing counselling as a force for social and attitudinal change when working with deaf people is stressed throughout.

Chapter 2 continues with the themes introduced in Chapter 1 from the individual's perspective. It shows how the wider influences can manifest themselves in the unconscious agendas of counsellors and their deaf clients. It investigates the underlying psychological and social roots of these agendas and the processes whereby they can emerge within the counselling relationship. Chapter 3 takes these themes into the counselling relationship and explores the range of effects of different counsellor behaviours on deaf clients when professional role boundaries and counsellor–client boundaries are transgressed. It introduces an array of counsellors who work with deaf clients and views the resulting 'healthy' and 'unhealthy' counselling relationships in terms of the core values of counselling and the concept of empowerment.

Chapter 4 begins the exploration of positive counselling agendas and styles through its focus on the concept of 'Language for Growth'. It identifies language as being the most important aspect of the deaf challenge to traditional counselling practice and explores the joys and the hazards of counsellors working in a multi-communicative environment with deaf people. It suggests different ways of viewing language infrastructures and their significance for counselling core values, and challenges the assumptions that counsellors can make about the language and language choices of different deaf clients. Chapter 5 concludes this section by addressing issues of methodology, and aims to develop a positive framework which will be useful to all counsellors, whether deaf or hearing, who work with deaf people.

CHAPTER 1

THEMES, CONTEXTS AND DEFINITIONS – THE PREVAILING WINDS

'Identity as a concept is fully elusive as is everyone's sense of his (her) own personal identity. But whatever else it may be, identity is connected with the fateful appraisals made of oneself – by oneself and others. Everyone presents himself to others and to himself and sees himself in the mirrors of their judgments'.

(Strauss, 1977)

Before we can begin our journey, we need to look at the structure of and the baggage carried by each of our boats as their occupants wait in the harbour, preparing to embark, and the contextual agendas which provide the energy for the journey under the influence of the prevailing winds. Boats may be made of straw, wood or metal, for example, each material donating a certain quality to the speed of the path that can be navigated and the energy that is required to power the journey. Likewise, a boat of the proportions of a cruise ship and built like a battle cruiser will doubtless convey the impression of security, but may require enormous force to lift the anchor and sail with the winds of change, and be staffed by a battalion of personnel, drilled in matters of conduct to perfection, and not easily swayed from the call of duty. Our boats, as we have indicated, are symbols. Their structure represents the context of counselling, as it is determined by a number of factors which, in varying combinations, represent the initial ingredients which will determine whether the journey can commence. In this chapter we are concerned with those factors which could be defined as institutionalised predispositions of both counsellors and deaf clients to think about deaf people and counselling in particular ways, which can determine trends in the provision of counselling available to deaf people. These are the prevailing winds, and, as we shall see, they can, in some circumstances, compete with the winds of change which are needed to blow the client on course for personal growth. Prevailing winds are not always of the individual's making, for they reside in the corridors of institutional power, and the annals of history. Thus they can be enticing and wily in their strength of persuasion and vice-like in their stranglehold over process and attitude.

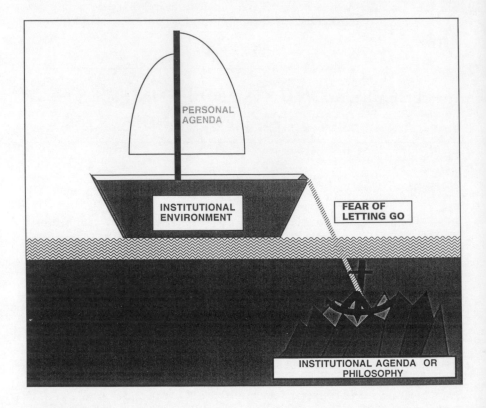

Figure 1.1 The Prevailing Winds

COUNSELLING PROVISION FOR DEAF PEOPLE IN BRITAIN

Counselling provision for deaf people in Britain could best be described as ad hoc, piecemeal, lacking in clear philosophy and relevant structure and often dependant on a chance encounter in the institutional corridor. A key factor is restricted access, and this can be seen in a number of spheres. For example, there are eight telephone lines nationwide which are accessible to deaf people with minicoms[1] within the Samaritans service and Childline, as compared to the hundreds available for hearing people on a regional or local basis. At present, there are six centres which offer counselling to deaf adults on an individual basis and can guarantee that deaf people's varying communication needs can be met directly or that communication support will be available (Katz, 1993). These are either institutionally-based within the Health or Education Services, or within the voluntary sector. There are also three sources of support, relating to specialist issues such as AIDS/HIV, vocational counsel-

---

1   A minicom is a telecommunications device which enables deaf people to communicate with other minicom users over the telephone by means of a text keyboard.

ling and child abuse and neglect in the voluntary and private sectors. There has been no specific reference to counselling for people with disabilities within the provisions of Section Three of the Disabled Person's Act 1986, which relates specifically to the assessment of need. This is generally the case with legislation affecting 'welfare provision' for deaf adults overall, unless they are identified as having a 'clinical disturbance' or 'psychiatric disorder' requiring specialist care within an institution or in the community. However it is important to make a distinction between this group of deaf people (the minority) and the majority whose 'problem situations' do not belong within these categories by any definition of the terms. For a variety of reasons, there are few accurate statistics relating to deaf people in this position.

The Royal National Institute for Deaf People (RNID) estimates that 1.4 million adults of working age have a 'clinically significant hearing loss'. The majority of these people have become deaf in varying degrees, although about 50,000 of the working population were born profoundly deaf. 0.2 per cent of the entire population under 30 are deaf. This gives some idea of the potential demand on existing services, even more so because these figures do not include deaf children and young people under the age of eighteen. We have no concrete information on the availability or quality of counselling provision for this group, which is a sizable and important population, but we do know that provision, again, is confined largely to institutional frameworks, in particular Health, Social and Education Services and the voluntary sector. Within statutory services, the quality of provision is often linked to the legislation of the Education Act (1981), the Education Reform Act (1988), the Children Act, (1989), and the provisions of the Education Bill (1993) currently passing through Parliament. Clearly it is difficult to see how existing services could meet even a small fraction of this potential demand, especially if on-going counselling is required. However, as some deaf counsellors have pointed out, it is important to distinguish between *need* and *demand* for counselling, and to separate *rehabilitation* from *empowerment* in viewing service structure. These terms have very different meanings for many deaf people. As empowerment is linked to education or re-education, it could be said that there is a great need for counselling services which empower deaf people. Conversely, however, because poor education suggests limited knowledge, skills and understanding, there may not be a great demand for counselling because of a lack of information or uncertainty about what counselling means and why it may be an important response to need. This can give counselling deaf people an added educational role or dimension, which Egan describes:

> 'Learning takes place when options are increased. If the collaboration between helpers and clients is successful, clients learn in very practical ways. They have "more degrees of freedom" in their lives as they open up options and take advantage of them...helping is a forum for social-emotional reeducation.'

> (Egan, 1990, p.6, p.58)

In addition to limited availability, there are other factors which restrict deaf people's access to counselling. It is evident from this list that there are some factors which may not be specific to deaf people, but which have an added deaf dimension, and others which are deaf-specific (Box 1.1). It is extremely important to distinguish between the two.

BOX 1.1 BLOCKS TO ACCESS

ADDED DEAF DIMENSION

Institutional frameworks and philosophies

Mistrust of professionals or 'experts'

Power and control issues

Fear of stigma

Perceptions of 'helping', both client and counsellor

Lack of choice

Perceptions of need

Societal or archetypal blocks to listening; alienism, attitudes, assumptions and labels

DEAF-SPECIFIC

Counsellor skills and personal agendas; audism, avoidance, tendency to rescue or protect client.

Confidentiality issues

Cultural issues

Mistrust of or limits to skills of Human Aids to Communication

Language mismatching or language barriers

Rehabilitation and empowerment issues

Methodological issues

For example, the experience of abuse, whether it is psychological, emotional or sexual, is often more complex for deaf children and young people because deafness adds its own dimension of power, through denial, stigma, self-blame, self-esteem, confusion, body perception, helplessness and loss. The sexual offender must choose a victim who will remain silent or who will not be believed in the event that she or he tells. In many instances, particularly in the past, deaf young people have been essentially barred from reporting sexual abuse because of language difficulties and the restrictions they impose on relationships and existing channels of support. If disclosure did occur, the offender could, with relative ease, claim 'misunderstanding' or 'miscommunication' (Westerlund, 1990). Further, because restricted communication creates blocks to access to information, deaf young people have often remained unaware that sexual abuse is unacceptable behaviour, however much they are hurt by it (Phoenix, 1987). The sense of betrayal, pain and powerlessness which can be felt by a victim of sexual abuse is at times beyond belief. The added dimension to counselling deaf victims of sexual abuse could therefore be described more explicitly in the following terms (adapted from Westerlund (1990):

BOX 1.2 THE ADDED DEAF DIMENSION TO THE EXPERIENCE OF CHILD ABUSE

Breaches of confidentiality have frequently been part of the experience of growing up. In educational contexts where a sense of 'family' exists (e.g. special schools), information may be passed from one professional to another. Similarly, in mainstream schools, hearing teachers may find it easier to talk to a deaf young person's parents than to the deaf young person themself, which may have horrendous consequences if the abuser is one of the parents. The deaf young person might well ask 'Why should I trust the counsellor?'

Deaf young people may have been taught by other professionals to view counselling as discipline for naughty children through inappropriate use of language or ignorance of what counselling is. They may approach counsellors with added suspicion if they have experienced betrayals in relation to their deafness.

Abuse is fundamentally the abuse of power. A deaf young person faced with a hearing counsellor or a hearing interpreter may experience a decreased feeling of power and control linked to being deaf. But, in addition, the hearing helper may be identified with a hearing sexual offender.

The counsellor may experience difficultly in directly discussing the abuse, particularly if dialogues take place in sign language which is visually explicit about sexual activity. The counsellor's avoidance can be rationalised as the client's inability to handle the issues, which can then be transferred to the client through conscious and unconscious messages such as: 'Maybe it's not really so'; 'It's true, but how much difference could it make'; 'It's true, but it's too unpleasant to confront'; 'We don't use words or signs like that here'.

We might also view counselling provision in terms of who delivers the service and how the service is defined. The vast majority of providers of 'support' for deaf people are hearing. Some may have training in counselling skills, but many are not qualified professional counsellors. There is also evidence of a widespread lack of deaf awareness on the part of providers of counselling training (Katz, 1993) which means that counselling training does not necessarily imply that a 'qualified' counsellor has the necessary attitudes or skills to work with *deaf* clients. This block to access becomes a double bind when we consider that there are, at the time of writing, only three specialist counselling courses aimed at training deaf people in England and Wales, two of which are psychodynamically orientated, and two of which are in their first year, offering training in basic counselling skills and theory. These courses tend to be 'discrete courses' aimed at deaf people who use sign language as a preferred or natural means of communication and are designed to minimise the kind of stress which deaf people can experience in integrated training with hearing people, or indeed, in integrated group counselling:

'In any situation, the decision to join a group that is homogeneous or one that is mixed should be made by the deaf client. It is inappropriate for a counsellor to view any decision as more appropriate than another. The decision may vary depending on the client, the composition of the group, and the purpose of the counselling. Having said that, it should be borne in mind that communication will normally be clearer in a situation where all the members of the group are deaf. The presence of hearing clients may place additional stress on communication.'

(Miller and Moores, 1990, p.86)

For those deaf people who prefer the option of mainstream courses access is patchy, dependent on the limited degree of deaf awareness amongst trainers and their willingness to include deaf people, and is usually confined to those deaf people who use spoken language or the availability of suitably qualified Human Aids to Communication (sign language interpreters, note takers and lip speakers). Training provision tends to reflect the structure of service provision for deaf people overall, with the exception that those deaf people who are 'in the middle' in terms of communication – that is, those who use both spoken language and sign language with varying degrees of fluency or who use English language but need signed interpretation to provide access to spoken language – are given a wide berth. The limits imposed by rigidly dividing spoken language and sign language can, in the case of counselling services, prohibit clear understanding of the terms of counselling contracts, counselling terminology and process, and standards that can be expected for both deaf clients and deaf trainee counsellors, because, in individual counselling in particular, the communication preference of the client must be used. This point is explored further in Chapter 4. Within this limited range of provision, good practice can of course be observed, but the inequalities between deaf and hearing people in terms of access to a wide range of choice of genuine counsellors and experientially relevant counselling processes and training must be taken on board if the influence of the prevailing winds in blocking access is to be avoided.

COUNSELLING PROVISION FOR DEAF PEOPLE IN THE USA

How does this provision compare with that available in other countries? It is of course difficult to make direct comparisons as policies in other countries vary as do population sizes. But published documentation seems to suggest that the range of services potentially available to deaf people is wider and is given more emphasis elsewhere, even if the communication base for provision and the stereotyping of deaf service users by linguistic preference and/or cultural identity remains similar. By way of comparison, we might consider the range of services available in the USA. Here, there are many examples of deaf people accessing a range of counselling approaches from psychotherapy (Harvey, 1989; Sullivan and Scanlan, 1990) and Rational–Emotive Therapy (Gough, 1990), psychodynamic play therapy (Urban, 1990), through art therapy (Henley, 1987; Cohene and Cohene, 1989; Horovitz and Ellen, 1991) and psychodrama (Barrett, 1986), to family counselling (Sloman *et al.* 1987; Luterman, 1987) rehabilitation and vocational counselling (Danek *et al.* 1989; Foster and Walter, 1992), peer counselling (Strong and Day-Drummer, 1990) and group therapy (Miller and Moores, 1990). We will come back to these different approaches in Chapter 5, but, for the moment, we need to acknowledge the diversity and its implications for deaf people seeking counselling. These publications also contain many references to *deaf* counsellors who have been through counselling training, and emphasise that all practitioners involved acknowledge the importance of fluent communication for the success of counselling. The authors have shown a willingness to investigate issues such as counsellor identity, the use of interpreters in counselling, and client culture and identity.

Although the services described in these accounts tend also to be institutionally based, there is an observable difference in emphasis. For example, the *College Career Programs for Deaf Students* (Rawlings *et al.*, 1988) lists 156 different programmes of post secondary education for deaf students in the USA which have 15 or more full-time deaf students enrolled. Whatever the size of the programme, personal and vocational counselling (which are listed as separate activities) appear to be given as much emphasis as communication support as reflected in the percentage of programmes with these services, · although it is later pointed out that 'many counselling resources may not ordinarily be accessible to deaf students because of communication barriers' (Saur, 1992). In Britain, we know that many deaf students do not have access to appropriate communication support in Further and Higher Education; indeed they may not have access to Further and Higher Education at all (RNID, 1990). The debate over which approach to communication to use in educating deaf children continues to rage as fiercely as it did a decade ago (Corker, 1990c) which means that, from the child's perspective, the possibility of having access to an acceptable standard of communication in any language and in any environment is seriously diminished. If access to appropriate communication support of high quality and standards is difficult to obtain, we can only imagine the situation for effective counselling services, given the widespread tendency to view counselling only in terms of a 'talking through of problems'.

Without wishing to portray the American experience as perfect or as a standard with which all other experiences must be matched, it is, in contrast, rare to find specific reference to counselling practice with deaf people in Britain, except in unpublished studies such as those of Tesni (1991), Dixon (1993) and Katz (1993). When reference is made to 'counselling', it is not always clear what definition of counselling is being used or whether the service is one providing emotional support through the use of counselling skills or whether it is a counselling service where the counsellors in question have professional qualifications in counselling. From the deaf client's perspective, it is extremely important to make a distinction between the two.

INSTITUTIONAL CONTEXTS AND ENVIRONMENTS AND THEIR RELATION
TO PERCEPTIONS OF NEED

If we look at the history of the counselling services available to hearing people,
it is possible to see their roots in clinical and educational psychology, social
work, psychiatry and psychoanalysis. There was a corresponding emphasis
on the inferiority of counselling when compared to the might and experience
of these 'professional' disciplines, proponents of whom tended to monopolise
training (Dryden and Thorne, 1991). Under the influence of American practitioners, counselling became a rapidly expanding profession in its own right
which has permeated many existing professional support services and institutions (Mearns and Thorne, 1988; Egan, 1990). We can see this trend beginning in relation to counselling deaf people, but it has not yet permeated service
provision for deaf people in Britain in a way which influences service development overall. Institutions, on the whole, have traditional strategies of
support in relation to deaf people which have formed the bedrock of their
philosophy of professional practice for many years and this, in itself, has
blurred the boundaries between counselling practice and other more generic
support services such as advice, guidance and pastoral care. Moreover, as
these strategies are very familiar to the practitioners who use them or work
within them there can be anything ranging from a reluctance to a very great
fear of letting go of them, which may or may not be disguised as scepticism
of counselling values. This can lead to the isolation or marginalisation of
counselling practice and professional counsellors, and sometimes to a block
to the psycho-emotional growth and well-being of deaf people because under
institutional influences, counselling services become a form of social control:

> 'In a list of activities, also including informing, advising, assessing and
> referring under the banner of Careers and Educational Guidance, coun-
> selling seems in danger of becoming part of an imposed manipulative
> process, rather than being an umbrella term for a process offering
> variety of assistance in the control of the client. Do words such as
> "advice", "guidance", "recommend" carry overtones of paternalism,
> judgment or direction of choice? Some clients openly seek guidance to
> decision rather than information to open up choice. Such a short-cut
> may bring immediate relief both for pressurised guidance officer, and
> student of low self-esteem. For the latter however, the long term out-
> come may be unwanted, and the imposed decision regretted.'

(Veasey, 1993, p.107)

Fourteen years earlier, practitioners involved in the provision of counselling
and emotional support to deaf people attempted to clarify the difference and
open up the debate, but it does not seem as if the views expressed have been
taken on board within the institutional context:

> 'Guidance differs from counselling in that the person receiving the
> guidance is given a number of options and through discussion comes
> to decide on certain modes of action. It also requires a knowledge of
> both statutory and voluntary helping services. Counselling and guid-
> ance are in practice inseparable, for in the course of counselling ques-

tions arise which require discussion. Counselling and guidance should be undertaken by professionals trained in counselling, but also with experience of all aspects of deafness – including the psychosocial implications. Guidance is also confused with giving advice which is a more directive form of help. The giving of advice does not proffer a choice of options – indeed, in the field of deafness it is often more than directive, it is dogmatic.'

(Denmark *et al.* 1979, p.57)

The British Association for Counselling (BAC), which is seen as the lead body in establishing professional codes and standards of practice has also made statements about the difference between counselling and support in terms of function:

'Only when both user and recipient explicitly agree to enter into a counselling relationship does it become "counselling" rather than the use of "counselling skills"...training in counselling skills is not sufficient for users to consider themselves qualified counsellors. The dividing line between the counselling task and *ad hoc* counselling...is the major safe-guard of the rights of the consumer.'

(BAC, 1984, 1989,1990)

BOX 1.3 WHO PROVIDES 'COUNSELLING' FOR DEAF PEOPLE

INSTITUTION	IDENTITY OF 'HELPERS'	TYPE OF HELP
The Family	Parents, siblings, grandparents	Befriending
The Community	Friends, the police, priests	Befriending
The Voluntary Sector	Advice workers, Samaritans, HIV counsellors, child abuse specialists	Semi-formal/ formal
The Health Service	GPs, audiologists, health visitors, speech therapists, nurses	Befriending
	Clinical psychologists, hearing therapists, psychiatrists	Formal
The Education Service	Teachers of the deaf, mainstream teachers	Semi-formal
	Classroom assistants	Befriending
	Educational psychologists	Formal
Social Services	Social workers with deaf people	Formal

In a book which is concerned primarily with counselling, it may seem strange that we are devoting the initial pages to activities which are linked to counselling only on the surface level. The reason is simple. If we look at the primary sources of support available to deaf people (Box 1.3) and the identity of the providers of support within these sources, it is possible to see a risk that counselling provision offered to deaf people will be confined to:

- existing institutional frameworks and environments which may have aims and objectives which conflict with those of counselling
- ad hoc provision of counselling skills
- well established counselling contexts and approaches which may or may not be appropriate to working with deaf people.

In such environments, it is possible that there will be a general resistance to placing counselling 'at the Heart of the Institution' (Rogers, 1993), where it needs to be if it is to be legitimately known as counselling, or, more importantly, if client growth can be encouraged through the *affective climate* of the institution.

Within existing institutionalised services there is a tendency to view deaf people as generally needy (they have 'special needs' or 'communication needs', for example), and in need of 'care' or remedial treatment (they need 'special provision' or 'specialist language teaching'), or as social casualties who are in need of support. Thus, there is a trend towards both the definition of need and the way in which needs are met to be very narrowly conceived within existing helping services, and at odds with the way in which deaf people perceive their neediness in human or individual terms in common with all human beings.

This concept of individual human needs has been enshrined in the work of Abraham Maslow (1943) and his theories about what motivates human beings. He contended that every person is born with a set of basic needs, including the needs for safety, belongingness or love, and self-esteem, and that these needs are essentially ordered in a hierarchical fashion. When needs at different levels of the hierarchy are satisfied they no longer motivate the person's behaviour, and the person can proceed to the next level unimpeded. If a deaf child is not loved or does not have a feeling of belonging, she may sacrifice her need for self-respect, but once she feels loved, she is more likely to seek to satisfy other more advanced needs such as self-actualisation:

'We may still often (if not always) expect that a new discontent will develop, unless the individual is doing what he is fitted for. A musician must make music, an artist must paint, a poet must write, if he is to be ultimately at peace with himself. What a man *can* be, he *must* be. This need we may call self-actualisation... It refers to man's desire for self-fulfilment, namely, to the tendency for him to become actualised in what he is potentially. This tendency might be phrased as the desire to become more and more what one is, to become everything that one is capable of.'

(Maslow, 1943, p. 382)

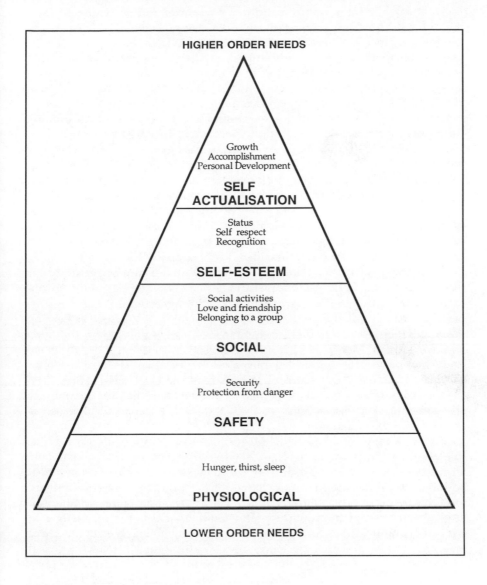

Figure 1.2 Maslow's Hierachy of Human Needs

This way of viewing needs, whilst it may be of little relevance within an institutional context which is based on making provision for *perceived* needs or needs which can be easily assessed or measured, is of relevance to the individual who feels that he or she is not loved or is prevented from being who he or she must be. But human needs can often become veiled by the professional needs of institutions.

How can the influence of institutional contexts and environments and definitions of need be observed on a human level? Obviously the degree and level of influence will vary with the context or environment, but it might be worthwhile looking at two examples. Within the Health Service, counselling is usually one of a range of services referred to under the heading of 'mental health', which, in the layperson's mind, is associated with mental illness. Similarly, the fact that support services are provided within a hospital environment and are commonly delivered by staff with medical or clinical training can present the image of a medical problem being 'treated' in a medical way. The layperson's definition assumes importance for many deaf people because the quality of their education has prohibited them from achieving a language level which will enable them to move beyond the layperson's definition (Sacks, 1989; Powers, 1990). They may see the source of counselling as a place where 'mad people' go, and, since they do not view themselves as 'mad' (as in 'has a mind that is considered not to work in a normal way, so that their behaviour is very strange and sometimes frightening'[2]) or 'mental' (as in 'someone whose behaviour is considered shocking, foolish or frightening'[3]), they may stay away from such a service and miss a rare opportunity for receiving genuine help. Alternatively, they may associate hospital environments only with audiology, hearing aids and poor communication and be unable to accept that different and more responsive services such as hearing therapy, which offer help on a more human level, can be provided within such an environment. Mental Health practitioners such as the groups who have been responsible for setting up purpose-built facilities such as the John Denmark Unit (National Centre for Mental Health and Deafness) in Prestwich are increasingly aware of these problems in educating the deaf community about mental health issues, and seek to use the skills of deaf people themselves in improving the situation.

Within the Education System, however, we have a different scenario. The role of counselling in education has been the subject of a great deal of debate within the mainstream sector, and has led to the development of professional bodies such as the National Association for Pastoral Care in Education and the Counselling in Education Division of the British Association for Counselling, which attempt to establish professional standards for counselling in education and provide a forum for teachers and others involved in the use of counselling skills to share experiences. Special education, which includes deaf education has, historically, been viewed separately from mainstream education and this has led to a two tier education system, as defined by policy and practice (Corker, 1993). In fact, it could be said that special education is the Cinderella of mainstream education. There is not, as yet, evidence that deaf education has been influenced by this debate sufficiently for 'support policies' to be reexamined. As a consequence of the mislabelling of deaf experience which we will explore in more detail later in this chapter, a large section of deaf education is founded on the normalisation of deaf people and the

---

2   Source: The British Deaf Association (1992) *Dictionary of British Sign Language/English*.
3   Ibid.

remediation of perceived deficiencies, sometimes at the expense of the broad-based education enjoyed by hearing people. Within such a philosophy, education can become confused with 'caring', which in turn, can be confused with 'benevolent humanitarianism' (Tomlinson, 1982; Lane, 1992) or paternalism (Lane, 1984):

> 'Benevolent humanitarianism is to do good to certain children; to the dominance of a narrow psychological viewpoint and therefore excessive individualisation of the "problem" of disability and handicap; and to the pervasiveness of the medical model of disability as a deficit in the child requiring remediation.'

> (Wood, 1988)

Counsellors who have attempted to take the core values of counselling into special education, have found themselves in an increasingly isolated position in part because of the structure and philosophy of specialist teaching. Teachers often find it difficult to deal with assertive, self-aware children whom they have become accustomed to viewing as weak or dependent and in need of care, as such children create further challenges for a teaching profession which gravitates naturally towards authoritative interaction and intervention, and which has not been adequately prepared for other alternatives. Some practitioners have pointed to the tendency for perceptions of authority to result in the the child's meaning being located only in the teacher's frame of reference (Edwards, 1980), which is the exact opposite to what we would hope to find within a counselling relationship. Counsellors, in their emphasis on confidentiality and the rights of the child, pose problems for a structure based on case conferences and professional sharing, and a philosophy which views the child as the problem. Moreover, counsellors are bound by their code of ethics to make explicit any conflicts:

> 'Counsellors who become aware of a conflict between their obligation to a client and their obligation to an agency or organisation employing them will make explicit the nature of the loyalties and responsibilities involved.'

> (British Association for Counselling, 1984)

SOCIETAL AND ARCHETYPAL BLOCKS TO LISTENING

Authors of books about deaf people are often compelled from the outset to explain exactly what they mean by the term 'deaf'. If we accept the rigours of this task, we soon find that we are not helped by the preponderance of contradictory definitions which continue to grow as a result of a compulsion to label something which is not easily understood, or is exceedingly complex and requires simplification in order that we can begin to understand it. We may also find that, in the final outcome, our particular definitions or perceptions are more about the language we use to label our own feelings than about the changeable nature of the reality that stands before us. That is not to say that labelling is always subjective, for we have the prevailing winds to contend with. We will explore the issue of labelling in more depth in Chapter 4.

Society at large is full of 'official versions' of the truth. We are all familiar with the tendency of politicians to be economical with the truth because they believe it to be for the good of all or because they wish to disguise a truth which is too awful, outrageous or painful to be believed or too embarrassing to the perpetrators of that truth (Pilger, 1992; Lane, 1992). Most human beings engage in such behaviour because it feels safer to go with the prevailing winds of the outspoken majority view, which are set in their exposition of 'rock logic' or 'I am right and you are wrong' (de Bono, 1991). It is easier to do this than to challenge from the position of the minority, or even from that of the silent majority, and flow with the 'water logic' of listening to and acting on unpleasant truths. Under the influence of the prevailing winds, labels can be used collectively by a group of people to disguise the 'multiple realities' of individual members of the 'pluralistic society' in which we live, and therein lies the danger:

> 'Kept in perspective as just another form of pretending, communal innocence offers a collective shelter against individual disenchantment. However, uncritical acceptance of the feeling of belonging and the mutual dependence offered by such consensual validation involves risking the closed-minded constraints of mistaking the group's parochial outlook for the one true vision of what is normal, natural or real. Communal innocence may blind a person to the equivalence of the multiple realities that can otherwise be experienced in a pluralistic society...'

(Kopp, 1981, p.153)

When a group of people, and that unfortunately can include counsellors, harbours an unconscious urge to behave in a certain way towards another group who has been stereotyped by a parochial world view or a predisposition to label this urge can appear as an *archetype*. With respect to deaf people this 'collective shadow' can show itself in the inner experience or historical trend in society to label deaf people as 'bad' or 'sick' and this becomes the prototype – the literal meaning of the word archetype – for society's subsequent behaviour towards deaf people. The archetype therefore acts as a block to listening which can prevent the understanding of deaf people's realities:

> 'The problem of the shadow is not only significant in an individual's own development and in his capacity to form personal relationships; it is also extremely important in a collective sense. Were we more cognisant of this darkness in ourselves it is entirely possible that collective phenomena which exhibit the projection of the group shadow – such as persecutions, inquisitions, purges, racial intolerance and prejudice, and other phenomena which involve the sacrifice of a scapegoat would never occur.'

(Greene, 1976, p. 93)

The underlying source of all oppressive behaviour of this kind has been referred to as *alienism*:

> 'Alienism is based on the hypothesis that all forms of oppression are derived from the exploitation of the weaker by the stronger... Such exploitation sets up forces deep within the psyche that predispose a person to export fear and anger upon some other person or group. Simultaneously, leaders and figures within the group that the person belongs to are idealised... We have a *propensity* to reproduce a puritanical and essentially hateful process upon people who stir up opposition to some deeply held view of our own. At an emotional level they literally *are* an *alien*. What happens is that our intellectual understanding is side-tracked by the *archetype* (of experiences which are perceived to be life-threatening for example) into an attack on people which is less than rationally based. This process is usually unconscious and out of awareness so no one is exempt.'

> (Southgate and White, 1989, p. 35)

This is an important concept which will be explained in more detail and at the level of individual counsellors in the following chapters. What we need to understand for the moment is that through alienistic urges, attitudes or assumptions, counsellors can label deaf people as the disabled victims of oppression to such an extent that they 'bear the mark of oppression' (Thomas and Sillen, 1972) and perceive themselves to be powerless unless they undergo fundamental change. In counselling, such attitudes can be dehumanising for deaf clients.

THE QUESTION OF IDENTITY

It is precisely these societal blocks to listening which make it difficult to come up with a description of deaf people which is meaningful for them, because the reality of the deaf community is that it consists of a continuum of individuals, each of whom has his or her choices or preferences and each of whom may harbour a dichotomy between the feeling self and the expressive self. As counsellors are concerned with *both* the feeling *self* and the expressive self, there is a need to make a distinction between a community identity or consciousness and the individual identity, whether fragmented or not, which the deaf client may bring to counselling.

Part of the difficulty faced by those who attempt to support deaf people, whatever approach they use and whether they have been invited to help or not, is that it is often assumed, both by the deaf person and the provider of the support, that an individual deaf person will conform to some kind of preconceived view or model of what a deaf person is. Indeed, models are often devised for the very purpose of fitting deaf people into boxes in order that their diversity appears more manageable. Having said that, counsellors do need to be aware of the different ways in which deaf people are described because many of these descriptions emanate from the societal matrix in which deaf people are embedded and have become deeply ingrained in the minds of deaf people and those who live and work with them. The necessity of

guarding against communal innocence and other blocks to listening is in
many ways the central theme of this book whether it is applied to deaf people
or counselling. It is in part because of wishing to maintain this guard that I
am wary of assigning definitions to the term 'deaf', in particular, because this
would be to play into the hands of those who divide and rule the deaf
community, and prevent different deaf people from developing an understanding of each other on a basic human level. In counselling, I have encountered deaf people who face acute struggles with the question of identity,
which, in essence, is about what they perceive 'being deaf' to mean; indeed,
as a client, I have faced these struggles myself. It is my experience that many
of these difficulties stem from the external pressures which surround deaf
people to take on a certain identity, and the conditions which are associated
with these pressures which play on the individual's deep-rooted desire to
belong to a group of people. These influences can be both positive and
negative in reality, or they can be perceived to be positive or negative by the
individual who is given no alternatives.

Deaf People's Multiple Realities and Identity Pressures

By way of analogy, we might consider the increasing number of workshops
which aim to strengthen 'the deaf identity' by exposing deaf and hearing
people to Deaf[4] culture, history and language. These workshops aim to
remedy the imbalance in the lives of deaf people as a result of their having
been deprived of this information because of hearing–speaking dominance,
and in this role they fill a significant gap in the lives of deaf people. The way
in which identity subsequently grows will, as is the case with most workshops, depend in part on the identity of the workshop organisers, how they
view deaf people and their relationship to hearing people, and how they pass
on this information to workshop participants. The processes whereby this is
achieved can involve the use of counselling skills; indeed, the processes may
parallel counselling in many ways. But most workshop organisers know that
their workshops take place over a few days, and can, at best, hope to plant
seeds of productivity. For the rest of the month, the year, even the person's
lifetime, there will be other influences which affect the growth of identity –
community, educational, political and media influences to name but a few.
This is because the reality of all deaf people is that they are suspended in a
network of complex systems most of which are controlled by hearing–speaking people. All deaf people, whether they choose to affiliate socially with other
deaf people or not, work within hearing systems, use hearing interpreters,
teachers, doctors and solicitors, teach sign language to hearing people and
have (usually) hearing parents. Despite the fact that all systems begin and end
with the individual, the power and influence of the majority system cannot
be ignored or denied.

---

4   Deaf people who identify as culturally deaf or as part of a linguistic minority who
       use sign language as a means of communication are commonly ascribed an
       upper-case 'D'.

Aside from these wider influences, there will also be individual differences as to how workshop participants respond to the contents of a workshop which are based on deep-rooted individual characteristics and behavioural preferences which may or may not be culturally linked, and these differences may remain hidden for a variety of reasons. As the emphasis of workshops is on education or reeducation, and the hidden agenda is therefore change, individuals will work in different ways and at different speeds towards change. Some may be too frightened to start the journey or reject the possibility of change unless it is on their own terms. So, at the end of the workshop, it is likely that there will be a range of *expressed responses* such as those shown on the left hand side of Box 1.4.

BOX 1.4

EXTERNAL EXPRESSED RESPONSES	INTERNAL FEELING RESPONSES
'That was mind-blowing – I've got to do something more!'	'I feel hearing people have sick minds'
'I like the idea of it all – it feels good, but I'm not sure about actually living that way because:	'I feel good about the deaf way; being deaf feels good inside, it feels right'
…my parents may not understand	'Sometimes I feel deaf and sometimes I feel hearing, but they both feel OK inside in different situations'
…I'm not comfortable with being so physical	
…I'm not happy about going to new places and meeting new people alone	'Nobody seems to understand me when I act deaf, so it feels as if it's easier to be hearing'
…I'm happier with just a few close friends'	'I'm frightened of being rejected again'
'I don't think I'll ever fully understand'	'I feel good about being hearing and I can't imagine any other way'
'I can't change how I was born'	'I'm fed up with being made to feel guilty. What's wrong with being hearing'
'It means nothing to me'	'I feel the deaf are retarded'

The first and last responses are fairly clear-cut, showing complete acceptance and complete rejection. However, the vast majority of workshop participants are likely to experience some inner doubts or insecurities and, when they leave the environment of the workshop, will be prey to the forces, both positive and negative, of the systems network and, because of their individual make-up, will experience different kinds of inner reinforcement and make different choices about subsequent activities. In the world outside our workshop microcosm, and at a very fundamental level, individual feelings about identity are very similar to expressed responses but more finely tuned and closer to the essence of the self, as we can see from the right hand side of Box 1.4. These *internal feeling responses* are subject to the same external forces, because these forces act as what I will call *identity pressures*, but expressed responses and internal feeling responses are like the cover and the contents of a book. The former are clearly observable whilst the latter cannot be gauged until the book has been read.

IDENTITY FORMATION

All people, whether they are deaf or hearing, acquire or form their identity, and the social groupings and contacts that people make, most especially in the early years, have a large influence on who they become as adults and how they behave in different contexts. Because identity is ultimately forged out of the environments in which individuals find themselves, to acknowledge the characteristics of these environments brings us a long way towards understanding what lies within the core of a deaf person's sense of self, and, more importantly, gives us the knowledge with which we can begin to challenge any assumptions we may be making.

There are a number of different theories of how identity develops, and the above description indicates that I have chosen that group of theories which suggest that identity is 'constructed'. This is because these theories, such as those of Erikson (1968), seem to convey an awareness of the individual as part of a system. The use of the word 'system' may send some more experienced practitioners of certain professions into a panic, but I would emphasise that I am not using it to detract from the individual, or to imply that the systems of which we are all a part are somehow the source of every human predicament. This qualifier is typical of the way in which 'symbolic interactionist' theories (Mead, 1934), can allow for the integration of constructionist theories with more abstract psychoanalytic and cognitive theories which distance people from their subjective origins. Individuals, whoever they are and whatever personal resources they harbour, do not live in a vacuum. A professional counsellor may work hard on using the client's foundations to build the framework of the client's inner resources, which will form the basis for a more enlightened future. But that counsellor can also guarantee that other forces will be in operation outside of the counselling relationship which are equally intent on flattening the house of cards. It is not until bricks replace the cards that the client will feel secure enough to withstand these forces.

Erikson (1968) argues that to understand an individual's actions or feelings, we have to take into account three factors which he calls somatic process, social context, and ego process or identity. The last of these is the way in which a person resolves conflicts and makes sense of him or herself. He identifies four important stages in personality integration or identity formation.

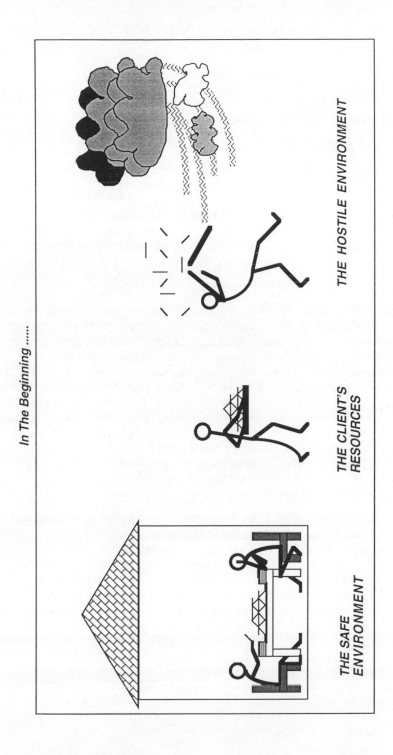

Figure 1.3 House of Cards

BOX 1.5 ERIKSON'S STAGES OF IDENTITY FORMATION

Identifications with significant others (childhood)

Role diffusion (early adolescence)

Role experimentation (adolescence)

Achievement of identity (adulthood)

The process of healthy identity formation which Erikson describes could be represented as is shown in Figure 1.4. It is possible to see from this description where Erikson's work fits the theories of Maslow that were referred to earlier.

DEAF CULTURE AND DEAF IDENTITY

The cultural identity of Britain's Deaf community hinges on socialisation, and this suggests that, within Erikson's framework, our understanding of deaf people's social context does indeed have an important role in its partnership with identity formation. The Deaf club and the Deaf school have become identified with the furtherance of Deaf people's desire to socialise with each other, and, as the home of Deaf culture, they form the network of channels through which cultural information is passed. These institutions are clearly an important part of Deaf people's heritage, particularly so for those Deaf people who have the benefit of a Deaf family environment. To thrive on the opportunities created by these networks, an individual has to be Deaf; that is, they need to have a Deaf 'centre' and sign language as a native or preferred language. Padden and Humphries have described the concept of the Deaf centre in cultural terms:

> 'The sign HEARING[5] has an official English translation, "can hear", but in ASL HEARING is aligned in interesting ways with respect to DEAF and HARD-OF-HEARING. In ASL as in English, HARD-OF-HEAR-ING represents a deviation of some kind. Someone who is A-LITTLE-HARD-OF-HEARING has a smaller deviation than someone who is VERY-HARD-OF-HEARING. In this way, ASL and English are similar – and yet the terms have opposite meanings in the two languages. The reason for this is clear: for Deaf people, the greatest deviation is HEAR-ING. This is the crucial element in understanding these "backward" definitions: there is a different center, a different point from which one deviates. In this case DEAF and not HEARING, is taken as the central

---

5   English glosses for the signs of sign language, in this case American Sign
     Language (ASL), are usually written in capital letters with hypens connecting
     glosses that are one sign in sign language. Glosses do not convey the grammar of
     sign language and they are not word-for-sign translations.

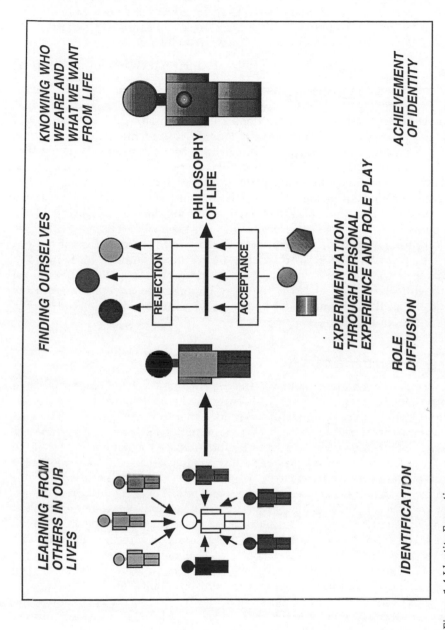

Figure 1.4 Identity Formation

point of reference. A-LITTLE-HARD-OF-HEARING is a small deviation from DEAF, and thus is used for someone who is only slightly
hearing. VERY-HARD-OF-HEARING is someone who departs from
the center greatly, thus someone who can hear quite well.'

(Padden and Humphries, 1988, p 41)

The different centres described in this quotation arise from different individual and group perceptions based on cultural assumptions, and we could
therefore say that these assumptions are the basis for differentiating Deaf
people from HEARING[6] people by means of a cultural model. The core of the
Deaf community is formed by Deaf people who come from Deaf families
which sometimes go back generations. It is therefore possible, because all the
elements are in place for healthy identity formation, that this group of Deaf
people will develop an identity which is, in essence, Deaf, and also that others,
because all the ingredients are accessible, will join them by acquiring a Deaf
identity by way of Deaf consciousness. In this they will be like hearing people
who are exposed to 'the right' ingredients for healthy identity formation, and
may well follow the path to identity formation as outlined by Figure 1.4.
However, this is only one means of differentiating deaf people, as the cultural
model itself implies, and it is therefore important to understand from the
outset that the cultural model is a valid representation of *one* Deaf reality,
though not the only reality.

THE DISABLED IDENTITY

Erikson's theory, along with the theories of many others, emphasises the
importance of events which occur in early childhood, in particular the significance of the child's relationship with his or her immediate family. The vast
majority of deaf people are born to *hearing* families and while in the formative
years are effectively shut off from the possibility of experiencing, let alone
living, Deaf culture. Any routes to the possibility of access are frequently
closed by educational trends to mainstream deaf children in a hearing cultural
milieu. It should be stressed that there is rarely, if ever, a question of choice
for the individual deaf child, especially in the early days when any choices
that are made are capable of determining subsequent life patterns. Choices
are made by adults, not children, and the compulsion of parents, in particular,
to make 'the right choice' can be both manipulated and strengthened by the
power of professional doctrine, as we have seen. However, it is usually the
deaf adult who has to bear the lifetime's responsibility for choices made for
or about him or her in childhood, and in accepting such responsibility, the
deaf adult can also become the focus of negative labelling intended initially
for those who made ill-advised choices and linked to negative assumptions
about the label 'disabled'.

---

6   There are many people who can hear and are culturally Deaf, having shared in
        Deaf heritage through familial connections. Children of Deaf Adults (CODAs) or
        HMFDs (Hearing Mother Father Deaf) as they are known in Britain, are good
        examples.

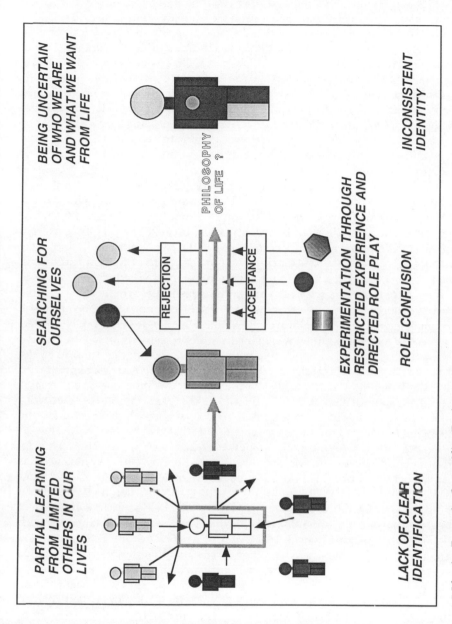

Figure 1.5 Identity Formation in an Alien Environment

It is somewhat inevitable that there will be other individual and group perceptions amongst the so-called 'successes' (positive labelling of 'deaf') and 'failures' (negative labelling) which are based on different assumptions arising at least in part from expectations placed on them. In a recent Australian television documentary, the situation of CODAs was described as being equivalent to having 'A Passport without a Country', and, in many ways, this is the situation in which these deaf people find themselves – they become torn between the world of their parents where there may be linguistic and cultural demands which are difficult or impossible to meet, and the world of Deaf people, where there is a chance of belonging at the cost of some degree of segregation from mainstream life. This can produce a different pattern of identity formation:

CODAs, in common with 'newly arrived deaf persons', are two groups who present particular problems for Deaf culture (Padden and Humphries, 1988), and the culture finds subtle ways of granting them an unusual or distinct status. The division between worlds, because it tends to be seen in terms of differences rather than areas where the two worlds may find some mutual agreement, is particularly taxing in the realm of human feelings, in part because it relates to another common perspective which gives rise to different centres. This revolves around the question of whether deaf people perceive themselves or are perceived to be disabled or not, which, on one level, is connected to the more painful debate about whether deafness can be viewed in terms of a medical model which incorporates the search for 'a cure'. I have thought long and hard about this emotive issue, coming as I do, from the segment of the deaf community that consists of deafened people, who are commonly said to identify as disabled and who 'therefore' desire a cure. It is true that many deafened people identify as disabled, but, in common with other disabled people, the qualifier lies in who or what constitutes the disabling factor, and not necessarily in the fact that they regard themselves as being not 'normal' in some way, or view deafness solely in negative terms. As there is Deaf culture, there is also disability culture, which, on one level, has similar origins, but which does not have linguistic or institutional foundations. Disability culture is born out of disabled people's common experience of oppression, and their desire to project and rally behind the positive face of disability. Disabled people share, for the most part, a common language with the hearing–speaking world, but it is in the way in which they use this language and the meaning which they ascribe to it that they can differ. In this we can see evidence of a disabled 'centre' which is also passed between disabled people through socio-cultural activity. Thus we have Deaf folklore and disability humour, for example, both of which have important roles to play in the maintenance of their respective cultures, and are quite distinct from the negative medical image of disability, which, it must be stressed, is also characteristic of some deaf people.

Despite this commonality, Deaf people are not as a rule happy about identifying with disabled culture, perhaps because of linguistic divisions which create a hierarchy within disabled culture and lead to the possibility that Deaf people can be oppressed by disabled people who are part of the hearing–speaking world, and therefore prey to language errors and misrepresentations which define oppression:

> 'If being called disabled is thought to inhibit employment prospects and a better social status, there could be an incentive to distance the possession of the particular condition from those thought to be lower down the scale. This, it is falsely believed, frees the individual, or group, to consider themselves as only a variation in the pattern of normality while the others, lower down the scale, can be regarded as really disabled. For example, people with spinal injuries may see themselves as normal (restricted only by barriers which limit wheelchair mobility – that is, they are mobility oppressed) whilst those with learning difficulties are "really" disabled. Similarly people with hearing impairments may think of themselves as normal (restricted only by barriers to British Sign Language as a form of communication – that is, they are language-oppressed) whilst those with a spinal injury are regarded as "really" disabled'.

(Finkelstein, in Swain *et al*. 1993, pp. 13–14)

Many Deaf people, as we shall see in Chapter 4, resent the use of the term 'hearing impaired' because, in stemming from the need of professionals to have an 'accurate' blanket term for deaf and hard-of-hearing people, it defines them in relation to the hearing centre with the outcome that they are substandard hearing people. Many deaf people object to the use of the label Deaf on the grounds that it creates divisions in a wider community which needs a unified voice in the face of oppression. But this view can often be labelled as having 'a bad attitude' by Deaf people because they feel it means that the deaf person does not accept being deaf.

Thus we have some idea of the array of individual feelings which exist within this very diverse group of people in relation to the label 'deaf'. This is without the complexity of other factors which influence self-perception and affiliation to other people:

> 'Self-identification with the group and skill in ASL should be important diagnostic factors in deciding who is Deaf. But the bounded distinction between the terms *Deaf* and *deaf* represents only part of the dynamic of how Deaf people talk about themselves. Deaf people are both Deaf and deaf, and their discussions, even arguments, over issues of identity show that these two categories are often interrelated in complex ways.'

(Padden and Humphries, 1988, p.3)

There are of course Black people who are deaf, gays and lesbians who are deaf and women who are deaf, and all the evidence suggests that membership of more than one group of people with a history of stereotyping and oppression produces a complex identity which cannot easily or simply be explained by assumptions such as 'Black–Deaf people are Deaf first and Black second', when the reverse is often true (Aramburo, 1989; Royal Association in Aid of Deaf People, 1991). This is surely why Black–Deaf people and gay–Deaf people have developed their own variations of sign language which reflect both their oppression as Black or gay people and their Deaf identity. Similarly, there are other deaf people who are also blind (for example, those who have Usher's syndrome) or are physically challenged or mentally disturbed, or have learning difficulties, cerebral palsy or Down's syndrome. The extent to which they identify as disabled or Deaf cannot be predicted.

In the world of counselling, it is important not to become judgmental about a particular view, as can happen in other fields. There is, for example, a preparedness amongst some Deaf people and their hearing allies to refer to the deafness of psychology and to question whether there is a psychology of the Deaf which provides an accurate framework for describing the inner worlds and behavioural or cultural motivations of Deaf people (Lane, 1992), whilst asserting that negative psychological labelling attributed to deafened people, for example, is accurate, because they *are* disabled (in the negative sense) and conform to a medical stereotype of defect or impairment and suffer as a result of their disability:

> 'An embarrassment for the medical model of cultural deafness heretofore was that this "pathology" had no medical treatment. With cochlear implants[7], however, the medical specialty of otology has been expanding its traditional clientele beyond adventitiously deafened hearing people who seek treatment, *for whom an infirmity model is appropriate*, to include members of the Deaf community, for whom it is not.'

> (Lane, 1992, p.206, italics added)

The implication of this is that deafened people are not Deaf and they are not hearing therefore they must be disabled as opposed to deafened. With respect to identity formation, this is a curious, some would say innacurate view to take, as it belies both the experiential base of identity formation and the different perceptions of disability. From the counselling perspective, it is also a very unhelpful way of attempting to justify the experiences of one group of people at the expense of the feelings of another, when their experiential baselines are quite different and not necessarily derived from their need to be deaf or hearing.

On the basis of the above explorations of deaf identity, I am not convinced that looking at the question of identity formation will produce a definitive statement which will be acceptable to all deaf people, or, indeed, that counselling experiences support the idea of 'a deaf identity' which is singular and finite. Identity, which is very firmly rooted in the individual self and its subjective experience, has come to be confused with consciousness or a common set of values and beliefs that *groups* of deaf people hold. The latter is, of course, extremely important from the cultural perspective, and, because some Deaf people have embraced a cultural identity, hearing counsellors have to be vigilant for the possibility that oppression will become part of the counselling relationship. But the concepts of self and *social* identity are two sides of the same coin and so must be considered within the same framework

---

7   Cochlear implants are electronic devices which can be implanted surgically to
      allow direct electrical stimulation of the nerve of hearing (the auditory nerve) to
      give a sensation of hearing. Their use has attracted a great deal of controversy.

of symbolic interactionism which is described by Strauss (1977) in the opening quotation of this chapter. Psychoanalytic and cognitive accounts of the development of self have an increasing emphasis on the primary role of relationships that an individual forms and can be seen to be compatible with this framework. Individual psychological factors must be presumed to be an active accommodation to a particular social climate of the individual. Social factors such as those described above, must be seen as facilitating or hindering, but not determining individual experiences (Honess, 1992).

Why focus on the concepts of self and identity at all? In the world of feelings, which is the world of counsellors and clients, there is no right way. I hope I am not alone in my belief that a strong ego, a strong identity, and an awareness of others from a position of strength is central to a human being's existence. Counsellors in general are concerned with making every effort not to violate a person's sense of independence, self-respect and resourcefulness, and this is what places counselling apart from other helping professions. Such is the complexity of identity formation and the development of the self that, in their inner world, most deaf people will have an identity which assumes different meanings and different levels of significance for all its component parts. That is the uniqueness of the self:

'Deaf people should never be regarded as a class apart, as a group with special curious characteristics, and there should never be attempted any research into the psychology of the deaf as if they all had some special traits in common. The fact of the matter is that each deaf person, whether deaf at birth or later, is a unique individual. He or she differs from all other people, both deaf and hearing, as does anyone else.'

(Sutcliffe, 1990)

Frameworks, such as that presented in Figure 1.6 are useful insofar as they are frameworks, but they should not detract from this uniqueness. In human terms, the individual's deafness is not always the most significant or relevant factor, but *being* deaf may be. Their identity and sense of self-worth, or lack of it, can be vital. From the counsellor's perspective, whether they themselves are deaf or hearing, it is crucial that this identity, whatever its nature, can grow from positive reinforcement and that it feels comfortable or natural, for only then can it be the basis for the development of self-esteem. But if this identity is adopted or acquired because of negative reinforcement it cannot rest easily within because it is linked more to the will of others than to the feelings of the individual. It is a contrived identity.

It is for these reasons that I will use the term 'deaf' to refer to people who are deaf or Deaf throughout this book, and allow individual deaf clients and counsellors to define what being deaf means for them in their own terms. Where there are clear distinctions between the two groups of deaf people which are relevant for counselling process and practice, I will make it clear which group I am referring to in order that confusion can be avoided. I wish to emphasise, however, that 'deaf' is not used because of my own particular allegiances or preferences. I would, if it were possible to develop my own terminology, prefer to use Deaf People throughout, the upper-case letters signifying the importance I attach as a counsellor to *all* deaf people regardless

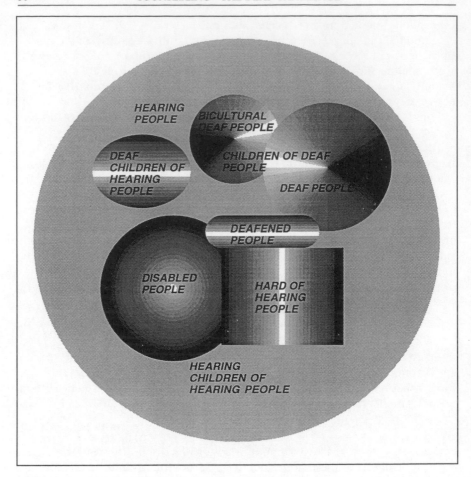

Figure 1.6 Identity Pressures

of their group identity; but this would be to go against established conventions and perhaps confuse the issue further. Similarly, I use the term 'hearing' to mean people who have full use of their auditory facility and spoken language, and who willingly incorporate this way of being into their everyday lives. The emphasis here is on 'willingly', as this, I believe, is what sets hearing people apart from deaf people who identify as disabled. This usage does not carry with it any assumptions of oppression, but rather an acknowledgement that there is always a strong possibility of alienism when two people come together, and one is perceived to be a member of a dominant society, the other of a society which has, historically, been oppressed by the dominant society. I would further suggest that the dynamics of such a situation, though complex, are more likely to appear within a counselling relationship because of the nature of counselling.

Towards a Definition of Counselling

I have used the term 'counselling' repeatedly throughout this chapter with reference to both positive and negative practices. Some reading this book may ask why I choose to use the term counselling as opposed to psychotherapy or even psychoanalysis. I have already made it clear that it is important to distinguish between the task of counselling and the use of *ad hoc* counselling skills. This is one of the primary aims of this book. However, the debate about the differences between counselling and psychotherapy is not yet resolved and this is not the place to air it further. Whereas I am clear that deaf people have a right to access counselling because counselling skills on their own may be of limited value, it is also true that for some deaf people, counselling will not be enough to effect lasting client growth and change. One of the premises on which counselling is frequently differentiated from psychotherapy is to do with the depth of therapy and, consequently, for which clients it is appropriate. Psychotherapy is concerned largely with people who may be psychologically disturbed in some way, as opposed to people who have, for example, low self-esteem, and has its roots in psychodynamic theory. Some of the case studies and experiences of deaf counsellors demonstrate a psychodynamic way of working with clients, and I will leave it to the contributors to explain what they mean by this. I have, myself, drawn upon the theories of psychotherapists and psychoanalysts on occasions, because I have found them to inform the framework within which I work.

I think that all of the contributors to this book would agree that 'severely psychologically disturbed' deaf people (those who have schizophrenia or chemically induced manic-depression, for example) are in the minority within the deaf community in the same way that their hearing counterparts are within the hearing community. Often the disturbance which causes deaf people's problem situations is rooted in the collective shadow of hearing people which is exported onto deaf people, and in deaf people's limited access to appropriate help which can result in problems accumulating. In my work as a counsellor, I have seen much evidence of the machinations of this collective shadow and of the emotional and psychological strength of deaf people in the face of its onslaught. I have therefore come to the conclusion that the vast majority of deaf people have the inner resources to respond to the counselling process and to the core values of counselling in a way which goes considerably beyond the solving of problems.

Counselling can, of course, be both a positive and a negative experience for counsellor and client, but the success of counselling must ultimately be measured by the client. In order that the client can assess their experience of counselling accurately, he or she needs to have some idea of what counselling sets out to achieve and what he or she can therefore expect from the counsellor in the way of values and skills. The client needs to be able to distinguish between those practices which keep power in the counsellor's hands and are mistakenly labelled counselling and those which acknowledge the client's personal power and inner resources and oversee an equalising of power within the counselling relationship. This is especially so because of the natural tendency of clients to see their counsellors as all-powerful, particularly at the beginning of a counselling relationship. From the outset, then, it is important to be clear that the counselling processes described throughout this book are aimed primarily at setting professional standards where they may be seriously lacking. In setting such standards, we need to establish precisely what counselling is within the context of the following chapters; that is, we need to have a clear idea in our minds of the core values of counselling process and to be able to distinguish these core values from counselling methodology and counselling style which are the subject of later chapters. The British Association for Counselling describes the activity of counselling as follows:

> '(Counselling is)…when a person, occupying regularly or temporarily the role of counsellor, offers and agrees explicitly to give time, attention and respect to another person or persons, who will be temporarily in the role of client. The task of counselling is to give the client an opportunity to explore, discover and clarify ways of living more resourcefully and towards greater well-being. The counsellor provides a secure and facilitating atmosphere for this to occur…'

(BAC, 1977)

BOX 1.6 COUNSELLING CORE VALUES

Empathy 'A continuing process whereby the counsellor lays aside her own way of experiencing and perceiving reality, preferring to sense and respond to the experiences and perceptions of her client. This sensing may be intense and enduring with the counsellor actually experiencing her client's thoughts and feelings as powerfully as if they had originated in herself.'

Unconditional positive regard 'The label given to the fundamental attitude of the…counsellor towards her client. The counsellor who holds this attitude deeply values the humanity of her client and is not deflected in that valuing by any particular client behaviours. The attitude manifests itself in the counsellor's consistent acceptance of and enduring warmth towards her client.'

Congruence 'The state of being of the counsellor when her outward responses to her client consistently match the inner feelings and sensations which she has in relation to the client.'

Though this is only one definition, it contains many of the characteristics which are common to the array of definitions, and forms a useful starting point. To complete this definition, however, we need to draw attention to how the counsellor fulfils the task of counselling through the use of counselling skills and upholding the core conditions or core values of counselling which enable clients to trust their counsellors – empathy, unconditional positive regard and genuineness or congruence. For those who may not be familiar with these terms, Mearns and Thorne (1988) have provided useful descriptions of these core values (see Box 1.6).

This book places the emphasis firmly on these counselling values because it has at its core the belief that the use and abuse of counselling skills is at the heart of the ongoing problem situations which many deaf people experience. I feel that the institutional bedrock of rigid beliefs and misguided concepts of 'normality' which surrounds deaf people clings to the anchor so fiercely that counselling does not receive the respect or the professional value that it deserves in its capacity to engender a better quality of life through the empowerment of the individual and in its aim to prevent problem situations occurring and recurring. Deaf people are given precious little time within the framework of institutional beliefs and attitudes to explore their feelings, their perceptions, their ideas and their values, and it is only within a counselling relationship, where the counsellor is bound by professional ethics and standards, that they can hope to deal with problem situations through building a strong identity and a sense of self-respect in spite of the many forces opposing such developments.

Counselling is not 'a cure', but when counselling skills are used within an institutional framework which has as its foundation the aim of 'curing' through benevolent humanitarianism, counselling can come to be perceived as being 'a cure'. As accurate listening is the cornerstone of counselling practice, these wider and more generalised influences are of great significance within the counselling relationship, for both client and counsellor, because they can both enhance and inhibit listening. These influences cannot be avoided unless we live in some fantasy world where the counselling relationship, far from representing a journey to a place where growth can occur which connects with the mainland of the client's status quo, is likened to an island, surrounded by tides of immunity and cut off from the mainland of trends, tradition and history. Counsellors and clients are suspended in a system with a convoluted and changeable fabric, and core values which can be suspect since they hinge on inequality, an aversion to the truth, rock logic and communal innocence.

CHAPTER 2

The Challenge of the Unconscious – Personal Agendas

'Effective helpers undertake the lifelong task – perhaps struggle is a better word – of fulfilling the ancient Greek injunction "Know thyself." Since helping is a two-way street, understanding clients is not enough. It is essential to understand your own assumptions, beliefs, values, standards, skills, strengths, weaknesses, idiosyncrasies, style of doing things, foibles and temptations, and the ways in which these permeate your interactions with your clients. The adage "He who knows not and knows not he knows not is a fool – shun him" is relevant here: Helpers who do not understand themselves can inflict a great deal of harm on their clients.'

(Egan, 1990, p.25)

Truth is a difficult thing on which to compromise. Counsellors are in a position to see the client's truth perhaps because it is part of their skills training to nurture it, but also, I believe, because feelings and their expression are closer to the core of the individual than ideas and their expression, whatever the route of the expression. The client's human truth can threaten the foundations of an institution or society which has a philosophy based on knowledge, intellect or moral values, for example, because these things are necessarily narrow in their conception. In the previous chapter, we looked at some of the institutional and societal trends which come together to influence the way in which we think and feel about deaf people. We saw how difficult it is for the individual within the institution or society to ignore or escape their influence. Many counsellors working with deaf people internalise these influences so that they become part of an unconscious agenda which dictates their attitudes and assumptions about individual deaf clients. Deaf clients may also have been conditioned by these influences to believe that institutional and societal trends are the source of their problem situations. Their unconscious agendas may run so deep that they may carry expectations of oppression into counselling, supported by the low sense of self-esteem which most clients present. In this chapter our boats have set sail, but unconscious personal agendas, of both counsellor and client can determine the course of the journey and the tempestuousness of the seas they traverse, as the tides of the mainland counter attempts by the deaf client to rebuild their house of cards using bricks of

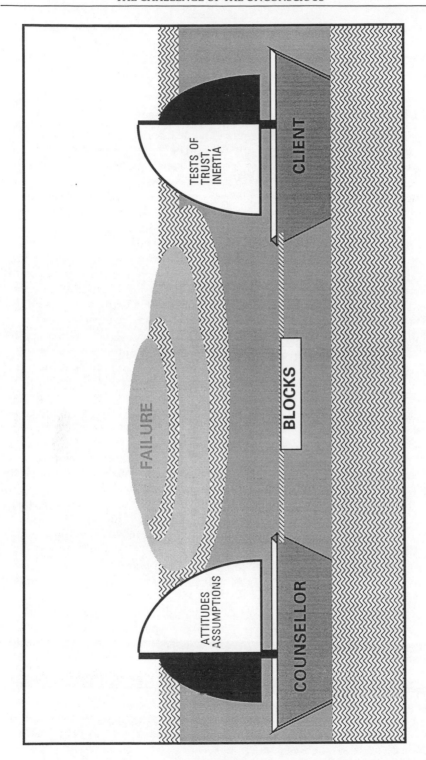

Figure 2.1 Early Tensions

self-awareness and self-esteem. It is important for counsellors to understand and work constructively with these agendas if counselling is not to become a battleground of negative and destructive feelings or the sandbanks on which our boats may be grounded.

THE STRENGTH OF THE SHADOW

Just as groups of people incorporate a great deal of diversity, every individual is a complex conglomerate of opposites. There can be no helper without helped, no power without powerlessness, no strength without vulnerability, no compassion without cruelty, no listening without ignorance, and no self without shadow self. It may be difficult for those of us who see ourselves as compassionate and good listeners to accept that we harbour the capability to be cruel or ignorant, but we must ask ourselves where sayings such as being 'cruel to be kind' and 'lying through one's teeth' come from. We may feel, for example that taking away another's responsibility for him- or herself is a form of caring because it makes life easier for him or her. It is after all hard work for us to take the responsibility, so we can feel immensely satisfied about our good deed and this reinforces our notion of caring. Caring is powerful. But what happens if, in the act of taking responsibility, we receive an angry rebuttal from the person whom we think we are helping? Instead of accepting without question their anger as theirs or considering the possibility that it might be justified, we may become aware of 'the devil on our shoulder' who taunts us with some somewhat unpleasant reasons for our motivation: 'She or he will never be able to manage that anyway', or 'It will be much quicker if I do it myself because I haven't got all day!' or even 'Deaf people need my help if they are to achieve anything at all.' When we become aware of our unpleasant companion, the most common reactions are that we *deny* his or her existence, *pretend* we haven't noticed him or her, attempt to *justify* his or her existence, or *blame* him or her for our beliefs and our actions. How often do we catch people saying: 'Of course, I don't *really* feel that way, but…' or 'Well that's what *all* the text-books say…' or 'There *is* more to life than work'? These are all attempts to explain away behaviour which we know to be unacceptable, but which we have not recognised as ours (Harding, 1965).

Unfortunately, blaming, pretence, denial and justification will not make our companion disappear altogether, because he or she is, like our shadow, a part of us which waxes and wanes with the light with which we illuminate and view our true selves. For some, the shadow rarely sees the light, and is so deeply suppressed that it works entirely through the unconscious. For others, it is worn like a mask which bears the smile of justification, and, for yet others, it stares its owner in the face gaining strength from the collective shadow of the archetype.

There are some differences amongst counsellors over the importance to attach to masks and shadows. For example, Jungian psychoanalysts fully integrate the shadow into their practice, whereas person-centred counsellors, in their belief that human nature is essentially constructive, are sometimes seen to be 'over-optimistic and naive' because they do not appear to take on board the strength of the shadow:

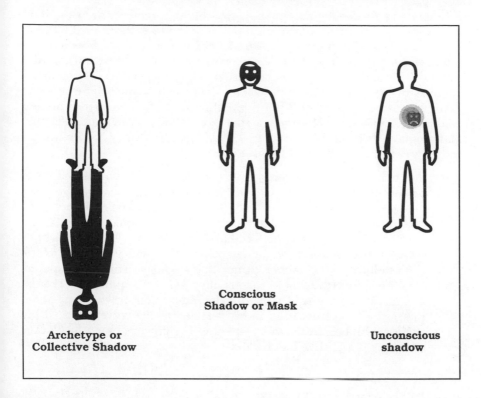

Archetype or
Collective Shadow

Conscious
Shadow or Mask

Unconscious
shadow

Figure 2.2 Masks and Shadows

'The person-centred counsellor, however, sees destructive behaviour and feelings as simply manifestations of the person who is by nature essentially constructive and self-preserving when that person is functioning under unfavourable conditions. Aggression and destructiveness are interpreted as resources which the person brings into play when his desire to grow is thwarted or threatened or when, in potentially terrible circumstances, his very existence is at stake.'

(Mearns and Thorne, 1988, p. 16)

It could be said that working with a client who is perceived to symbolise a threat to the *counsellor's* desire to grow may represent exactly the kind of unfavourable conditions which might lead the counsellor into destructive behaviour, for counsellors, in their quests to know themselves are in the business of personal growth and acceptance. For some and especially those who view counselling as a talking through of their client's problems, deaf clients may create unfavourable conditions as the counsellor's ability to empathise is apparently blocked. Yet a counsellor who is unable to communicate with their deaf client, might not be fully aware of the ways in which empathy can be developed. She has probably not ventured into the deaf community in an attempt to understand why she feels threatened by deaf people and how she might use this understanding in learning how to communicate with them. If she sees deaf people as a client group with whom she can suddenly and miraculously develop empathy and genuineness within the confines of the counselling relationship, she risks her counselling sessions becoming an arena for her own self-exploration at her client's expense. In such conditions, it might therefore be said that those who are of an impressionable and sanguine disposition or inexperienced in their trade may be pursued by the biggest and most threatening shadows:

> 'For many people, the shadow is a shameful secret that must at all costs be kept from view; and we have the extraordinary idea that we must not show our common humanity, which is after all half an animal, to each other for fear of moral condemnation. In consequence, we attempt to show each other only perfection, and the strain of the effort is both an intolerable burden and a guarantee that we will always fail in our expectations... One cannot change one's shadow, still less dispel or exorcise it, by criticism or condemnation; what is required is a change of conscious attitude. The more balanced a man in permitting some inferiority to express itself in his personality, the more balanced his shadow will be; but the more strenuously righteous he is, the blacker and more destructive the shadow.'

> (Greene, 1976, p. 97–98)

Jung (1959) stressed that our unconscious thoughts and feelings are strongly drawn towards conscious awareness only when our conscious behaviour 'adopts a false or pretentious attitude'. We react instinctively and defensively if the unconscious behaviour of our shadow, on seeing the light, is confronted. If I, as a deaf person, challenge hearing people about what I genuinely see to be their discriminatory behaviour towards me, their reaction in most cases will be denial in the form of 'extreme anger and an outburst of enraged justice grossly disproportionate to the observation, which may be a true one and constructively offered' (Greene, 1976, p.96). It is probable too that the sense of outrage will be thrown back at me with accusations that their behaviour is my fault because I have 'a problem with my deafness'. Yet I get angry because I care about relating. Because the shadow is the individual's personal unconscious, beneath the level of conscious awareness, it can be made conscious without too much difficulty, or with lack of insight, by slips of the tongue and other 'mistakes' which reveal feelings and motives which the conscious self disowns (Storr, 1983).

DISCOVERING THE SHADOW SELF

The shadow is often projected onto others; that is to say, in disowning it as ours, it is all too easy for us to treat it as if it were a part of another person or people. Thus, if a hearing person is afraid of being deaf he or she may become, by the process of projection, afraid of deaf people, and this inclination to see deaf people as frightening or even life-threatening determines his or her

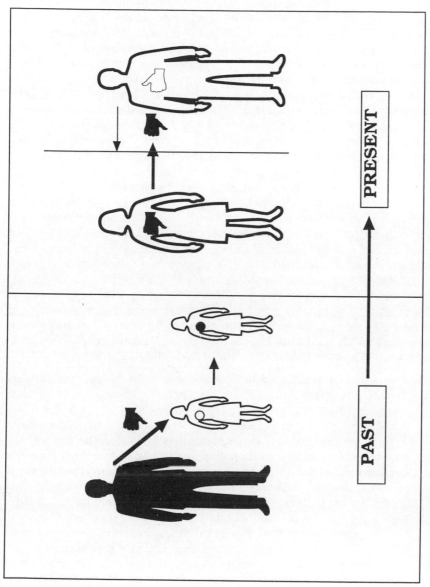

Figure 2.3 Transference

behaviour towards them. This person may not be aware of this behaviour in themself but it tends to be all too visible to deaf people who may then introject it and treat it as part of themselves. They become the hearing person's behaviour towards them. There is a risk that deaf people who have introjected such behaviour will then transfer it onto future relationships through unconscious and general assumptions that 'all hearing people are the same', regardless of whether or not it is appropriate.

The concept of *transference*, when described in this way, can be used constructively within a counselling relationship especially if the counsellor is seen by the client to be representative of hearing people and precipitates a transfer of client feelings. There are differing views, however, about the reciprocal counsellor behaviour, which is called *countertransference*. Truax and Carkhuff (1967) view countertransference as a lack of genuineness on the part of the counsellor, and express concern about the effect of the counsellor's unconscious, sometimes irrational, feelings on the client when the client has unwittingly aroused these feelings. Put simply the client does not know what has hit him or her, nor why. Jacobs (1988) takes the more balanced view that counsellor feelings, if they remain unconscious or subject to any of the denying behaviours outlined above, can become an obstruction through countertransference. When hearing counsellors work with deaf clients, the relationship is likely to be very similar to that which can be observed in transcultural counselling because, when counsellors work across, through or beyond their cultural differences, oppression can become part of the process. d'Ardenne and Mahtani warn against the very subtle ways in which countertransference can ambush the transcultural counselling relationship:

> 'Counsellors are unlikely to examine their own racism and cultural prejudice. As a consequence of this neglect, unacknowledged prejudice is reflected back unconsciously in the counselling relationship. When this occurs, the client no longer experiences unconditional positive regard, genuineness and empathic understanding in the counselling relationship, and may consequently withdraw. Worse than this, the unaware counsellor only perceives the client's withdrawal as non-compliance or resistance. This dissonance in the relationship results in both parties having their beliefs about the other's culture reinforced...counsellors tend to blame their clients as being unable to verbalise their feelings, unwilling to postpone gratification, or refusing to co-operate with treatment. Under these circumstances, counsellors communicate in an abrupt, critical and distant manner... Transcultural countertransference is not just about attitudes to other cultures. It touches our deepest fears as counsellors about being seen as judgmental and tribal.'

(d'Ardenne and Mahtani, 1989, pp.81–82)

The deaf world is full of examples of these processes, and they are particularly prone to appear in informal helping situations where helpers are off-guard or preoccupied. A common one, which I have also experienced in counselling, is that of a Deaf client who refuses to (as opposed to chooses not to) use their voice in the presence of people whom they perceive to be hearing, because, in the past, they have observed hearing people's reaction when they do and have internalised the view that their voice is 'bad' and a symbol of hearing people's rejection. These clients will frequently use their voice when with other Deaf people. An unaware counsellor can run the risk of projecting anger or irritation in countertransference because they may feel unconsciously that the Deaf client is deliberately not using his or her voice in order to turn the tables on the counsellor by introducing a block to communication. Conversely, a counsellor who has embraced the possibility of cultural differences between Deaf and hearing people may create difficulty for a client who has not, as happens when Fiona first meets her client, Tessa.

BOX 2.1 TESSA AND FIONA

Tessa turns up for the first session on time, though Fiona, having been waylaid by a Deaf student in reception, is ten minutes late. Tessa observes Fiona and the other student from a distance, but does not realise that it is her prospective counsellor she is watching. When Fiona finally comes to find Tessa, angry with herself for being late with a new client, she notices that Tessa is wearing hearing aids and, in part because she has not switched off from her previous encounter, greets Tessa with 'Hello Tessa, I'm Fiona. I'm so sorry I'm late. Let's go into my office so that we can talk without interruption', using BSL with minimal lip patterns. Tessa, who has become anxious about Fiona's lateness screams at her 'Don't use that stuff with me!' and storms out in tears!

Fiona manages to retrieve the situation by writing to Tessa and apologising for her mistake. She suggests that they might start again by talking about Tessa's communication needs, and sends her a further appointment. Tessa does return to see Fiona the following week.

There are of course deaf people who choose not to use their voice as a positive indication of their political and cultural affiliation to other deaf people,[1] but it is extremely important to distinguish between the positive and the negative roots of this behaviour, and how they may influence counselling process. If counsellor feelings are acknowledged for what they are, countertransference, like transference, can be useful within the counselling relationship. We will explore their use further in the following chapter and in Section 2.

Of course it is not humane nor even morally right for a hearing person to behave badly towards a deaf person because they may be deeply afraid of what that deaf person represents. We know that, and that is precisely why we deny such behaviour in ourselves. The shadow can therefore become a moral problem which challenges the whole self-concept. Recognising the darker

---

[1]   Because BSL and English cannot be delivered simultaneously as a result of their completely different structures, it is common for BSL users not to use voice or lip patterns, in order that BSL can convey its natural clarity and meaning.

aspects of our personalities as present and real is imperative for any kind of self-knowledge. This is why the shadow within meets with considerable resistance and why denying its existence can have catastrophic effects on the development of self and identity, and our relationships with others.

Because, at the same time, some of us may refuse to believe that we are even capable of behaving in such a way, or worse still, in communal innocence, we consciously justify our behaviour on the grounds that it is the majority behaviour, we can be successful only in revealing our inner motivation to have power over deaf people through our stereotypical behaviour towards them. These circumstances, which are created by the environmental forces of the collective shadow, can support the formation of archetypes – the predispositions to experience life in more or less stereotypical ways outlined in the previous chapter. Archetypes are not so easy to make conscious, but the collective shadow that they throw can be immensely destructive, because it is the archetype which is built into alienism or the root processes of all oppressive behaviour. The above discussion on projection, introjection and archetypes enables us to build up a clearer picture of the cycle of alienism.

UNDERSTANDING OPPRESSION

Because personal agendas are unconscious, the key to preventing them from becoming destructive blocks to counselling process lies in acknowledging

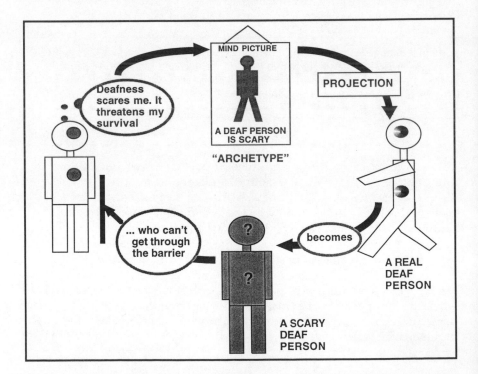

Figure 2.4 The Cycle of Alienism

when they exist within ourselves. An important starting point in achieving this is to look at our conscious behaviour, identify aspects of it which may be assumptive about or discriminatory towards deaf people and give a name to the thoughts and feelings which cause this behaviour. Most of us are familiar with terms such as 'sexism', 'racism' and 'prejudice', perhaps because they are enshrined in the law of the land and are therefore given the kind of exposure which enables and enhances understanding. By the same token, feminist counselling and transcultural counselling are given a place amongst the 'legitimate' or 'acceptable' approaches to counselling (d'Ardenne and Mahtani, 1989; Chaplin, 1988). Whether we fully understand what the terms mean both for ourselves and for those who are discriminated against by these behaviours, and are aware of whether we have a tendency to be sexist or racist towards women or Black people, is quite another matter. If we have experienced direct or indirect discrimination, we may only know it as something which gives us a bad feeling, because we are uncertain how to assign the labels 'sexist' or 'racist', or are reluctant to do so for fear of recrimination from those who make us feel bad and whom we generally perceive as being powerful. A lack of knowledge can, in turn, lead us to assume that if a person is both Black and a woman, the effects of discrimination will be cumulative rather than complex or simultaneous (Stuart, 1992), even though this may not be an accurate representation of what that person feels. This is perhaps a consequence of separating gender and race in legislation rather than acknowledging the root behaviours which lead to imbalances of power in our society, and which assume importance in the counselling relationship.

This lack of acknowledgement is symptomatic of the desire to view people in terms of their component parts instead of seeing them as a whole, and has led to the trends towards seeing deaf people's problem situations only in terms of their deafness, which this book sets out to challenge. Further, because deafness, like homosexuality, is seen by the majority as being 'not normal', terms such as audism, hearism and homophobia do not occur in most people's vocabulary. To paraphrase Dominelli's definition of racism (1988, p.6), audism or hearism is about the construction of social relationships on the basis of an assumed interiority of deaf people (the minority group), and, as a result their exploitation and oppression by the dominant hearing–speaking majority. Through this definition we can observe the links to alienism, but it is important also to establish why these terms are preferred as opposed to others which are commonly used. For example, the term oralism is traditionally afforded negative connotations by Deaf people because it has come to be seen as a representation of the linguistic centrism which signifies the oppression of Deaf people as a linguistic minority. 'Oral', in the layperson's terms, relates to spoken language, and, as we have seen, there are many deaf people who use spoken language themselves and experience linguistic oppression through the explicit or implicit attribution of different meanings to commonly used descriptive terms when they are ascribed to deaf people. These different meanings are often unconsciously conveyed through body language and facial expression or by undue emphasis on particular words in a sentence (which can be perceived in lip patterns), and this can result in the deaf person being left feeling that behaviour which is acceptable in most hearing people is not acceptable in deaf people (Anon, 1993). This wider definition of linguistic oppression allows for the possibility that all deaf people can potentially experience linguistic oppression, with the historical suppression of sign language as an extreme example. Just as there are different kinds of racist behaviour, there are different kinds of linguistic oppression which can lead to an atmosphere of harassment and intimidation or lead to an imbalance of power within the counselling relationship. However, in the same way that racial abuse and insulting behaviour are not the only examples of racism, linguistic centrism is only part of audism. Oralism therefore seems of limited use in this context. Hearing is vital for optimum speech development and full command of spoken language. It is therefore the dominant majority's ability to hear rather than their ability to speak, and the curious dichotomy which has been created between silence and sound which is the primary source of deaf people's oppression from which all other oppressive practices stem. 'Silent' or nonvocal language confuses those who are accustomed to space being filled with sound, such that members of some cultures who are in full possession of their auditory sense, and value silence by ascribing different meaning to it, are the focus of negative stereotyping in the same way that deaf people are:

> 'We hear people say that Athabaskans are "passive", "sullen", "withdrawn", "unresponsive", "lazy", "backward", "destructive", "hostile", "uncooperative", "antisocial" and "stupid". And these are not just the attributions of ignorant bigots… Athabaskans, at least, are building on a different metaphor. At Fort Chipewyan, Alberta, for instance, "quiet" is a term for knowledge, control, cooperation, attention to others, and a socially productive attitude. Basso (1979) has passed on to us the views expressed by some Apaches in their portraits of "Whitemen" of the "warmhearted", "talkative", and "outgoing" qualities as negative values in most contexts.'

(Scollon, in Tannen and Saville-Troike, 1985, pp. 24–27)

The Athabaskan conceptualisation of 'quiet' should be familiar in a different sense to counsellors, who often use silence to demarcate boundaries within the counselling relationship. But is this in full recognition of the double standards we may be setting in ascribing non-vocal communication or inner speech[2] a negative stereotype in the case of deaf people? What is the difference between expression in sign language and the written language in which I write this book? I suspect that the answer lies in the quality of presence. Through the words I write here, the reader is given only an essence, a flavour of my presence. But if I were before the reader peppering space with the sound of my silence, the effect would be much more immediate – I would be present and observable, as counsellors know from their experience of silence in the counselling relationship. Our concern as counsellors must be to pay attention to our unconscious tendency to attribute negative stereotypes to deaf people so that we can prevent this developing into a more overt and readily observ-

---

2   See Chapter 4 for further explanation of these terms within the context of communication.

able discriminatory practice, such as deliberately simplifying a complex communication because we believe a deaf person to be incapable of understanding the full version, or turning our back to continue a conversation with another hearing person when a deaf person enters the room.

It is important for me to understand both the whole person who is my client, and how the multitude of inner responses that I have to him or her can become the cover of my book or those which I overtly express to my client. I cannot easily place myself in a hearing–speaking person's inner world despite the fact that I lived there once and have its language, however much empathy I can muster, as we shall see in Chapter 7. But what I can do is examine the feelings that I have and place them in an appropriate context and in relation to particular individuals using the kind of knowledge generated by the above discussion. From this position, I can attempt to own my prejudices and face up to them. Two contrasting examples may help here.

The first example concerns one of my own painful awakenings to the fact that I harbour prejudice within. I was on a bus recently, going nowhere in particular and spending my time, as I am given to do, observing the scenery and my fellow passengers. At one stop there was a substantial bustling and changeover of passengers such that I could not get a clear view of who got on and off the bus. When the bus moved off, there were new passengers in the two rows of seats in front of me, whom I could only see the backs of. In the front row, there appeared to be sitting an elderly woman and a man and in the seat in front of me there was a middle-aged woman and a child. The elderly woman wore a woollen hat with a bobble on it, which was clearly a source of amusement to the child who periodically reached forward and knocked the bobble, much to her mother's chagrin. Eventually, the elderly woman moved to another seat because she was not enjoying this 'game', and so the child started playing a different game with the man who remained. She tapped him repeatedly on the shoulder and then sat back in her seat when she thought he was going to turn round. Her mother again tried to intervene unsuccessfully. At the next stop, the man got off the bus and was replaced by an elderly man with a humorous face. The child began her antics again, but this man turned round and grinned at her every time she touched him, so that she eventually stopped her game, happy and contented that she had got the response to her mischievousness that she wanted. The mother turned to speak to her and in so doing caught my eye and smiled at me, so that the child turned round and looked at the person her mother had smiled at. She was not a child, but a young adult with Down's syndrome, and I immediately felt the pit of my stomach plunge as I searched inside myself for an avenue of escape. I smiled at 'the child' through the mask of my shadow.

I always embarrass myself when I have this reaction to people with Down's syndrome or cerebral palsy. I know in my heart that they may be locked in the same kind of cage that I find myself in from time to time and that I can make assumptions about what I observe. That is my prejudice. I can hear my inner voice saying 'counsellor – heal thyself!', and as a result I always question myself about the source of my feelings. On a surface level, I was afraid that the mischief might turn her attentions to me, presenting me with a difficult communication situation. Accustomed as I am to dealing with such situations on a one-to-one basis, I am not comfortable with them in group settings or in public. But, on a deeper level, she represented for me something that I have an unconscious fear of – a sacrifice of all the things I have fought hard for and have come to value in myself. It was therefore much harder for me to recognise that I was unconsciously projecting this fear onto this young person, and at risk of not seeing or accepting her happy and mischievous demeanour in the way that her mother obviously could.

It is painful to acknowledge that I can give a home to prejudice, all the more so when the particular nature of the prejudice is like a mirror of and a contrast to examples from my experience with many hearing people. I have lost count of the number of times I have mutually muddled my way through a communication block with a hearing person without making reference to my deafness, and then, when it becomes necessary to refer to it, the word 'deaf' has a sudden sobering effect on the hearing person who then withdraws their co-operation having been given some kind of implicit permission that they are absolved of any responsibility for the communication block. It is as if the label 'deaf' acts as an unconscious trigger, a justification for them to change their behaviour towards me with a pitying look and 'I'm so sorry.' This is true of most of the labels which are used to describe deaf people, often inappropriately, for they can create a very misleading impression of the individual, as Catherine discovers when Robert is referred to her, accompanied by a written case history which is littered with negative stereotypes of deaf people (see Box 2.2).

Catherine misinterprets Robert's statement that he is unable to hear her, believing him to mean that he is unable to understand her because in the absence of any concrete information about Robert she makes an assumption that he won't benefit much from using hearing aids given the information about his hearing loss. Robert in fact makes good use of his residual hearing, and is dependent on his hearing aids.

This kind of unquestioning assumption is the reality of many deaf people's lives within the dominant hearing society. Whereas it could be said that my reaction to people with Down's syndrome is representative of how alienism might appear to the conscious, it is, within this definition, difficult to place my unconscious, automatic reaction to hearing clients I have worked with in counselling, because alienism has its roots in the exploitation of the weaker by the stronger through oppression. As deaf people are traditionally seen as 'the weaker' party in deaf–hearing interactions, my anger and despair at the discrimination I experience from hearing people is not oppressive, but a reaction to something in them which has touched me within the counselling relationship or through transference from the past. By being alert to experiences such as these in my life outside the counselling role, by broadening my experience of people generally through social interaction and reading, for example, I can begin to build what I have learnt into my personal agenda, and guard against its inappropriate or unexpected interference in counselling process. Feelings have a natural transience if only this were allowed to happen.

BOX 2.2 ROBERT AND CATHERINE

Robert arrives late for the first session. He refuses to look Catherine in the eye or communicate with her, and curls up on the chair in a foetal position, staring at the wall. Catherine has been told, among other things, that Robert is 'severely deaf', so, after allowing him some minutes silence and observing his body language carefully, she attempts to draw him out verbally, speaking clearly and calmly:

C:'Would you like to talk about it?'

Robert does not respond. More silence.

 C:(*more deliberately*) 'Robert, you seem a long way away. Would you like to talk about it?'

Prolonged silence.

C:'Robert, I need you to show me where to begin. Perhaps if I explain to you why I am here? Will that help? Sometimes counselling can be confusing if you've never done it before.'

More silence. Robert continues to stare at the wall. Catherine explains what happens in counselling clearly and briefly, watching for non-verbal responses or changes in body language. After fifteen minutes there is still no response. She moves her chair so that she is sitting within Robert's gaze, and mimics the position he is sitting in. She remains silent for a few more minutes, then notices that he is looking at her.

C:'Is this what it feels like Robert?'

Robert fidgets nervously.

C:'I feel sort of lonely sitting here.'

R:(*slowly and hesitantly*) 'I...can't...hear you.'

C:(*pauses*) 'How would you prefer me to communicate with you? Can you read my lips, or would it help if I signed?'

R:(Irritatedly) 'I *can't* sign... my battery is finished. *She* forgot to get me some more. I *hate* these things.'

CLIENT TESTS OF TRUST AND COUNSELLOR AGENDAS

As a counsellor, I am concerned with being genuine, and like most counsellors, there are times when I fail miserably to achieve this, or feel that I am unable to achieve this to such a degree that I cannot work with a particular client. Through listening to myself, I have learned to deal with my own alienating behaviour, and to recognise both the source of that behaviour and the processes whereby my clients become aware of the root feelings. If I fail to make the unconscious conscious, I know that there will be a block to empathy and trust. But I also recognise that I am not alone in my potential to create blocks. Deaf clients may also delay the start of the counselling journey or draw our boats in the direction of sandbanks through their own capacity to create blocks to listening. This happens either through direct and indirect *tests of trust*, or through *client inertia*. Again, this is largely unconscious behaviour which, though part of the counselling process with all clients, can be a result of how deaf clients have been taught to view themselves and the power imbalances that they have experienced in their lives through their oppression. There are times when the tests are more overt and have a quality which is specific to deaf clients.

Fong and Cox (1983) have suggested that there are three factors which seem to determine the form which tests of trust take with most clients. These are the time the client has been in the counselling relationship, the client's preferred mode of gathering information, and the extent to which the client prefers the direct or indirect approach to sensitive subject areas. My observations in working with deaf clients are that, in comparison to hearing clients, they pose more tests of trust, sometimes over a longer period of time. With some clients, it is not always clear whether their behaviour is a test of trust or whether it is cultural, or a consequence of living in a visual–spatial world. For example, I have had acute difficulties as a counsellor with the tendency of some Deaf clients to think in terms of linear as opposed to chronological time. They appear to think sideways rather than forwards or backwards, and to live very much from one event to the next rather than having a clear idea of natural time sequences, and the relationship between events. I know that there are reasons for this. Arnold (1990) cites three possibilities: a difference between the capacity of the auditory and the visual systems to process temporal information; a restriction in the amount of language which is available to describe the passage of time; and cultural deprivation as culturally deprived groups live more in the present than culturally secure groups.

But in practical terms this is still quite difficult to deal with because it means two things. First, these clients rarely keep to the time limits of the agreed contract, despite constant assurances that they have understood what these terms are. They may arrive late or at a time when they are not expected and will sometimes abruptly terminate a session before the agreed time is up, or expect me to prolong a meeting. They frequently fail to arrive for sessions without prior notification, despite the fact that I have a minicom. Second, they may have great difficulty with focusing, and will frequently take up much of the time within the session with a linear continuation of an event which has happened prior to the session. There does not seem to be any sense of having told a story before or any concept of counselling sessions being linked in time; therefore the same stories are told repeatedly without much variation. Sharon Ridgeway expands on this in Chapter 9. When I first began to work with Deaf clients, I felt as if it was not only trust that was being tested but also my patience. Through my own experience of being progressively deafened, I have learnt how much this has to do with living in a 'soundless' world, free from the many auditory and verbal indicators of the passage of time, and have begun to see this influence in my counselling style. I am told by hearing colleagues that I now have a tendency to become so focused on the present and so full of desire to see an event through to its natural conclusion that I am oblivious to time, and often irritated by forced or premature conclusions. When working with clients, I do not have the usual indicators that the next client has arrived and, regrettably, I have yet to work in an environment where visual indicators are standard or provided on request.!3•Moreover,aclockor watch is not sufficient because of the degree of focus and concentration on communicatiion required of me in the counselling situation, particularly when I am working with hearing clients and have to lip-read. Diverting my eyes to the clock for a split second may mean that I miss something important. Thus, with hearing clients, it always feels as if it takes me a great deal longer to obtain the same amount of information and absorb it in comparison to hearing counsellors, and this feeling is often reflected in deaf clients who are not receiving information through their preferred mode in counselling.

Deaf counsellors working with hearing clients will develop compensatory behaviours in dealing with this kind of situation, in particular by using a more direct approach in obtaining information from their clients. But this can conflict with the needs of clients who prefer a more indirect approach in sensitive subject areas or who feel more comfortable with a slower pace, and can appear didactic and directive when it is not intended that way. Likewise, some Deaf clients are very concrete in the way that they think and more direct in their expression of what they think, in part because they may have insufficient language to express abstract thought as a result of lack of relevant education, but also, for example, because of feelings of frustration connected to expression. This can be disconcerting for the unaware counsellor and may lead them into inappropriate ways of responding. A hearing counsellor I encountered recently said how frightening she found it when a Deaf client became angry. I asked her what it was about his expression of anger that frightened her so much, and she said that his facial expression was so directly aggressive that she thought he was going to hit her. It was as if he was nothing but his raw feeling of anger. She was uncertain of how to deal with it because she knew that on the one hand this client was always very direct with his feelings, and that the anger was not directed at her even if it felt that way to her; but on the other, her gut reaction was to self-disclose how threatened she felt by his anger at the risk that he would misconstrue her feeling as a rejection of his anger. She had insufficient experience of being with Deaf people to become familiar with the nuances of their communication and acclimatised to their directness, and harboured an unconscious desire to protect her client from other people's responses to his directness, which she risked projecting on to her client.

---

3   Deaf people generally require flashing lights which alert them to a door-bell, a telephone ringing or a fire alarm, for example. The latter comes under Health and Safety Regulations, and employers are therefore bound to provide flashing light fire alarms. The Department of Employment Special Aids and Equipment for Disabled People Scheme can supply other kinds of alerting devices in the work environment (as can Social Services in the home environment), but in practice, employers vary enormously in their knowledge of this scheme and their willingness to assist employers in this way, and many deaf people do not know how they can benefit.

Another example of client preference for directness or indirectness which may be based on cultural and linguistic differences, is where a client makes a direct statement to or asks a direct question of the counsellor which may be construed as a challenge or a way of inconveniencing. It is not uncommon for Deaf clients to ask many direct personal questions of counsellors such as 'You married?', 'Children have?', 'You sex like?',[4] or to issue direct statements which infringe the counsellor's personal boundaries: ' You bad attitude have!', 'She want you very bad fuck!'. If a Deaf client does not like you or your attitude, for whatever reason, he or she will generally tell you so, or walk out, and it will not always be easy to encourage him or her to return. It helps to remember that the feelings which result in this behaviour may be a projection of events past, where a Deaf person has learnt the hard way that hearing people will often turn their backs (a restrained form of walking out) rather than engage in stilted communication which makes them face up to their own fears and insecurities.

BOX 2.3 CLIENT TESTS OF TRUST

CONTENT: THE CLIENT'S TEST	PROCESS: THE REAL QUESTION	EXAMPLES (DIRECT AND INDIRECT)
Request for information	Can you understand me?	Is this room soundproof? You marry Deaf person?
Divulging a secret	Can I be vulnerable with you?	Father my, me sex have… Sometimes, I touch myself…
Asking a favour	Are you reliable and honest?	You tell mother my go Deaf Club OK? Will you come to the doctor's with me?
Self-denigration	Can you accept me?	There's no way I can become a teacher… Voice my horrible…
Troubling or annoying the counsellor	Are you consistent in the boundaries you set?	Help me phone? Minicom break I was talking to my friend (an excuse for lateness)
Questioning the counsellor's motives	Do you really care for me?	Do you think about me between sessions? You think sign language rubbish?

---

4   These are written as they would be signed.

BOX 2.4 CLIENT INERTIA

Passivity	Doing nothing, uncritically accepting others' goals and solutions, acting aimlessly, shutting down or blowing up (Schiff, 1975)
Learned Helplessness	Persistent and incapacitating failure to take responsibility for change (Seligman, 1975)
Disabling Self-talk	Excessive use of negative statements and reinforcements in communication e.g. 'I can't...' or 'It won't work' (Ellis and Dryden, 1987)
Vicious Circles	Communication or behaviour which goes round in circles and leads to defeatism and depression
Staying Disorganised	Continuous distraction with minor hassles and problems

BOX 2.5 ROBERT AND CATHERINE

C:(*pauses*) 'I have some batteries, Robert. You can change it now – if you want to, that is'.

Robert changes the hearing aid battery, fumbling, but remains sitting in a tense, foetal position, which Catherine continues to mimic.

C:(*reestablishing eye-contact*) 'Does that happen often Robert? Does she often forget things?'

R:(*flinging himself forward, angrily*) 'Don't talk to me about *her*. Typical bloody woman, always so bloody nosy and wanting the gossip. Poking your nose in when it's not wanted.'

C:(*pausing nervously, uncurling and leaning forward slowly*) 'You're right Robert; it is nosy to intrude into very personal things...I expect it makes you feel pretty angry?'

R:(*very quietly*) 'I feel bloody stupid, that's what. I never hear when I need to, not that it would make any difference to them anyway. They're not interested in *me*. They only really care about how easy life is for them...always taking the easy way out...everything's too much trouble. Sometimes I wish I was...*that* would be easy for them.'

C:'It sounds as if life is pretty hard for you at the moment Robert. Do you want to tell me more about it?'

Robert talks in fits and starts about what being deaf means to him. He uses expressions such as 'I *can't* do this because I am deaf...', 'They behave like this because I am *deaf*...', 'They *don't* understand...'. Every association made with his deafness is a negative one.

Fong and Cox (1983) have identified six common types of client 'tests of trust', which are shown in Box 2.3, together with examples which I have experienced with deaf clients. You will note that not all of these examples relate specifically to the client being deaf, but many have an added deaf dimension.

CLIENT INERTIA

Client inertia, or what stops clients from acting on their own behalf, can be a big obstacle when counselling deaf people. I have already pointed to the difficulty in coping with clients who tell their stories repeatedly, but there are some clients who have a way of telling these stories which can leave the counsellor feeling somewhat impotent. Again we need to reconcile the knowledge that many deaf people will have been on the receiving end of a power imbalance which has damaged their self-esteem and eroded their confidence in their capacity to act for themselves with that which suggests that the capacity for lasting change and growth lies within the client. Egan (1990) identifies five kinds of client inertia, though he stresses that these are not exhaustive (see Box 2.4).

Both Catherine and Fiona experience inertia early on with their clients Robert and Tessa.

BOX 2.6 TESSA AND FIONA

In the first session, and also in the subsequent four sessions, Fiona finds that she has to do a lot of listening, because Tessa talks at great length about herself and her experiences. Fiona listens carefully and with great attention, mentally noting recurring themes and issues which seem of particular importance for Tessa by listening for changes in Tessa's voice and watching changes in her body language. Tessa's themes and issues are, with Fiona's comments in brackets:

- longing for 'the past' and dwelling on memories ('distant looking')
- frequent use of the word 'But', followed by a statement which cancels out the statement preceeding the word ('disabling self-talk', 'learned(?) helplessness', 'vicious circles')
- a tendency to analyse even the smallest event in great detail as a means of avoiding focusing on major trauma ('sobbing intense'; 'rigid, withdrawn posture – like she's running away from herself'; 'looks terrified whenever really painful things begin to emerge')
- a desire to show Fiona how much she knows about life the attitudes and motivations of other people and how much she has read ('she knows more than I do', 'needs to control me – why?')
- persistent lack of eye-contact ('she seems afraid of mutuality and relating')

Throughout these sessions, Tessa cries a great deal ('she cries like she's crying for the world'), her monologues only interrupted when her sobbing becomes uncontrollable. Fiona manages to calm her by the end of each session (though she 'gets the feeling that the calm is from the exhaustion of continuous discharge of emotions'), but the crying starts again close to the beginning of the following sessions. In her own supervision, Fiona finds that she spends much of the time in tears when she talks about Tessa, and speaks of longing for some 'positive' counselling experiences and her 'powerlessness' in the face of the 'enormity' of Tessa's trauma. She feels 'overwhelmed by guilt' and 'desperate to break the stranglehold'.

Catherine notes that Robert accepts a variety of self-denigrating feelings, beliefs, images and thoughts without question, such that the 'disability' of his deafness has 'spread' to swamp his whole way of being and how he functions in relation to others. Harvey (1989, p.98) describes this process in another client (Mary) using the following analogy:

'Being hard of hearing became a noun for Mary, not an adjective; as if to view herself as "I am hard of hearing", rather than "I am a person who is hard of hearing".'

It is important to understand further that there may be an interaction between the client's culture or religion and their perceptions of themselves as a deaf or disabled person. In Chapter 5 we will look at native American attitudes towards and perceptions of disability, but there are some cultures where the perception of deafness or disability is extremely complex and multifaceted. For example, Jepson (1991) in a study of deaf people in India points to the system of attitudes and beliefs that structure the experience of deafness in the Hindu population. She found a range of attitudes from 'shame' and 'guilt' to the Hindi *prakritic* or concept of 'naturalness'. Clearly the former may produce a kind of inertia in some deaf people.

Egan argues that client inertia is unsurprising given that inertia is something of a fact of life, aimed at preserving 'an average' status quo:

'A friend of mine is a consultant to organisations. He told me about one larger organisation in which he worked with senior managers to transform the place. They did it right: diagnoses, identification of key issues, establishment of objectives, formulation of strategies, drawing up of plans. My friend went away satisfied with a job well done. He returned six months later to see how the changes were working out. But there were no changes: no one from the president down had acted on their plans. The managers looked sheepish and gave the excuses we all give – too busy, other things came up, couldn't get in touch with the other guy, ran into obstacles – the litany is endless.'

(Egan, 1990, p.95)

But Carl Rogers tells a similar story with a rather more sinister ending, which suggests that inertia can be the result of conditioning or dominance. It would therefore be wrong, in any circumstances, to blame deaf clients for inertia, but more appropriate to recognise how inertia finds a natural home in the deaf client's battered unconscious world:

> ' Recently I talked with this consultant. He told me that while the experimental plants continue to do extremely well, and he feels pride in the work he has done with them, he regards his work with the corporation as a failure. The top management, though appreciative of the increased profits and good morale of the experimental plants, has not moved to follow this model in their other plants, even though it appears evident that overall profits would be increased. "Why not?" I enquired. His answer was most thought-provoking. "When managers from other plants look closely at what we are doing, they gradually realise how much of their power they would have to give away, have to share with their employees. And they are not willing to give up that power." When I stated that it appeared that power over people was even more important than profits – which are supposed to be the all-important goal of industry – he agreed.'

(Rogers, 1983, p.250)

Inertia, like most behaviour, is learnt. Given the institutional, social and identity pressures on deaf people, which we discussed in the previous chapter, it is not difficult to see the implications that the above accounts might have for inertia in deaf clients, and for counselling process, when unconscious past learning is projected on to present situations. We will explore ways in which Fiona and Catherine dealt with this situation constructively in later chapters.

ACKNOWLEDGING COUNSELLOR AGENDAS

The skill of the counsellor lies in how far they are successful in minimising the inappropriate effects of their personal unconscious. A counsellor who does not 'know themself', or refuses to look at who they are and what they feel about deaf people both subjectively and objectively, is unlikely to change in the act of moving from practising as a person-centred counsellor to practising as a psychoanalyst, for example, though the different methodologies they employ may well change how they express their inner self and how this affects their relationships with their clients. This is especially so when, as we have seen, the odds are stacked heavily in favour of the stereotyping of deaf clients within society according to normative assumptions. Thomas and Sillen (1972) have developed a continuum of attitudes which white counsellors have towards black clients, which may form a useful basis for exploration of our personal unconscious. They suggest that most white counsellors are placed between two extremes of the continuum, though I have expanded this model in order that it can be more relevant to counsellors working with deaf people.

BOX 2.7 COUNSELLOR ATTITUDES

ATTITUDE CONTINUUM

Counsellor Attitude:

deaf people have 'the mark of oppression'; they have "chips on their shoulder", and their behaviour is pathological

deaf people become:

disabled victims of alienism

in counselling, deaf people feel:

dehumanised

Counsellor Attitude:

deaf people are no different from hearing people, so the consequences of alienism can be minimised

deaf people become:

hearing people with deaf ears

in counselling, deaf people feel:

they are the focus of assimilation

Counsellor Attitude:

deaf people are different; they have a right to be who they are and to have a strong sense of self-respect as deaf people

deaf people become:

people for whom being deaf is part of their identity

in counselling, deaf people feel:

accepted

The task of the counsellor

Attitudes towards and assumptions about deaf people are borne out of unconscious processes, and though it is rare to find a counsellor who engages in open display of their personal agenda, many counsellors will reveal subtle reminders of their inner world which will come to light in the 'unconscious supervision of the counsellor by the client' (Casement, 1985). Moreover, counsellor personal agendas cannot be dismissed lightly with the promise that the core values of counselling will be adhered to. Smith (1985) says that counsellors who protest that the only essential attitude required in counselling is one that contains empathy are 'burying their heads in the sand'. Empathy is of course a necessary requirement, but it is not sufficient on its own when, for example, hearing counsellors are working with deaf clients whom, historically, they have oppressed. d'Ardenne and Mahtani (1989) suggest that counsellors who insist that they are non-judgemental with all their clients may be "rationalising and avoiding different cultural and racial conflicts' within themselves. Using their transcultural model as a foundation, counsellors working with deaf people must address certain questions to themselves, and listen to the answers, if they are to be genuine with their clients.

BOX 2.8 KNOWING OURSELVES

Am I afraid of being deaf?

Does the fact that I am deaf or hearing affect my attitude to my client?

Do I see my client being deaf as the cause of their problem situation?

Do I see my client being deaf as part of the solution to their problem situation?

Do I accept, acknowledge and understand my client's interpretation of being deaf?

Do I have expectations about my client being deaf which affect the outcome of counselling?

Does my prejudice in relation to deaf people have a bearing on the counselling relationship?

Does my prejudice in relation to deaf people affect the counselling relationship?

Once unconscious personal agendas become conscious, and we still fail to see what these behaviours do to our clients, we risk becoming more deliberate and contrived about the way in which we work with deaf clients in counselling. We no longer experience unconscious alienism so much as we *are* audist or paternalistic towards our clients. And such is the power imbalance within the counselling relationship – whether it is a result of the deaf client perceiving the counsellor as the professional expert, or the counsellor being perceived as 'hearing' – that our clients may not realise that we are abusing their trust in us. Through their own self-defeating personal agendas, clients can inadvertedly encourage audist or paternalistic behaviour in counsellors through the awakening of their unconscious urges. This combination of factors and the different levels of responsibility assumed by counsellor and client will cause the counselling relationship to move in a particular direction with respect to client growth and counsellor power, as we shall see in the following chapter.

CHAPTER 3

MAKING THE UNCONSCIOUS CONSCIOUS –
ROLES AND RELATIONSHIPS IN
COUNSELLING DEAF CLIENTS

'We might in fact compare roles with musical scores. In some scores the composer has indicated not only every note of the melody and harmony he wants played, but also every nuance of expression he wants brought out. In others, there is simply an unfigured base-line and the performer is left to add his own melody, harmony and expression.'

(R.S.Downie, 1971, p.133)

In the previous chapter, we explored the psychological processes whereby the unconscious agendas of counsellors and deaf clients can come to light within a counselling relationship to different levels of awareness. These processes can seem somewhat ethereal, almost to the point where they are forced to remain unconscious unless we can examine how the interplay of personal and professional agendas occurs within the counselling relationship between different deaf clients and their counsellors. Reaching such an understanding has a number of different dimensions. At a basic level, we need to build a practical picture of the counselling role, as distinct from an advisory or guidance role, for example. Because deaf clients and counsellors are *people-in-roles*, we need to identify different counsellor behaviours and counselling styles and how these interact with different client behaviours to influence the development of a counselling relationship. This means that we also need to look at the people themselves, their *professional identity*, their own *internal role conflicts*, and the *role boundaries* which are established within the context of the counselling relationship. Our boats are steered not only by self-knowledge and understanding, but also by our awareness of what we do, and how we behave in different professional and personal roles and in different kinds of relationships consciously or unconsciously, as this may influence our work with deaf clients in different ways. This awareness ultimately determines whether the deaf client perceives the counsellor to represent an iceberg with two-thirds, perhaps the most dangerous two-thirds, out of sight below the water line, or a rock which provides firm anchorage, safety and containment when the client is floundering.

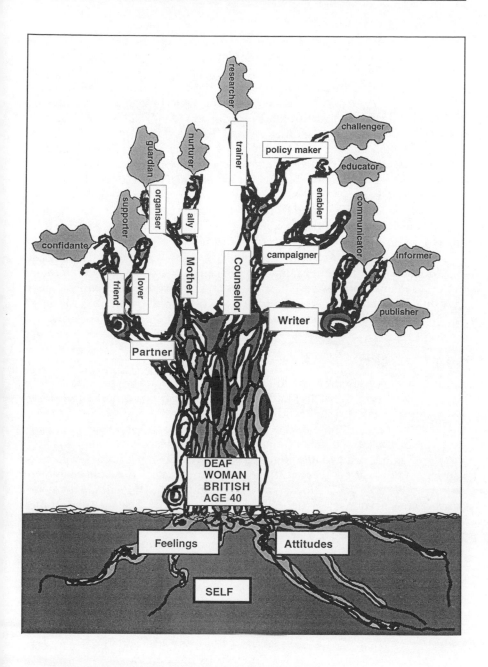

Figure 3.1 Role Tree

THE CONCEPT OF ROLE

We have made many implicit references to roles. On the one hand, counsellors are not always solely counsellors (though they may, for the most part, be hearing) and clients are deaf *people*, which implies that they will have many characteristics other than being deaf. Role definitions may therefore range from 'teachers', 'managers', 'social workers', 'psychologists', 'researchers' (*achieved, primary roles*), through 'pastoral providers', 'advisers' (*achieved, secondary roles*), to 'men', 'women', 'gay', 'lesbian', 'Black' (*basic* or *ascribed roles*) and so on. Banton (1965), who developed the above role terminology, has also pointed out that people have *independent achieved roles*, for example, voluntary work or being a school governor, and to this Ruddock (1969) adds *transient roles* because people can change roles in the course of a single conversation and have different ways of behaving which point to different roles. So, as Ruddock continues, a person could be seen in terms of a role tree. My role tree, for example, might look something like Figure 3.1.

I have found this a useful way of getting to know and understand myself as a functional, multi-dimensional human being; it also serves as a reminder of the part of me which exists below the surface of the ground, to which I must give due attention if it is not to become the two-thirds of the iceberg, for these are my roots, the fundamental *me* which influences all the roles I occupy.

ROLE DEFINITIONS

It must be obvious by now that the concept of 'role' is not always clear, nor is it consistent, and I think it would be fair to say that professionals working with deaf people are not generally encouraged to explore the different roles that they occupy and how these might compete or conflict. The average job description of a 'trained professional' working with deaf people demands that they be all things to all people, perhaps because of the shortage of people who can work with deaf people in different roles, and the lack of resources which might enable role separation and a more efficient use of skills. However, counsellors and counsellor supervisors working with deaf clients *are* required to be more accountable from this perspective:

> 'Because there is a distinction between line management and counsel-ling supervision, where a counsellor works in an organisation or agency, the lines of accountability and responsibility need to be clearly defined, between: counsellor/client; supervisor/counsellor; organisa-tion/client; organisation/supervisor; organisation/counsellor; super-visor/client.'
>
> (BAC Code of Ethics and Practice for the Supervision of Counsellors, 1988, C(2.11))

It is therefore important that we begin to understand the concept of role, and why clarity, and therefore consistency, is sometimes difficult to achieve. There are a number of ways in which we can view the concept of role. One useful framework is that developed by Downie (1971).

BOX 3.1 DEFINITIONS OF ROLES

ROLE DEFINITION	EXAMPLES
A class concept or the label attached to a group of individuals in virtue of certain properties they have in common.	We might use the label 'counsellor', 'teacher', 'social worker', 'psychologist', (professional labels) or 'deaf person', 'man', 'woman', 'Black person', 'disabled person', 'gay', or 'lesbian' (socio-cultural labels).
A part in a play subject to audience expectations.	A deaf person who plays the role of 'victim' may see themselves as a victim and expect people to respond to them accordingly.
The projection of an image or the adoption of a style of behaviour.	A councellor who believes Carl Rogers to be the doyen of good counselling practice may adopt Rogers' 'style' in modes of communication, dress and general mannerisms.
A set of causal–functional activities in a social system.	When deaf people are expected to underachieve in comparison with their hearing peers they are viewed as second class citizens (*de facto* concept); counsellors belonging to particular schools of thought are expected to adopt particular styles of counselling and therefore cannot be held responsible for the effect that their style has on individual deaf clients (*de jure* concept).

Adapted from R.S. Downie (1971)

The core values of counselling will be common to most counselling frameworks, and are enshrined in the British Association for Counselling's Code of Ethics and Practice for Counsellors (1984). They could therefore be seen as an example of the characteristics which counsellors have in common (Downie's first role definition). The 'how' of process and delivery, and the emphasis on particular theoretical considerations may differ from framework to framework because roles become defined in terms of the attributes of Downie's third role definition. From the counsellor's perspective, it is usually the case that counselling style is underpinned by its own dogma of knowledge, expertise or prejudice, and embodies its own set of attitudes and assumptions. These can act to generate a feeling amongst their followers that there is no alternative to the role presently occupied. We can divide psychodynamic counselling into the approaches developed by Freud, Jung and Klein, for example, but we could not so easily envisage separating the practice of Kleinian psychoanalysis from the particular orientation of psychodynamic theory proposed by Melanie Klein. When we begin to doubt this approach to theory, we begin to change how we practice, sometimes to the extent where what we do could only be very loosely defined as Kleinian psychoanalysis. Indeed, the Kleinian approach developed under Klein's guidance after she herself abandoned the polemics and hostility of the Berlin Psychoanalytic Society in favour of the support given by the British Psychoanalytic Society (Cooper, 1984). When professional counsellors support radical change within their own discipline, they tend to end up being ostracised or marginalised, some to the point where they are forced to dissociate themselves from their colleagues; the same is true of professional teachers or professional social workers. Counsellors, like all providers of support, are human and will always have a vested personal and professional interest in the 'success' of the counselling relationship; this is, after all, where counsellors gain their sense of professional respect and the trust of their clients. In this sense, the personal and the professional roles are inseparable. When this happens, counsellors may be tempted to adopt Downie's second and fourth role definitions because their personal uncon-scious comes into play. But perceptions of counsellor success can be very subjective, especially if success is measured in terms of an inappropriate model or standard. For example, Finkelstein says of the relationship between helpers and disabled people:

> 'The existence of helper/helped builds into this relationship normative assumptions. "If they had not lost something, they would not need help" goes the logic and since it is us, the representatives of society, doing the help, it is society which sets the norms for the problem solutions.'

> (Finkelstein, 1980, p.17)

Counsellors, whether in their counselling role or not, are representatives of society. They can therefore set the norms for perceptions of 'success', and, more importantly, the boundaries of the counselling process. Client 'success' is awkward to assess, however, primarily because objectivity is not helped by the difficulty in finding a measure of client experiences of counselling, and the reluctance of some counsellors to accept the challenges that their clients may pose to the counsellor's view of the counselling task because of their own deeply held beliefs, as we shall explore further in Chapter 5:

> 'Even though asking clients what their counselling was like for them may appear to be an obvious and highly common-sense course of action to anyone outside the world of counselling, it can be seen that it threatens some of the most fundamental assumptions held by counsel-lors about the nature of their craft, and by researchers about the nature of their enterprise. In addition, it is also essential to recognise that there are serious ethical and practical difficulties involved in doing research of this kind.'

> (McLeod in Mearns and Dryden, (1990), p.2)

Each of the roles we occupy will have different boundaries, different role expectations, different levels of involvement of individual, personal attributes and different socio-cultural assumptions. Professionals working with deaf clients, as we saw in Chapter 1, often end up working with deaf people in a counselling role after having first encountered the deaf client through some other role. There are a number of reasons for this, all of which are linked to perceptions of the qualifications required to interact with deaf people or to understand them, and the availability of 'suitably qualified' people, rather than to a clear understanding of the nature of the counsellor's task, the quality of their client's problem situations and their status as a complex individual. Thus if we believe that a teacher of the deaf, a social worker with deaf people or a Registered Sign Language Interpreter (SLI)[1] can 'communicate' with deaf people, we can fall into the trap of believing that only they can work as counsellors with deaf people, in just the same way as some of us believe that Deaf people cannot be teachers or counsellors. This may be an accurate, though somewhat simplistic belief, *if* there is a clear understanding on the part of the professional involved that the role expectations of 'teacher', 'social worker', 'SLI' and 'counsellor' are quite distinct from each other, as are the kinds of relationships formed with clients when in these roles, and the particular quality of the personal attributes that are brought to these roles. More often, however, these beliefs are a fallacy in professional terms, because they also belie the personal qualities which enable optimum skills in communication or counselling to be developed. Kyle and Pullen (1988) point out, for example, that it is possible to become a 'trained professional' working with deaf people without ever being assessed in ability to communicate with deaf people. It is certainly possible to 'counsel' deaf people without ever having received any counselling training or without having a knowledge of communication as an *interactive* activity. If we consider the qualifications of registered SLIs, we would discover that SLIs are trained to translate one language into another. This training does not necessarily indicate a skill in interaction with deaf people, but a skill in *translation*. The mental processes required to achieve accurate translation are immense because of the movement between a visual–gestural–spatial language and an auditory–vocal one. Hence, if an SLI is asked to recount the content or detail of something that they have translated, they are often unable to do so. This implies that the quality of listening required in the interpreting role is different from that required in the counselling role, though both kinds of listening are different to the listening that most of us engage in from day to day. The common emphasis on confidentiality with the respective codes of practice of interpreting and counselling, plus the promise of fluent communication can nevertheless lead SLIs in the direction of counselling either individually or as part of a counsellor–client–interpreter triumvirate; it can also lead clients to believe that interpreters may be 'good' counsellors. This is perhaps the underlying reason why deaf people often choose to share their problems with professionals whom they perceive to be 'caring' or 'nice', and why hearing professionals often become resentful of the role demands placed on them in deaf–hearing relationships (ADSUP, 1993). But whereas confidentiality is guaranteed, empathy, genuineness and unconditional positive regard, as the core conditions of counselling, may be unfa-

---

1   A Registered SLI is one who has undergone full training and has justified inclusion in the Central Register of Interpreters held by the Council for Advancement of Communication with Deaf People (CACDP) through rigorous assessment.

miliar to professionals working with deaf people in roles other than counselling.

Teachers are also drawn towards 'counselling', because they are involved in educating and communicating with deaf people, but they frequently fail to see the difference between a directive and a non-directive activity; and social workers with deaf people may see their 'caring' role as being compatible with the counselling role, without recognising that there are fundamental differences between this and the counsellor's perception of 'caring'. Barrie Rogers provides us with a graphic account of the difficulty this might pose for professionals working in education and their students:

> 'In a homogeneous educational unit...the personal tutor may have functioned as a "house parent" to a small number of students. These students would probably be on the same or similar courses, from the same or similar background, with the same or similar values with the tutor and each other. The tutor of such a group advised primarily on academic performance when required but would safely leave students alone, if that was his or her style. Working in that manner, the personal tutor reduced pressures on Counselling Services and may, indeed, have had the effect of making such services largely unnecessary. With loss of homogeneity this is no longer the case. Personal tutors continue to exist, however, – but for what purpose? Answers to that question differ. Some become no more than academic advisers; others become the first line of defence, the first port of call in personal crisis. This creates problems of stress for them. How, for example, are students allocated to personal tutors, (= ethnicity, sex, gender preference, value systems shared, subject choice, counselling skills of tutor)? Is it any wonder that staff in personal tutorial roles, and students who may have as personal tutors their teachers and assessors, experience role confusion and role diffusion, finding it difficult at any particular moment to answer those questions:"Why am I here?" (and) "What am I anyway?". These questions now appear, in this context to be questions of Role confusion – v – Identity.'

> (Rogers, 1993, p.38)

ROLE BOUNDARIES

In our counselling role, the question of who we are for our clients is a key one as is how and whether we establish appropriate role boundaries with our clients. There is of course a very important distinction between having a role and *being in* a role. This is because people occupy roles and to a large extent are moral agents in these roles. Indeed Existentialists such as Jean Paul Sartre argued that people who continuously take refuge in a role and ignore their moral agency as human beings are insincere, using the role concept as a means of evading personal relationships and pretending to themselves that they are not responsible for their own decisions because their role is defined for them by others. Such people often show stereotyped or rigid role behaviour.

In the professional domain, a teacher of the deaf would be showing stereotyped or rigid role behaviour if they adhered to a particular approach to communicating with deaf students and refused to try a different approach when their approach with one student is clearly not working. They are effectively allowing this particular student to fail before all possible options have been explored. They may exonerate themselves of blame for this failure by pleading LEA Policy, the 'right' approach, or their terms and conditions of employment, without considering the student's perception of the situation. The same may be true of a Head teacher who cuts resources for a secondary PHU[2] based in his or her grant-maintained school leading to lower standards of education for deaf students. He or she may say they have no choice because Section 2(3b) of the 1981 Education Act says that integration of pupils with special needs must be compatible with 'the efficient education' of the children with whom they are educated, and the education of the majority therefore required more resource priority. This Head teacher is at risk from placing a narrow interpretation of his or her legal responsibility above the needs of the deaf students. Another example in this category may be a College Principal who, on receiving a complaint from a deaf student about discrimination by staff at the college, chooses to ignore the College's Equal Opportunities Policy or pleads that the Policy is an ideal to be aimed for, though its provisions can rarely be achieved because it is not compatible with the efficient management of personnel or resources, or the maintenance of the good will of the majority of staff and students in the college. He or she is taking refuge in the stereo-typical role of 'detached manager', but in so doing is providing a poor *moral* role model for personnel.

The above appear to be examples of insincerity, though it is not immediately clear whether this is because the personal role of each of the individuals in question is played down or ignored. A professional who occupies a role that is more impersonal and detached may be in that role because they *are* impersonal and detached themselves or because they believe that the role expectations demand these characteristics of them when they are in the role. The former are less likely to accept their role as moral agents, though they may well see themselves as agents of social control. If we look at the last example again there is another approach that the College Principal could take which involves playing the role of 'manager', but not insincerity. If the Principal were to take the Equal Opportunities Policy as 'an ideal set of behaviours' which can be viewed as morally correct and therefore worth aiming for he or she can still play the role of 'involved-manager' by valuing people instead of resources. He or she may then find that his or her personnel are more aware, make better use of existing resources and meet higher professional standards so that the deaf student has no risk of discrimination and, therefore, no need to make a complaint. This involves choosing a different interpretation of the role of 'manager' which takes account of his or her

---

2   PHU - Partially Hearing Unit. These Units are located on the site of a mainstream school, with the aim that deaf children can experience 'integrated education' with their hearing peers for some or all of the time, using the specialist expertise of Unit staff.

function as a moral agent. The person-in-the-role is therefore acknowledged alongside professional role demands.

It may seem at first sight that these descriptions are not relevant to the practice of counselling. Surely counsellors would not bring such behaviour to the counselling relationship? Regrettably, many counsellors working with deaf people can and do because transferable personal characteristics lead to the *role confusion* and *role diffusion* that Rogers describes above. This is distinct from the role stereotyping or rigidity that we looked at earlier, and is important because of the nature of a person's general or basic role, which, as we saw earlier, represents the main trunk of the tree and the link between the roots (self-identity) and the branches which often determines whether a person's roles become 'a framework or a cage' (Reynolds, 1992). When the roots of the tree are diseased, it is not hard to see how the infestation can invade the person in *all* their roles. I have discussed boundary issues at length elsewhere with respect to professionals working with deaf young people in education (Corker, 1993b). The principles, which apply to all professional roles, are summarised in Figure 3.2, and are based on those used by Handy (1976, pp. 54 – 60). Most people experience role conflicts, overload, ambiguity and incompatibility, and some manage them better than others, but when counselling is a secondary achieved role, as is often the case with professionals who counsel deaf people, the difficulties with role management can intrude on the development of the counselling relationship, because the core values of counselling are abused in some way.

Roles and the Core Values of Counselling

In Chapter 1, we highlighted the core conditions of counselling – empathy, unconditional positive regard and genuineness or congruence, which create the conditions for client growth by allowing the client to feel safe in their trust of the counsellor. We also pointed out the importance of considering a 'transcultural' perspective in our work with deaf clients, in particular those who identify as a cultural minority. These issues will be explored further in Chapter 5 from a methodological perspective, which will enable us to develop our practice in the counselling role. The core conditions of counselling are not necessarily the core conditions of the other roles we occupy, though, as various authors have pointed out, there is no reason why genuineness, empathy and unconditional positive regard cannot become a foundation for other roles that counsellors working with deaf people occupy – in education (Rogers, 1983) or management (Hore, 1983) for example. Hore (p. 9) says that although managers are perceived, in simple terms, to be people who must achieve results through others and counsellors are concerned with the non-directive process which helps people to help themselves, 'there is enough overlap between the role of manager and the process of counselling to guarantee some common ground.' We saw above, how a College Principal might find this common ground and use it in a way which would benefit everyone.

Possibly the biggest factor preventing greater use of the core conditions of counselling in other roles lies in the assumption that these core conditions can

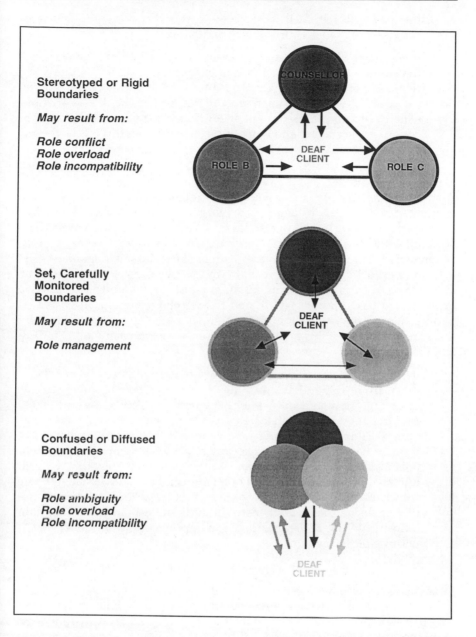

Figure 3.2 Boundaries

be maintained with very little work on the part of the counsellor. This is far from true, as Mearns and Thorne (1988) emphasise:

'The core conditions are simple enough to state, but for a counsellor to develop and maintain such attitudes involves a lifetime's work and demands a commitment which has profound implications not only for the counsellor's professional activity but for her (sic) life as a whole. (There are) complex issues involved when a counsellor attempts to be congruent, accepting and empathic.The words can trip off the tongue but their significance can be little short of awe-inspiring.'

(Mearns and Thorne, 1988, p.15)

At times, especially when the going gets tough, counsellors can slip into complacency which leads them to take refuge in another role which is not so demanding or taxing on their personal resources, and does not require them to examine the deeper parts of themselves, which as we saw in the previous chapter, are not always easy to live with. In practice, this might manifest itself in the counsellor becoming judgmental in their counselling role because anger, attempts to seize power and moral judgments, for example, are easier to express than to work with within and these feelings are indeed expressed within friendships. Counsellors are also under a great deal of pressure from their clients to express these feelings because their expression may be indicative that the counsellor cares about them:

'Users[3] often work very hard to elicit moral judgments about themselves from workers.[4] It is as if they are saying "Tell me you regard me as an important person by telling me how you dislike me", or "show me I'm important enough to be angry with." One of the major problems of establishing counselling relationship(s) is that few counsellees have been trained in counselling. They often misunderstand non-judgementalism as uncaring or evasive and work very hard to subvert a counselling relationship into the kind of relationship they understand, where shows of anger, attempts to control and moral judgments are evidence that someone cares about them. In addition, a thorough-going non-judgementalism denies the user the opportunity to find out what is permissible behaviour.'

(Gomm and Woolf, 1992, p.64)

Deaf clients, as we have already indicated in Chapter 1, are even less likely than hearing clients to have an understanding of the counselling process and why non-judgementalism is important. But there is an added deaf dimension to this for counsellors working with deaf people. A Deaf client who identifies with and engages in direct expressive behaviour may see *failure* to express such feelings as 'a bad attitude' on the part of the counsellor. A deaf client with low self-esteem or a disabled identity, however, may be completely demoralised by such expression, especially if it occurs in a negative way and at the

---

3   Receivers of helping services, or, in this context, clients.
4   Providers of helping services, or, in this context, counsellors.

beginning of the counselling relationship. Displays of such behaviour are, in their perception, *not* indicative of caring and they may perceive the counsellor to be uncaring if the counsellor drops their non-judgementalism. It is issues such as these which must be taken into account when establishing the boundaries of the counselling relationship with deaf clients. We will explore this further in later chapters.

Just as it is possible to transfer the core conditions of counselling between roles, it is also possible to transfer beliefs and values which work against the core conditions from other roles. A professional who, in their basic role, assumes that deaf people are 'weak', 'unintelligent' or 'unskilled' may unconsciously have difficulty with the idea that a deaf client can reclaim their personal power as a deaf person when contained by the boundaries of the counselling relationship. Through vague role boundaries, they continue with these unconscious thoughts and feelings in the counselling role, where such judgmental perceptions are inappropriate, and this results in their deaf clients feeling dehumanised or that they are disabled victims of oppression. Correspondingly, a deaf client may have a great deal of difficulty in trusting a professional in their counselling role because they are perceived by the deaf client to be unsympathetic, cold or authoritative in their role as a social worker, for example, and are apparently representative of one of the many layers of mistrust which have developed as a result of experiences with hearing people. This will clearly have implications for the client's perception of the counsellor's genuineness and ability to convey unconditional positive regard. Further, because empathy is fundamentally about feeling and communicating a deep, empathic understanding, using the kind of language described above will not encourage empathy with deaf clients, as we will see in the following chapter.

A deaf client may be unable to understand that hearing people bring different personal attributes to different roles because they have been encouraged to believe by past events that all hearing people are the same whatever role they are in. Indeed, this difficulty may be exacerbated with deaf clients because of particular characteristics of the Deaf community, for example, and the environments in which many deaf people have lived and been educated:

> 'Breaches of confidentiality have frequently been part of the experience of deaf women growing up. In school settings for deaf children, where a sense of "family" sometimes exists, administrators or teachers may be given access to information from counselling sessions. In hearing schools, confidentiality may be breached simply because hearing teachers and administrators find it easier to talk to hearing parents than to a deaf child. Such occurrences may contribute later on to concerns on the part of deaf women that confidentiality will not be respected by the therapist.'

> (Westerlund, 1990, p.106)

Counselling Relationships

The concepts of 'relationship' and 'relating' have a unique quality in counselling, not least because client growth, change and improvement are closely correlated to interpersonal counsellor characteristics, in particular empathy, genuineness and unconditional positive regard. A client may think they are being 'helped' by a counsellor who does not display these characteristics but who perhaps has a warm personality because clients generally approach counsellors when their sense of self-worth is low and they are more gullible to the kind of 'caring' and 'sympathy' which comes from such personalities. A deaf client may be unable initially to distinguish a counsellor from a friend and because they perceive the counsellor in this way, they may look for qualities associated with friendship. Again, this may be a result of the deaf community being small in comparison to the hearing community with the increased likelihood that the counsellor and client have encountered each other through some other kind of relationship. If the counsellor then fails to set and monitor the boundaries between friendship and counselling, the client, in the final outcome, will often *experience* counselling as an extension of friendship. In such circumstances, the client may be left with an uneasy feeling at the end of the counselling relationship that they have not moved from the position they were in at the start of the counselling relationship, because friendship, by itself, rarely effects *lasting* change in the individual.

The counselling relationship is different from a friendship and other kinds of professional relationships not only in its core values, but also in the way in which different kinds of relating can be used constructively to assist the client in discovering their internal resources and personal power. Clarkson (1990), for example, has identified five different kinds of relationship which are potentially available for constructive use in psychotherapy, though they may be equally applicable to other kinds of counselling. Using Clarkson's framework, I have tried to suggest examples of how these five kinds of relationship may manifest themselves in working with deaf clients (Box 3.2).

Power and Boundaries in Counselling Relationships

The relationship between a counsellor and a deaf client is often established on the basis that the counsellor has been handed power in another role and another context, which is in addition to the power that is automatically bestowed on the counsellor as a result of the counselling process. From the above discussion, it must be clear that the locus of power in counselling, that is the activity or the person in which power can be found, has several interpretations when working with deaf people. Power can be located in professional status, professional methodology, counsellor identity, the cultural matrix, hearingness and the use of the communicative infrastructure, the latter three being unique to working with deaf clients both directly and indirectly. For example, in very simple terms, a power inequality can be generated by the tendency of a deaf client who uses sign language to see a hearing counsellor who uses speech as more powerful. This can inhibit *client understanding* of counsellor styles and counselling processes and it can also limit the *effectiveness* with which the counsellor can work with the deaf client through such processes as transference. We saw in Chapter 1 that work with deaf people who have been abused presents particular issues in respect of power. If the counsellor uses his or her power to preserve a power imbalance, power becomes more akin to a form of social control.

BOX 3.2 COUNSELLING RELATIONSHIPS

TYPE OF RELATIONSHIP	EXAMPLE
The working alliance	When a deaf client first encounters a hearing counsellor, the client may be unsure of whether they can work together. The formation of a working alliance enables this to happen, through the counsellor setting clear boundaries, for example.
The transferential/countertransferential relationship	The experience of unconscious hopes and fears moving between counsellor and client. This kind of relationship may be forged when a hearing counsellor is unable to accept their deaf client's view that because they are hearing, they are part of the client's oppression. The client may then feel rejected and the possibility for deeper exploration of the client's oppression may be overlooked.
The reparative/developmentally needed relationship	The counsellor may consciously and deliberately become the nurturing hearing parent when the deaf client's real parents have been abusive or over-protective, or he or she may challenge the client's negative view of themselves in relation to hearing people in order to repair or replenish the client's distorted or damaged experience of hearing people and their low self-image.
The person-to-person relationship	This is the real or core relationship, how the counsellor and the client actually see each other and interact.
The transpersonal relationship	'The spiritual dimension of the healing relationship'. It is the particular and undescribable quality of the counselling relationship which allows the client to change and grow.

Adapted from Clarkson (1990)

Power can also be located in people within the counselling relationship, particularly when counselling becomes more than a one-to-one activity, and each of the people occupies a different role. For some Deaf clients, there will be no such thing as a one-to-one counselling relationship because, with the shortage of Deaf counsellors, communication between client and counsellor can only be achieved through the skills of an SLI. There is the possibility that the power in this triumvirate lies with *the interpreter*, as the receiver and translator of client stories and counsellor responses, because the effectiveness of the counsellor can be reduced by working through a third party, and the power of the client can be reduced by mis-translations, in particular, of the deeper nuances of counsellor responses and the language of feelings (Harvey, 1989; Roe and Roe, 1991; Steinberg, 1991). Similarly, if a hearing counsellor is working with hearing families where there is a deaf child or young person, or facilitating integrated groups, the power of 'hearingness' can be multiplied for the deaf family or group member by the presence of other hearing people. The deaf person can unwittingly become 'the victim', who is 'persecuted' by hearing people, and the counsellor can be placed in the role of 'rescuer' in an attempt to equalise the power. Power can of course work in reverse in some circumstances when the counsellor begins to feel disempowered by their client's situation or threatened by the client in some way. Abuse invades personal boundaries so totally that counsellors often encounter difficulties with their own boundaries especially when they become overinvolved, wanting to give more and more to the client (Walker, 1992). They can develop powerful 'rescue fantasies' which can undermine the client's sense of independence and competence. Preventing power imbalances of this kind requires careful management of boundaries by the counsellor; indeed, counsellors have *responsibility* for 'setting and monitoring' the boundaries of the counselling relationship (BAC Code of Ethics and Practice for Counsellors, 1984, A(2.4)). We will explore detailed practical examples of these issues in the second section of this book.

The 'States' of Counselling Relationships

Some social scientists believe that a social group or institution will generate the functional roles necessary to maintain it in a 'healthy state'. Clearly there can be different views as to what constitutes a 'healthy state', and the aims and the objectives whereby this can be achieved. There are, as we have suggested, two primary perceptions of 'the healthy state', one in which a deaf–hearing power imbalance is preserved and one in which deaf–hearing equality is aimed for. These two 'states' will generate and determine different roles in counsellors and deaf people, and chart the course of the counselling relationship to the point where it can be seen that they diverge into healthy and unhealthy, from the client's perspective. On the one hand we may see counsellors who assume a high level of responsibility for the client's problem situation, often showing paternalistic or audist behaviour or counselling style, and dependent, self-denigrating clients. On the other we may see empowering counsellor behaviours and counselling styles and independent, self-valuing clients who are given a high level of responsibility for growth and change.

The levels of responsibility assumed by counsellor and client within the counselling relationship have been shown to be an important marker to the client's ability to trust the counsellor. These two 'states' are reflected in the counsellor agendas shown in Box 3.3. They are distinguished from each other by the aims and objectives of counselling process, the behaviour of counsellors and the counselling style they adopt when working with deaf clients.

BOX 3.3 COUNSELLOR AGENDAS

THE UNHEALTHY STATE

THE HEALTHY STATE

Conditional feelings and actions
Placing conditions on positive expressions and actions such that they become linked to reward

Unconditional positive regard
Unconditional acceptance

Sympathy and conference
Colluding in and disseminating low self-image

Empathy and confidentiality
Being with and containing the client

Paternalism
Patronage disguised as caring; encouraging dependence

Congruence, genuineness and openness

Over-protectiveness
Preventing the client from exploring possibilities for themself for fear that they might get hurt, or preventing them from seeing the world as it really is; taking responsibility from the client

Experiential learning and client self-awareness
Identifying and developing client awareness of their strengths, weaknesses, potential ability, skills, and independence of action; being responsible to the client

Negative images and stereotypes of deaf people

Counsellor self-knowledge and awareness of prejudice

Discrimination (audism)
Giving deaf clients less favourable treatment than hearing clients primarily because they are deaf, but also because they are young, Black, female, gay or lesbian

Equality
Valuing the client's difference, and desiring the client's freedom to be themself

Dominance, tyranny and manipulation
Keeping deaf people in their perceived inferior position by all means possible, including manipulation

Respect and clarity
Dispensing with political, social, emotional and psychological hierarchies based on flawed conjecture and opinion

Normative assumptions, attitudes and low expectations Making value judgements about ability and potential of deaf people based on fictitious norms and generalisations	**Searching for the client's truth** Non-judgemental, direct knowledge of client
Restriction of learning opportunities, life choices and alternatives Forcing 'black and white' thinking on deaf people by unneccesarily simplifying, modifying, biasing or withholding information	**Client agency and counsellor consultancy** Giving accurate information or acting as a consultant to clients when asked
Segregation Narrowing life contexts, maintaining the client's sense of isolation	**Integration** Developing the client's awareness of relationships and contexts
Authority Reinforcing images of power and status	**Facilitation** Focus on the client's personal resources

Deaf people require accessible and accurate information about the counselling process in order that they can understand the terms of the counselling contract or how counselling works, and what the purpose of *effective* counselling is. Counsellors who embrace both of these agendas, despite the heavily-loaded language, will claim that their aim is client change and growth. They will all say 'I care' and be seen as powerful in their clients' eyes. But there are differences, some subtle and some not so subtle, which delineate the role of the counsellor in this process and how far the counsellor's agenda influences the direction of change and growth. From this it is clear that there can be a very fine dividing line between counselling which is aimed at rehabilitation (in the negative sense) and counselling which empowers.

The unhealthy counselling relationship, through its association with treatment or cure, is clearly more aligned to medical models of helping or *rehabilitation*. But, as is the case with most helping terms, the use of the term rehabilitation can be confusing. This reflects different perceptions of what the aim of rehabilitation is and how it is to be achieved. If rehabilitation is viewed as an activity which aims to restore an individual to their 'proper condition', the objectives of rehabilitation can become linked to perceptions of what 'the proper condition' is. For example, if it is perceived as the deaf person's integration into hearing society with its accompanying assumptions about the benefits that this may bestow on the deaf person, rehabilitation can become focused on skills which are seen by the helper, not always appropriately or accurately, to enable integration (for example, the development of spoken language), or on the development of a strong sense of self which provides the deaf person with a secure base for integration. The latter focus moves the individual in the direction of empowerment only if the sense of self in question is the true one as opposed to a contrived one. If, on the other hand, 'the proper condition' is seen from the outset as improving the deaf person's sense of self and the quality of their life, there is apparently more flexibility from the deaf person's perspective on the surface, though this flexibility can carry a hidden agenda. In all of these situations, there is a risk that interventions interfere with natural processes so as to prevent or modify natural outcomes from the deaf person's perspective, because, at least initially, the counsellor holds the power in the counselling relationship. The rehabilitation agenda can be an unconscious or passive one which presents itself to conscious awareness unexpectedly in a particular set of circumstances, for example, when a hearing counsellor meets with a deaf client. It can also be conscious from the start, with the counsellor working with the deaf client in full awareness that their intention is to rehabilitate the deaf client to 'normality'.

COUNSELLOR TYPES AND COUNSELLING STYLES: THE DANGEROUS COUNSELLORS

We can now take a tongue-in-cheek look, heavily influenced by the work of Virginia Satir (1988), at counsellor 'types' and the counselling styles they use with deaf clients within counselling relationships. Dorothy Rowe (1993) in an article in the *Independent on Sunday* newspaper brings together the strands of the above discussion:

'The great men (sic) of psychotherapy have abused their power, and far too many therapists continue to do so. A therapist is invested with immense power by his clients who want him to be able to take their pain away but not change them. They want happiness without effort. Good therapists, right from the beginning, disabuse their clients of this foolish notion. They say: "I have no magic wand or magic word. Your pain is part of you and for you to lose your pain you must change. I can help you, but I cannot do your work for you." Bad therapists try never to let their clients make this discovery. They want to keep the power their client has given them, (because)...they are in love with power...greedy...[or] like to think of themselves as being exceptionally empathetic, sensitive and caring.'

I would suggest that the 'dangerous therapists' that Rowe refers to are dangerous because they come to believe that they know their deaf client group and what their deaf clients need better than they know themselves or their motivation for doing what they do. In this, they perpetuate unhealthy counselling relationships with their clients. Doubtless, many practising counsellors reading the following descriptions will be outraged, because the practices described bear no resemblance to counselling. Others may be amused, because these characters and what they do are vaguely familiar. Therein lies the purpose of this exercise. *Deaf clients* know these 'counsellors' only too well, and they may have been encouraged to believe that the treatment they receive at their hands is 'counselling'. We must dispel these myths, and remove the confusion if deaf people are to understand what counselling really is, because deaf clients can and do have a greater chance of encountering 'dangerous therapists', some of whom we will now expose.

The Benevolent Humanitarian

The first type is a variation of the counsellor that Rowe (1993) would describe as the 'Earth Mother', although she points out that they do not always appear this way. The *Benevolent Humanitarian* sees herself as so caring and understanding that she appears to bear a permanent smile on her face. This smile is often but a mask. Inside, she is deeply insecure and needs her clients desperately to confirm her sense of purpose, perhaps even her very existence. She believes that her own needs must always be subordinated to the needs of her deaf clients, but this is simply a way of avoiding her reasons for feeling insecure. Her attachment to her clients is so strong that she cannot bear the thought of separation, and therefore encourages her client's dependence on her. Indeed, if the *Benevolent Humanitarian's* clients fail to recognise how selfless she is, her sense of martyrdom is instantly projected and this further damages her clients' sense of self-esteem. She may be a very lonely person, or someone who has experienced failure in another profession, who cannot succeed in equal relationships or lives with a sense of failure, so she actively seeks out a counselling role where there is a guarantee that she can live behind a personal façade of being successfully benevolent with clients whom she perceives to be 'weak' or 'needy'. In her counselling style, she may be gentle, maternalistic and unable to deal with challenges and confrontations. Her instinctive reaction to the latter will be to 'placate' her clients, trying to please, constantly apologising and never disagreeing, always seeking her clients' approval. In this she is using one of the four universal patterns identified by Virginia Satir (1988) to overcome deep-rooted worries about the threat of rejection. She will give her deaf clients the utmost sympathy, thereby reinforcing their sense of injustice and inequality, but she does not understand the difference between sympathy and empathy and is totally unable to be objective or to maintain a meaningful emotional distance from her deaf client. Whereas she may do anything to help, including taking full responsibility for sorting out the deaf person's 'problems' with others, she will not recognise the source of the problem situations and is quite unable to say 'No!'. Concrete examples of the *Benevolent Humanitarian* are counsellors who give deaf clients their home minicom number or who will accompany a deaf adult on a difficult visit or excursion because of their belief that, because deaf people were *always* accompanied as a child and adolescent on visits to the doctor and so on, they will *never* be able to do anything alone. In short, the *Benevolent Humanitarian* will not allow her deaf clients to grow up, nor help them to identify the skills and resources whereby they can become independent. The irony is that it is her own independence that she craves, but because she is unable to achieve this state, she prevents her clients from doing so. In doing this, she exercises a mild form of social control.

Figure 3.3 The 'Benevolent Humanitarian'

The Expert

This is the counsellor that Person-Centred practitioners love to hate (Mearns and Thorne, 1988) – the counsellor-diagnostician, the know-all, who knows everything there is to know about deafness, Deaf culture, linguistics, psychology and so on but absolutely nothing about people and their individualism. She is obsessed with showing her clients how knowledgeable and wise she is, with finding answers or solutions, and with putting her deaf clients into boxes. She will say that because a particular client has identified as x,y,z, then he must endeavour to do a,b,c to achieve the outcome p,q,r. When the client doesn't deliver, the *Expert* is confused and tries to 'compute' a different strategy, usually based on the piles of literature which adorn the floor to ceiling bookshelves. If she can't find an answer she labels her client as an anomaly. Satir says of the 'computer':

> 'The computer is very correct, very reasonable and shows no semblance of feeling. The person seems calm, cool and collected. She or he could be compared to an actual computer or a dictionary. The body feels dry, often cool, and detached. The voice is a dry monotone, and the words

are likely to be abstract. When you are a computer, you use the longest words possible, even if you are not sure of their meaning.'

(Virginia Satir, 1988, p.89)

The *Expert* makes their living out of her knowledge of deaf people, but she is almost always hearing, and may question deaf people's ability to be objective or doubt the value of subjective experience. She believes, in short, that she knows deaf people better than they know themselves. The *Expert* nevertheless feels vulnerable deep inside, and lives in constant fear that one day deaf people will increase their own self-knowledge and understanding such that the *Expert's* livelihood is diminished or taken away. Unlike the *Benevolent Humanitarian*, the *Expert* hides behind a professional façade. She can therefore be intellectually manipulative with her clients, stunning them with her knowledge and her cleverness, but failing to check out whether her clients have understood what she is saying. Indeed, she loves to impress with her knowledge of the jargon, and often communicates with her clients using a poetic style coupled with many abstract thoughts and theories. She will frequently do most of the talking in the counselling relationship, trying to keep the ball in her court all the time, so that the client is never given the opportunity to see themselves outside of the *Expert's* models or frameworks or as an individual.

Figure 3.4 The 'Expert'

The Power Broker

This counsellor is often a crueller version of the *Expert*. The *Power Broker* has fervent beliefs about a particular philosophy of deaf education or 'the psychology of the deaf', and is often obsessed with 'cures' because she fundamentally believes that deaf people are 'inferior', 'ill' or 'not normal' or, alternatively, she believes that deaf people are all the same and if a client rebels, they will be forced back into their box without a second thought. The *Power Broker* has an image of herself as superior, expert and omniscient, but there is something quite contrived about the way in which she makes her clients realise this. Common words in the *Power Broker's* vocabulary are 'ought' and 'should', and using 'methods developed by evangelical religious leaders' (Rowe, 1993), she will indoctrinate her clients into believing that only she is right. The *Power Broker* is a 'blamer' (Satir, 1988), who blames deaf people for her problems, and sometimes, the problems of the world. She is constantly trying to insinuate that deaf people are the cause of all their own problems because they won't conform, and so her clients remain trapped and in pain, believing that they are disabled by a chip on their shoulder or because they are deaf. The *Power Broker* is quite unable to view her client as a whole person choosing to relate only to that part of her client's experience which enables a power imbalance to be preserved in the counselling relationship, and satisfies the *Power Broker's* pursuit of authority and control. A common example of this would be the *Power Broker* who insists on the use of speech in counselling because of her belief that the deaf client will never be part of the hearing world if they can't speak, when the client has sought help *because* they are unable to communicate with their hearing parents, partner or children using speech. The *Power Broker* takes the side of hearing people or the hearing way of doing things, and often refuses to accept that the problem situations that deaf people face are any different to those that hearing people face, as a means of assimilating her clients into a hostile world and making them feel guilty for having problems. She will say, using a didactic and forceful approach, 'We *all* have difficulty hearing at parties', or 'Do you think *I* don't have problems too?' instead of 'I had much the same problem myself, and, although I understand that you may be different, I found it helpful to look at it this way...' She may also adhere to a particular counselling methodology, and will not even consider alternative approaches or that her approach may be of limited value in working with deaf people. In reality, the *Power Broker* does this because she is lonely and unsuccessful, and wants to be the opposite. Unlike the *Benevolent Humanitarian*, she chooses to work with deaf people because she believes she *can* control them in satisfying her lust for power. She may find the use of sign language abhorrent because she has been unable to learn it in three hours or even one year, usually because of lack of commitment and a great deal of anger that she has even been put in the position of having to attend classes. She knows that if she is with sign language users her inability to understand them will mean that she must relinquish power, and she hates that prospect. She may refuse to acknowledge transcultural counselling because she holds audist beliefs. She is more dangerous that the *Expert* because she disguises her true face with a mask of love and caring, but unlike the *Benevolent Humanitarian*, this mask is a long shadow that stares her in the face. The *Power Broker* is

Figure 3.5 The 'Power Broker'

so sure of herself on the surface that she will not even consider alternative scenarios or search for new frameworks. She sees *all* her clients as anomalies.

The Counsellor for the Advancement of Normalisation (CAN)

This counsellor is of two distinct types: she either believes that deaf people can only survive by adopting hearing values or she believes that deaf people can only survive by becoming Deaf. She specialises in potted histories of what, why and how deaf people *can* achieve, for she does believe that achievement is possible. She is distinct from the counsellor types we have discussed thus far in that she usually insists on working in groups, which she orchestrates according to her own beliefs. So, if the *CAN* opts for hearing values, her deaf client may well find themselves in an all-hearing group having been refused a sign language interpreter on the grounds that it will spoil the dynamic flow of the group. In reality the *CAN* has a problem with interpreters because, to her, the presence of an interpreter defeats the purpose of the therapy and involves a certain amount of power sharing. *CANs* will encourage a form of group dynamics where the deaf client's deafness becomes the focus of the group and they are repeatedly forced into a situation where they must admit that they are having problems with communication. This is for the alleged purpose of building confidence and assertiveness and reflecting group situations as they are in the outside world. In practice the deaf client feels oppressed, but this is not a word which exists in the *CAN's* vocabulary, and the other group members get fed up with the constant interruptions.

Figure 3.6 The 'Counsellor for Advancement of Normalisation'

The second type of *CAN* will view Deaf culture as the 'norm', and her target clients will usually be 'oral' deaf people, deafened people and deaf people who prefer to use Sign Supported English (SSE).[5] This *CAN* will, like the *Expert*, often be hearing and have adopted 'the Deaf cause'. She will often declare, with a pitiful look on her face, that the deaf client 'is hearing inside' in a way which implies that this is some sort of defect, rather than accept the realities of that deaf client's education or family background. In group-work, she will isolate the deaf client in an all-Deaf group and *will* use a sign language

5   SSE is English-based use of signing. Spoken English is supported by signs used in the order that words are spoken, but not every word is signed. In practice, many deaf people use SSE or move between SSE and BSL depending on their contact group. Some Deaf people and their hearing allies see SSE as 'defect' BSL or take its use as an indication that the deaf person cannot accept that they are deaf.

interpreter, but will insist upon a BSL interpreter whom the target deaf client is unable to understand fully. Again the client becomes the butt of the group's jokes and the object of their frustration. The *CAN* will usually be indignant or angry on behalf of Deaf people, but fail to accept that Deaf people are also human, and can indulge in discriminatory behaviour. She fails to see the wider meaning of oppression or the diversity of the deaf community.

The Stockbroker

This counsellor is greedy. Unlike the *Expert*, the *Stockbroker* is emotionally manipulative, withholding information and actively preventing her client from reaching the island of growth. Instead of knowledge and understanding, the goal is to make as much money as possible out of the client. Rowe (1993) says of this type:

> 'They encourage the client to investigate his past, not in terms of seeing connections between events, but in terms of blaming parents, siblings, teachers and society. This is a seam which can be mined forever. The client remains a child with a ready excuse for his behaviour, which is "can't help what I do. I had a terrible childhood."'

(Rowe, 1993)

The *Stockbroker* is looking for something unique, 'a specialism' she will say, and she identifies the deaf 'cause' as presenting exciting possibilities – for her. She says 'the plight of deaf people is truly horrendous' or 'deaf people have problems of a depth yet unexplored' when she means 'deaf people will swell my bank balance if I can find a way to tap (or sap?) their energy'. Like the *Benevolent Humanitarian*, the *Stockbroker* finds it difficult to form meaningful relationships, though is less warm and loving and more detached. The *Stockbroker* transfers blame but will not allow either herself or the client to take responsibility for doing something about change, because she also has some of the characteristics of Satir's fourth universal pattern used by people to avoid the threat of rejection. The *Stockbroker* can be a 'distracter', which means that in her counselling style she doesn't respond to what is real and present for the client, but to her own need to reinforce the negative in the client. If she succeeds in getting the deaf client to blame their (usually hearing) parents for everything bad that has happened, the *Stockbroker* will never suggest that the parents may have been innocent victims, trapped in their own unhappy webs of denial and frustration, created by the circumstances of the time. If she transfers the blame to the education system or the Government for her client's problem situation, she distracts the client by putting the alleged cause out of their reach in the echelons of power and policy, reinforcing the client's sense of outrage at the inaccessibility of possible solutions. The *Stockbroker* has no original answers, other than those provided by her deaf clients, and these she keeps to themself – until another opportunity to increase her income presents itself.

Figure 3.7 The 'Stockbroker'

The Panic Broker

This is the counsellor who is completely without boundaries, and unable to deal with confidentiality or containment. Although the *Panic Broker* harbours nothing deliberate in her thoughts or actions, she is so unsure of herself, both as a person and as a professional, that she becomes acutely anxious in the face of the unexpected 'intrusion' of dimensions to the deaf client's problem situation which indicate that the client is someone other than a *deaf* person. The very mention of 'sex', for example, can throw her into panic and she feels in instant need of reassurance because, as she will sometimes say, she 'has received no training in that area', or she 'is not very experienced in that subject'. The reality is that the *Panic Broker* finds talking about sex deeply embarrassing. Or perhaps she may have an insatiable curiosity about other people's sex lives which may compensate for her own unhappy sex life. It is as if the *Panic Broker* longs for her clients to be straightforward with simple problem situations that can be solved. The real difficulty with the *Panic Broker*, however, is that instead of confining her panic to her relationship with her deaf client, she spreads it around, often to anybody and everybody who will listen, until the walls of an institution reverberate with the echoes of the story of a deaf client who is identified in every way but a name. The *Panic Broker* thrives on counselling conferences, therapy groups, supervision groups, staff meetings, case conferences, chance encounters with friends or colleagues – any opportunity to gain 'more information', 'another angle' or 'another side' to her client's story. She craves the centre of attention in these settings. Frequently, she becomes so confused by the multitude of angles she discovers that she forgets what the client's story was in the first place. The problem then becomes her own. If she is in individual therapy herself or has individual supervision, which is unlikely because she does not recognise any need, the *Panic Broker* cannot contain these relationships either. She has been known to explore these relationships with her clients in such a way that the client becomes the counsellor. Indeed this is common practice, for the *Panic Broker* is an expert in self-disclosure and the discharging of emotions and, like the *Benevolent Humanitarian* is completely unable to maintain emotional distance, be non-judgemental or non-evaluative. Her trade mark might well be 'But that's absolutely *awful...*'. She will often claim that she is in need of constant education by her clients. Because the deaf world is small in comparison to the hearing world, and gossip or rumour are less containable, the *Panic Broker* rapidly finds herself without a client, if she hasn't referred her client already that is, and becomes perpetually engaged in the briefest of 'brief counselling' (Dryden and Feltham, 1992). The sad thing is that the *Panic Broker* does not really want to be a counsellor; she is not sure who she is or what she wants to be, except that she wants to 'help' deaf people, or make other people more 'aware' of deaf people when she herself does not understand deaf people nor appreciate deaf people's individualism.

THE SEARCH FOR EMPOWERMENT

With all these dangerous people around, it is no wonder that many deaf clients become confused or suspicious about the purpose of counselling and have no concept of what a 'good therapist' is. It may be helpful to look at the process of empowerment and to give a face to the *Empowerer*, the counsellor who is given the unenviable task of creating conditions which enhance client growth through 'healthy' counselling relationships, by highlighting and learning from the above accounts.

The healthy state described in Box 3.3 is equivalent to an empowerment agenda. It can be a positive conscious response to the knowledge of the darker, more passive unconscious, but for this to happen, the counsellor must first make the unconscious conscious and work with it. The true empowerment agenda cannot therefore be passive in any sense of the word, since it requires constant education, monitoring of counsellor and client behaviours and of counselling process. But, as Mitchell (1989) suggests, without the recognition of the links between conscious and unconscious forces and without understanding of the powerlessness and loss which results from the material and ideological oppression of deaf people by hearing people, the language of empowerment trips too lightly off the tongue and is too easily used merely as a synonym for 'enabling', or an approach to practice which is 'colonised or domesticated in the service of the (normative) status quo' (Ward and Mullender, 1993, p. 148). One important aspect of empowerment is that the helper is

Figure 3.8 The 'Panic Broker'

in a supporting role, identifying, encouraging and nurturing the deaf person's inner resources, which moves the counsellor – client relationship away from 'helper–helped' and towards *partnership*. Williams (1993) emphasises the importance of partnership:

> 'This approach recognises that knowledge is socially constructed, and acknowledges the value-laden nature of the definition and transmission of knowledge. No longer is the professional seeking to impose her view of what constitutes knowledge on her clients, with the goal of attaining compliance... The goal of the professional becomes the personal growth and development of the client. Thus the professional–client relationship changes from one of superior–subordinate to one of partnership; it becomes, in Jarvis' terms (1975) the "education of equals".'

(Williams, 1993, pp. 11–12)

At the beginning of the counselling relationship, an empowerment agenda will necessitate the counsellor and the client exploring the implications that being deaf has for the client, and looking at the parameters of oppression through the 'education of equals'. This must be seen as part of the whole

Figure 3.9 The 'Empowering Counsellor'

process rather than a desire of the client to focus on their deafness, and identify their problem situation solely in terms of their deafness. The client may need to find a way of being sure of the counsellor and to establish how safe they are before they can begin to discuss any problem situations, most especially if the counsellor is hearing. Testing out the counsellor's attitudes and assumptions about deaf people and also their knowledge of deaf issues is one way of doing this. Asking personal questions is another. Being mindful of the empowerment agenda, assists the counsellor in defining their role, in setting counselling boundaries and in navigating the course for client growth:

'It is important that the therapist does not fully take over the ship and navigate for his or her own needs. This, I think, often happens when the ship might be in stormy waters and the therapist needs to steer towards quiet waters because of personal fears. The opposite can also happen – the therapist feels the ship is moving too quietly and prematurely pushes the client into more dramatic situations. Navigation means that there may be times when the therapist needs to point out to the client that there are other possible directions to choose than the one they have chosen... I have worked with people who have been stuck in the mud or lost in the dark, but the human capacity for transforming chaos into beauty has never stopped amazing me.'

(Minde, in Jennings and Minde, 1993, p. 41)

The *Empowerer* strives for healthy counselling relationships. She does not lie to herself or to her clients. She is transparent in her genuineness such that her client gets a sense that it is perfectly acceptable to be who they are. She does not hide behind façades of any kind and, unlike the *Expert*, prefers to broaden her horizons of self-knowledge and knowledge of her deaf clients by reading novels, poetry and autobiography and mixing socially with deaf people.

The *Empowerer* is not confined by roles. She believes that the best route to genuineness is to be 'role-free', and so she strives to achieve the qualities shown in Box 3.4, because she acknowledges the usefulness of these qualities in establishing clear boundaries between herself and the deaf client. She refrains from using the role or facade of counsellor to protect herself, like the *Benevolent Humanitarian*, to substitute for competence, like the *Expert* or the *Panic Broker*, or to fool the client, like the *Power Broker* or the *Stockbroker*.

BOX 3.4 BEING ROLE-FREE

The Empowerer...
- communicates clearly and honestly
- listens to the client without evaluating or making judgements about what they say
- is clear and honest about *why* they say what they do
- avoids using habitual or planned strategies and cultivates spontaneous, easy and natural communication
- cultivates immediate responses to the client's need or state instead of waiting for the 'right' time or giving themselves enough time to come up with the 'right' response
- knows and accepts themself, in particular the parts of themself which are deeply buried in their unconscious
- works to challenge their own alienism or prejudice and owns these behaviours
- lives in and communicates about the here and now instead of dwelling on the past
- strives for interdependence rather than dependence or counterdependene in their relationship with their client
- learns how to enjoy psychological closeness
- is concrete and direct in their communications
- is willing to commit themselves to others

(after Gibb, 1968, 1978)

The *Empowerer* recognises the dangers of becoming complacent, and is prepared to make her unconscious conscious – to recognise the darker side of herself which hijacks the counsellor's core values and leads her in the direction of prejudice and alienistic behaviours perpetrated by negative transference and countertransference:

> 'Self-acceptance should not be confused with complacency or a kind of weary resignation. The complacent or resigned person has usually called a halt to self-exploration so that he can rest on his laurels or give up the effort. He can *turn a deaf ear and a blind eye*[6] to the responses of those around him. Such a person is no longer growing, and is unlikely to assist the development of others. Self-acceptance is without meaning or value unless it is accompanied by the desire for growth and a willingness to face the truth. Unfortunately, the truth about ourselves often involves feelings of guilt and it is then that self-acceptance seems a particularly difficult accomplishment.'

(Mearns and Thorne, 1988, p.24–25, italics added)

It *is* easier to seize power than to share it or give it up, for example. In such circumstances, it is perhaps useful to consider the difference between being and expert and having knowledge and understanding of our clients as they perceive themselves to be. Using offensive language or seizing power will not create an appropriate climate for growth, as we shall see in the following chapter. In practice, counsellor styles which have their origins in oppressive unconscious agendas or methodological rigidity can be as much a problem as those of the client who is deaf. Where there are problems within the counselling relationship, it may be difficult for clients to tackle their counsellor's alienism and subsequent expectations of outcome. The power difference between them makes this an unlikely scenario. It is therefore up to counsellors to take responsibility for their own audist tendencies and to understand, for example, the effect that low expectations may have on the deaf client's search for inner strength and growth:

> 'Alice Miller was against what she termed "poisonous pedagogy" – the teaching and advising of "patients" by therapist/teacher expert for "their own good". Poisonous pedagogy perpetuates the role of therapist as all-powerful and the client/patient somewhat submissive, therefore malleable to treatment. Many adult survivors have said to me that in the previous course of "therapy", their therapeutic relationship was based on an unequal power-submissive dialogue which replicated the original power-victim dynamic they experienced in childhood... The Institute for Self-Analysis in London who use an advocacy approach and base their work on that if Alice Miller describe the function of the therapist as being "the advocate of the inner child". There are five aspects of this role: Nurturer (offers warmth and care), Witness (validates the experience – believes it happened), Protester against what has

---

6   This is discussed further in the following chapter.

been done, Translator (translates meaning), Supporter of the person's inner advocate and creativity.'

(Kennedy, 1990, p.8)

In fulfilling some of these roles, Catherine begins to establish an empowering relationship with Robert, and, in being open to this possibility, she surprises him. We will explore this further in Chapter 8.

BOX 3.5 CATHERINE AND ROBERT

Catherine, who has initially been surprised and caught off-guard by the violence of Robert's feelings, discovers that he feels angry about having been sent to counselling. He feels that 'everyone is talking about him'. She affirms his feelings with direct statements such as 'That *is* an impossible situation to cope with...', 'I can see why you feel like that...', 'People *can* be very insensitive sometimes', and shows that she is attending to him by maintaining eye-contact, nodding her head periodically. At the end of this session, she asks Robert how he feels about writing down some more of what he feels about being deaf, and bringing it to the next session. Robert's reaction is:

R:(*surprised*) 'You mean you want to see me again?'

C:(*smiles warmly*) 'Of course I want to meet with you again. (*pause*) Shall we fix a time now?'

Having defined the characteristics of and made clear the necessity for creating an environment which nurtures the conditions for client growth, we now move on to the part of this book which attempts to repair this damage.

CHAPTER 4

THE COMMUNICATIVE CHALLENGE – LANGUAGE FOR GROWTH

'"We are our language", it is often said; but our real language, our real identity, lies in inner speech, in the ceaseless stream and generation of meaning that constitutes the individual mind. It is through inner speech that the child develops his own concepts and meanings; it is through inner speech that he achieves his own identity; it is through inner speech, finally, that he constructs his own world.'

(Sacks, 1989, p.73)

The quality of human existence has always been founded on language and communication. We all recognise that relationships with other people can be made or broken by how we communicate with each other and the content of what we communicate. Our motivation for expressing what we do is more deeply hidden, along with the instinct which moves us to that expression; but this too has significance for our success or failure in communicating with others, for language can be both a direct expression of truth and a disguise for the truth, language can be muddled or clear, language can empower or manipulate. Indeed, at the most fundamental level, the substance of language and communication has a crucial part to play in identity formation, and the creation of meaning in an individual's inner world.

Ultimately, within a counselling relationship, we might expect to see the power of language and communication in full flow, as counsellors draw upon an ever increasing repertoire of skills or ways of listening, attending and responding to their clients' stories. Further, there is an element of interpretation in most counselling relationships, with the counsellor attempting to translate accurately the inner world of the client in order that it can be become conscious. In the hands of experienced and genuine counsellors, counselling has to be seen, in outcome, as a formidable linguistic and communicative tool in creating social change through client growth, as counsellors join with clients on their inner journeys through the development of empathy and trust. Counsellors enter the inner worlds of their clients, and in so doing, they become party to the construction of the client's 'own world'. It follows from this that in ignorant, unskilled or unscrupulous hands, counselling can be devastatingly damaging for the unsuspecting client who, in placing their trust in the 'wisdom' of the counsellor, finds themself lumbered with a false reality,

'Good' counsellors will strive to develop linguistic awareness and skills, and in doing so will receive a great deal of conflicting information about the language choices that deaf people make. If this leads them to form an opinion about the 'right' way of communicating with deaf people, and this opinion is brought to the counselling relationship, it may interfere with the development of the core values of counselling process. Counsellors must have communicative skills which are of a sufficiently high standard to demonstrate empathy with their client, whilst remembering that there are limits to how far communication skills serve the counselling process, as we will see below. It is common to consider the language that deaf people use *only* in terms of its structure and fluency, but this is useful to counsellors only insofar as they are able to recognise which language, language form or language variety their client is using and to gauge whether a deaf client shifts between different ways of expressing themselves to emphasise different meanings or reinforce different feelings. This recognition will enable the counsellor to match or mirror their client *when appropriate* and to gain access to their client's inner world of meaning, and can only be achieved through a preparedness to commit oneself to learning the range of languages, language forms and language nuances of deaf people. Clearly, it is not within the scope of this book to educate sufficiently in this area, but we can begin to explore aspects which are of particular relevance to counselling.

LINGUISTIC DIVERSITY

Some of the linguistic diversity that can be observed in the deaf community is equivalent to that which we might experience in the hearing community. There are deaf Urdu, Bengali and Punjabi speakers, deaf users of European languages, deaf women and deaf gays and lesbians who have developed their own vocabulary of meaning which is quite specific to them, and deaf artists for whom their creativity is the ultimate channel of expression; there are also a multitude of regional dialects, accents and communicative preferences. In the Deaf community, there are also Deaf people who use sign languages in various forms – French Sign Language, Irish Sign language, British Sign Language, American Sign Language, and Scottish dialects, Black varieties, and gay sign language, for example. The Deaf community has been described as a bilingual diglossic community in that its members are a linguistic minority functioning within a larger English-speaking society. Their language therefore shows features which are common to BSL, English and/or another language which has a spoken or written form, or a mixture of these. How this ultimately manifests itself will depend on the dominant social contacts deaf people make or their language competence, which is more commonly a reflection of inadequate education and restricted learning experience than a lack of innate language ability. Thus we see some deaf people using Signed Exact English or Manually Coded English (MCE), fingerspelling, Pidgin Sign English (PSE), Sign Supported English (SSE) and creoles, in addition to the standard forms of BSL and English. To explain the differences between these, it may be helpful to look at a simple example using English glosses (capital letters) for signed components.

BOX 4.2 EXAMPLES FROM THE BSL – ENGLISH DIGLOSSIC CONTINUUM

English	She broke the hearing aid
Fingerspelling	S-h-e-b-r-o-k-e-t-h-e-h-e-a-r-i-n-g-a-i-d
Signed English	SHE BREAK + PAST THE HEARING AID
Sign Supported English	She BREAK the HEARING AID
Pidgin Signed English	Point FINISH BREAK HEARING AID
British Sign Language	HEARING AID POINT FINISH BREAK

LANGUAGE NUANCES, PERSONAL LANGUAGES, 'INNER LANGUAGES' AND COMMUNICATIVE INFRASTRUCTURES

Linguistic diversity, of course, is not confined to the form of the language used by an individual, and this is an issue which is of relevance to *all* counsellors, whether they are deaf or hearing, and for *all* clients. Because we tend to think in terms of whether or not counsellor and client share a language, we often overlook the interplay of different levels of the individual's *personal language* and their *individual communicative infrastructure*. All languages have a number of channels through which they are expressed and these *channels* come together to create the client's individual meaning:

> 'It's important to understand that every time you talk, all of you talks. Whenever you say words, your face, voice, body, breathing and muscles are talking too:
>
> Verbal communication – words
>
> Body/sound communication – facial expression
> (with or without words)   body position
>   muscle tone
>   breathing tempo
>   voice tone
>   gestures
>
> Discrepancies between verbal and non-verbal communication produce double messages. Your words are saying one thing, and the rest of you is saying something else.'

> (Satir, 1988, p. 80)

The conditions of worth created by counselling core values can illuminate the highly individual nature of clients' personal language so that communication becomes unique in the hands or voices of each individual. For example, I cry very easily, both in public and privately, and for many different reasons, but the most common one is that I am experiencing feelings at such an intense level that I cannot express them in any other way. The feelings can be anger, or frustration, or love, or empathy with another person, and so I may appear inconsistent. But I never cry when I am sad or depressed, because these feelings are so deep that even crying will not express them adequately. I had a client who rarely cried for or about anything and generally was able to express what she wanted when she wanted it in a clear, unmuddled way. She came for brief counselling because of the impression that others got of her as being unfeeling and calculated in everything she did, to the point where she was seen as being an 'ultra-professional robot' and attracted a great deal of jealousy. Her unpleasant experience of jealousy made her cry, for she was a very feeling person who had developed a thick skin in childhood out of self-preservation and, later, to allow her to manage her life better. She genuinely wished to share her feelings with others, but the professional jealousy she experienced as a result of her professional success and competence was preventing her from making contact with those around her, to the point where she felt ostracised and lonely. The meaning that tears had for her was different to the meaning my tears have for me, but her difficulties were added to because she felt that it was 'wrong' to cry. Once she was able to recognise that people's jealousy was their problem, and that she was not faced with a cause and effect situation where she was responsible for their feelings, she was more able to accept her tears as legitimate expression.

Mearns and Thorne emphasise the importance of personal languages for counselling core values:

'If the counsellor was working with a client from a different culture, and with a different language, she would probably be unusually patient, tolerant and concerned to discover the meaning of his language. She would be wary of forming early judgements, because she would know that those judgements might simply be based on her lack of understanding of his language and culture. For the counsellor who is trying to develop her attitude of unconditional positive regard it can be helpful to make the same kinds of assumptions about *all* her clients. She might start by assuming that each new client has his own "personal language" which he would use to express himself. The counsellor's task, principally through empathy, is to uncover and understand that language…concentrating on the question *what does this behaviour mean for this client?*'

(Mearns and Thorne, 1988, p.64)

Personal language is for the deaf client often a visible indicator of the presence of *inner language*, and this gives us yet another layer to the communicative infrastructure of counselling. Ultimately, it is the client's inner language that the counsellor is searching for because it is the most deeply personal way of communicating which is in touch with the core of the client's identity. Sacks (1989), in the opening quotation to this chapter, gives us an essence of the importance of inner language. For some deaf people, inner language is so important that it becomes an essential resource or synonymous with a place of safety where feelings can be explored and understanding can be reached apart from the machinations of a disabling society. Writing of his frustrations of being deafened in adulthood, Peter Wood says:

> 'There is a tendency, indeed attraction, in these circumstances to become introverted and subjective. Just as Beethoven claimed that the only time he could ignore his deafness was when he was composing music, so the deafened if intellectually inclined realise that the world of the imagination still exists for them. For myself, it has been to a large extent my safety net. Whether or not others feel this inward withdrawal as a positive response to deafness is of little concern. It has provided a new authenticity in my life and that is all that matters.'

> (Wood, in Jones, Kyle and Wood, 1987, p.196)

The evidence seems to suggest that deaf people in general are more instinctively aware of communicative infrastructures, but the meaning this holds for them and the way it comes to be received and interpreted varies enormously within the deaf community. In this context, it is important to look at the counsellor's search for a common language infrastructure with their client not only in terms of the *transcultural* counselling relationship, but also to consider what happens when there is apparently a *shared language* and when there is *language dissonance* which is based on different language competences.

THE IMPORTANCE OF LINGUISTIC MATCHING

It was mentioned in an earlier chapter that the expressive features of sign language *may* give the impression that thinking and feeling activities are much more up-front, and consequently, the risk of double messages is considerably reduced if there is *linguistic matching* between the counsellor and the client. However, counsellors cannot be complacent if there is *apparent* matching as in the case of a hearing counsellor and balanced bilingual, English-dominant bilingual or English monolingual deaf people. Furnham and Bochner (1986) suggest that language similarities may mask cultural differences which make it *more* difficult to negotiate appropriate communication strategies. For example, a CODA may mistakenly be seen as culturally hearing on the basis of their being audiologically hearing, or a deafened person's identity struggle can be masked by their ability to express themselves in spoken language by a hearing counsellor who is not fully aware of deaf issues and their cultural manifestation. Conversely, an English monolingual deaf client who has unconsciously developed a 'Deaf way' in her values about time-keeping may, because she is fluent in English and has clear speech, lead her counsellor to assume that she is always late for counselling sessions because she is uneasy with what is happening in counselling. The shared language of client and counsellor may disguise the client's inner adaptations to life in the deaf world, though it should be emphasised that cultural differences *within* the deaf community may be even more subtle or more heavily disguised by shared language, as we will see below.

On another level, as we have implied on several occasions, the language used by the client may reflect perceived counsellor expectations as opposed to cultural affiliation or experiential difference. Conscious or unconscious expectations on the part of the counsellor about the client's culture and language preferences and skills can mean that the client feels less free to trust the counsellor with their feelings, and the client will often experience an emotional shut-down or distancing in such circumstances. There is ample evidence to suggest also that deaf clients who feel they are under pressure to conform in some way to language expectations of counsellors may confuse unaware or inexperienced counsellors with learned behavioural and linguistic responses which do not represent the client's true feelings.

SHARED LANGUAGE AND 'SEEING SKILLS'

Research suggests that hearing people tend to develop a particular way of talking to deaf people, in particular deaf children, which is stilted and unnatural and where undue emphasis is placed on particular aspects of questions by way of *visual affirmations* of the response that is expected from the deaf person (Gregory and Bishop, 1989). Further, hearing people, as we have seen, often wrongly assume that if they speak more slowly, exaggerate their lip movements or speak louder, communication will occur naturally. In this situation, a deaf client may respond to a *visual interpretation* of the counsellor's communication because they have not understood the full meaning of what has been communicated. When counsellor and client share a spoken language, for example, the move towards visual interpretation in the wider sense (e.g. body language and facial expression) is in part because of the inadequacies of the visual stimuli from what is said (e.g. lip patterns). It has been suggested by a number of authors (e.g. Jeffers and Barley, 1975) that sixty per cent of speech sounds are obscure or invisible on the lips, including one half of the vowels and diphthongs and three fifths of the consonants. Thus a deaf person who is totally dependent on lipreading could be expected to distinguish only forty per cent of spoken communication in addition to being deprived of the meaning derived directly from vocal inflections and stresses (Roe and Roe, 1991). The resulting emphasis on accessible stimuli means that with all deaf clients, whether the counselling relationship is monocultural or transcultural, there is a risk, for example, of open-ended questions becoming leading questions. A simple example of this might be of the counsellor who asks a question and either nods or shakes their head at the same time as asking. The client then mirrors 'Yes' or 'No' depending on what they have seen, as opposed to indicating that they have not understood the question. We can imagine the complications which might ensue if the questioning has been in relation to sexual abuse, for example, where the practice of asking leading questions is generally discouraged.

If counsellors do not pay adequate attention to being congruent in what they actively express and what they think and feel, the client may also perceive a lack of genuineness:

> 'Seeming not to be genuine when you listen breeds insecurity in the client. Your clients may consciously or intuitively pick up more messages than you think. Assessing the matching of your words with your vocal and body messages is a major way in which they gauge your sincerity. If you say you are interested and you look bored, the latter

message will probably be the one that registers with them. If you say you are happy at their good news but seem to force a smile, they may receive the message that you can accept them more when they are depressed than when they are happy.'

(Nelson-Jones, 1988, p.39)

Figure 4.1 Visual Reflecting Back

All clients are of course capable of reading their counsellor's demeanour to some extent, and the likelihood of this occurring in a counselling relationship is greater because of the level of intimacy which can be reached. But with deaf people, this ability often becomes a natural skill, a *seeing skill*, which develops because of a renewed focus on their intact senses. This means that there is a possibility that a deaf client will be *more* skilled at reading their counsellor than a hearing client or, indeed, than the counsellor themself. What is 'read' or 'seen' in the counsellor may determine the client's responses and can take the counselling relationship on to a completely different plane, as the above example shows. This is perhaps why language fluency and linguistic matching, more than anything, are crucial in the development of counselling relationships with deaf clients. Because words can conceal as well as express, for it is the words that have the function of concealment and not body/sound communication, it is often the deaf person's responses that carry double messages for a hearing counsellor because they are responses to the *real* message given out by the counsellor when they fail to be genuine, and not the words or the silences that attempt to conceal it. The counsellor may not always be aware of the non-verbal messages they have been displaying, because of the verbal/vocal dominance in communication arising from the counsellor's understanding of shared languages, as these two extracts show:

BOX 4.3 DEAF PEOPLE'S 'SEEING SKILLS'

'Of course I had always known that sound is vibration, but I didn't know, until I stopped straining to hear, how truly sound is a refinement of feeling. Conversations at parties might elude me, but I seldom fail to pick up on moods. I enjoy watching people talk. When I am too far away to read lips I try reading postures and imagining conversations. Sometimes, to everyone's horror, I respond to things better left unsaid when I am trying to find out what is going on around me. I want to see, touch, taste, smell everything within reach; I especially have to curb a tendency to judge things by their smell – not just potato salad, but people as well – a habit that seems to some people entirely too barbaric for comfort. I am not claiming that my other senses stepped up their work to compensate for the loss, but the absence of one does allow me to concentrate on the others. Deafness has left me acutely aware of both the duplicity that language is capable of and of the many expressions that the body cannot hide.'

(Galloway, in Saxton and Howe, 1987, p.8)

'As Freud once put it, "If a man's lips are sealed he chatters with his figertips." For example, as somebody waiting impatiently for a friend to finish a telephone conversation with another knows when it is about to end by the words said and the intonation of the voice, so does a deaf man – like a person queueing outside a glass panelled callbox – judge the moment when the good-byes are being said or the intention formed to replace the receiver. He notices the shift of the hand cradling the instrument, a change of stance, the head drawing a fraction of a millimetre from the earphone, a slight shuffling of the feet, and the alteration of expression which signals a decision taken. Cut off from auditory clues he learns to read the faintest visual evidence. The deaf man can, if he knows his friend intimately, make a good guess at the identity of the caller at the other end of the wire. He will do this by noting his friend's expression, or the tempo of the animation in his countenance; the posture of his body (relaxed or tense); and what his hands are doing. (These) infinitesimal adjustments of the lineaments and carriage…are not generally observed, since most people are naturally attending to other sources for the same information. But the deaf person notes them because they are the only signals he can receive and interpret.'

(Wright, 1990, p.112)

Limited awareness on the part of some counsellors may also be a result of not knowing what additional steps they must take to minimise the number of 'unrewarding messages' (Nelson-Jones,1988) they send out to their deaf clients. Most counsellors have learnt to understand the effects of sitting in particular ways or modulating their speech or facial expression for particular effect. But they may not be aware of the unrewarding messages sent out by their wearing brightly coloured, multi-patterned clothes, dangling earrings or tinted glasses, having a heavy moustache or beard or working in poorly lit conditions. All of these things distract from or make communication difficult for most deaf people and are very easily remedied.

What is implied in the above discussion is that even when a deaf client and their counsellor share a language, this may mask differences between deaf and hearing people which, though they could not be described as being of cultural origin, are wide enough to influence the course of the counselling process if they are not recognised. In their ability to access the *counsellor's* 'hidden world' to a deeper level than the counsellor may be aware of, the deaf client also faces the possibility of misreading what they see, which may create a vicious circle because the counsellor may also misread the client's response. Harvey gives us this example of a client who gets drawn into the confusion created by his psychiatrist, who plays upon words which look similar when lipread:

> 'I found it very confusing. It would almost have been better if I hadn't gone. Because I found that he was almost trying to direct my thinking into certain channels. I used the expression "it didn't amount to pea-nuts" which was an expression that seemed to be used at the time. Although my speech was perfectly clear, he kept having me repeat that word "peanuts", "peanuts", until I realised he somehow was construing the word "penis" from "peanuts", and was drawing a relationship. And that kind of thing made me feel like saying "see you later". I just couldn't deal with that'.

(Harvey, 1989, p.122)

The difference in 'seeing skills' may be built in to the deaf person's way of behaving towards and responding to others which, as Galloway suggests, can result in a wariness on the part of the person who has been observed and they may consider the deaf person's behaviour to be inappropriate rather than acknowledge their worry about being caught out. The difficulty for many deaf people in this position is that they may not realise that their seeing skills are construed by a hearing person as attempts to invade that person's personal boundaries, in the same way that they may not realise that they have mis-lipread something, until the atmosphere becomes so uncomfortable that something is obviously not right. I recall an example of this which happened outside of counselling, but contains many of the elements of the resulting breakdown in communication that can occur.

At one time, I shared an office with a man who was recognised generally as a compulsive womaniser, who had broken many hearts out of his lack of consideration for the women who were unfortunate enough to succumb to his charms. We shared an uneasy working relationship because he knew that I had no time for his flirting. Relationships had become more strained when I realised that the latest object of his attention was a close friend, Pauline, but when he returned from a weekend away and announced that he had been to see Pauline, I blew. I tore the poor man apart with a lecture on his moral shortcomings, in part because I knew that Pauline was very happy with her existing partner, and that she had planned to spend two weeks with him. This man did not speak to me for the next two weeks, and it was only when Pauline returned to work that I realised why. He had in fact said that he had been to Sea Palling, which is a coastal town in Norfolk, and I had mis-lipread him. The problem for me, however, was that by the time I realised my mistake, I had already laid my cards on the table very clearly, and in the end we had to move into separate offices because of the unhealthy atmosphere between us. Pauline was also furious with me because I had apparently not trusted her, though fortunately, we were able to talk it through and our friendship remained strong. I have learnt, as a result of this experience, to be more cautious with the expression of my feelings, but it is also true that I cannot predict when such situations are going to happen. Complications of this kind can and do happen in counselling.

THE TRANSCULTURAL RELATIONSHIP

We will discuss deaf people's 'seeing skills' further below, but, for the moment we need to consider whether this means that if someone does *not* make use of sound in communication, the 'refinement' or fine tuning of feeling that Galloway refers to and the information content of their communication is reduced, or that 'gestures', for example, assume the same meaning. This is an assumption which is often made by those who see deafness as a symptom of 'language impoverishment'. Clearly, these are questions which have to be considered when clients are Deaf, and Deaf people's experience suggests that such assumptions can be highly misleading and judgemental. In sign language, hand movements, facial expression and body posture, for example, become an integral part of directly expressive language, and are developed in such a way that they become equivalent to 'voice tone'. The kind of incongruencies or double messages which can be observed in communication through spoken language become incongruencies between facial expression and body posture and what is signed. The latter are often more subtle and require a higher level of language skill to identify, but, correspondingly, they happen more easily in the act of transcultural communication because hearing people are not used to being aware of the messages that the face and body are giving out. Muscle tone and breathing tempo may well be similar in similar situations, but we have to take into account that just because a hearing client's pulse rate and breathing rate may become faster if they are angry, for example, this does not mean that a Deaf client will have the same physical changes in the same situation. Signing for some Deaf people is in itself a highly physical and emotional means of expression, and is loaded with metaphor about the growth of Deaf culture and language as a response to Deaf people's oppression. Communicating with Deaf people is not simply a matter of establishing non-verbal congruence, but having a deep understanding of how sign language is used in a culturally significant way. Sign language is not merely 'gestures'. Whereas non-verbal communication generally assists verbal communication by elaborating on what is stated directly, providing feedback from listener to sender and giving messages about turn-taking in speaking and listening (Furnham and Bochner, 1986), sign language is far more sophisticated, because it is a direct expression of a visual–gestural–spatial way of experiencing. Thus, if we look carefully, we see subtle changes in handshapes and movements to convey a slightly different emphasis on a particular concept or feeling, facial expressions which frame different kinds of questions, and a whole approach to language that, far from being iconic or pictorial, can give an essence of raw here-and-now experiencing, where spatial behaviour assumes more importance. The way in which sign language is used by individual clients may be extremely important for counselling process. Sharon Ridgeway points out in Chapter 9 that Deaf clients, for example, may move between different ways of expressing themselves which has particular meaning for the counselling process and the counselling relationship, and can signify complex transferences and countertransferences. This will happen more naturally when the client has a comfortable baseline for expression, and is not under pressure to communicate in a particular way where their meaning may become distorted.

Clearly, the way that clients structure the stories they bring to counselling will reduce the counsellors understanding of these stories, if there is limited or no linguistic matching between client and counsellor. Here are two examples of stories told by Deaf people, which have been translated literally on a word for sign basis because this is the approach to the translation of sign language that many hearing people use, particularly when they are in the process of learning the language. We can assume that this would be the case with most counsellors working with Deaf people, as hearing counsellors who are fluent in sign language are a rarity in Britain.

BOX 4.4 CLIENT STORIES

John

Me talk you work. Before foreman good me. he good friend he help me lot. he spell good hand both. Now change, new foreman, him come think him clever. He jealous of me. He me ask job about. explain he know me better him worse. He not friend, give me hard job all time, never smile. Me feel sad. But one thing good – boss know me work good want make me foreman – but me deaf – never will come., impossible. Me think best go now, find other job or stay which best?

Margaret

She is who at ask. Teacher me cross everyone. she bad and what you Teacher with cross another people Hear. she want you very bad fuck. We people you Teacher Hate bad you kill mad and dog's Food Teacher happy good and we people Hate Fuck people you Teacher me died, happy.

If a counsellor is unable to understand these stories, and others like them fully because, as a result of limited signing skills, they concentrate on the gist of the information they receive, it is probable that they are not be able to take sufficient steps to identify a common language with their clients, and they will not be able to establish empathy with Deaf clients. But focusing solely on the signs of sign language as described in this way can be as misleading as focusing only only the words of spoken language. There are visual clues and ways of behaving which many counsellors have been trained to interpret in a particular way when working with hearing clients, which have a totally different or deeper meaning for Deaf people. This presents the *possibility* of culture clashes between Deaf culture and counselling culture which the counsellor must be alert to. Examples which may be observed with some Deaf clients are given in Box 4.5.

BOX 4.5 LINGUISTIC AND CULTURAL CONFUSIONS

BODY MOVEMENT, FACIAL EXPRESSION OR BEHAVIOUR	HEARING INTERPRETATION	ADDITIONAL DEAF USE OR INTER-PRETATION e.g. NON-MANUAL FEATURES OF SIGN LANGUAGE
Nod of head	Affirmation, agreement	Punctuation
Slight frown	Disagreement, disapproval	Open-ended question
Raising eyebrows (with open mouth)	Surprise	Closed question
Hunched shoulders	Withdrawal, depression	Questioning
Eyes down	Avoidance, concealment	Thinking
Persistent lateness	Unhappiness with counsellor or counselling	Culturally based time values, linear time
Re-inventing the wheel	'Vicious circles'	Culturally based time values, thinking in linear terms
Silence at start of counselling	Uneasiness, uncertainty about where to begin	Need for direct communication from counsellor

It is important to remember that humanistic counselling culture, for example, is primarily non-directive, facilitative, passive (in the physical sense) and has clear time constraints, but these are *hearing* values. Culturally, Deaf behaviour tends to be more directive (controlling), direct and concrete (up-front), active (in the physical sense, though different kinds of touch may have culturally significant meanings) and operates within different time constraints governed by different values attributed to time, and the quality of information received from the environment which alerts Deaf people to the passage of time. Some common counselling skills such as reflecting back may bore Deaf clients (Callow, 1991) and be of limited use because of this cultural divide. They may also, if they are used insensitively, have the effect of negative reinforcement. The different expectations which result from culturally determined patterns of behaviour can therefore have implications for counsellor style which some humanistic counsellors may feel uneasy or uncomfortable with. These cultural differences are over and above those which we might observe in counsellor responses to the body language of Deaf people who are also Black. People from some Black cultures regard it as culturally inappropriate to make eye-contact with people in authority, and will often look down or away from such people. We have seen how there are several counts on which a counsellor might be seen as powerful and authoritative, and it is therefore possible that such body language might be misconstrued. I have explored the implications of 'double immersion' in two cultures for counsellors working with deaf young people in educational settings elsewhere (Corker, 1993b).

LANGUAGE DISSONANCE BASED ON DIFFERENT COMPETENCES

If the counsellor and the client are not matched in their language, the cultural or experiential divide can result in the counsellor's misinterpretation of both the meaning and the intensity of client responses which blocks the client's right to be understood (d'Ardenne & Mahtani, 1989). Anger, powerlessness or any other multitude of thoughts and feelings may be construed when in fact they are not present within the client or immediate for the client, and this is all the easier if the counsellor has difficulties in their attitudinal and conceptual communication. Because the counsellor will be seen as having professional, cultural and, in the case of deaf clients, *linguistic* power, difficulties which arise from language dissonance are that much more problematic from the client's perspective. A counsellor's unfamiliarity with the structure of their client's language, or a client's limited understanding of both their own and their counsellor's language, can mean that the intense focus and concentration required to understand the units of that language (words or signs for example) prevents the development of a relationship because the expression or reinforcement of feelings cannot happen. The often repetitive and cumulative nature of the problem situations experienced by many deaf clients means that anxiety and stress levels will often be acute. Mehrabian and Reed (1969) have suggested that even low levels of anxiety stemming from seemingly simple problem situations, if they are uncontrollable or persistent, can severly interfere with the quality of a client's life. Anxiety about disclosure of such problems is exacerbated if deaf clients are not communicating in their natural or most comfortable language, or if they have limited competence in that language. The additional stress can lead to less *fluency* of expression (Henley, 1979), increased pidginisation or bilingual interference between languages, for example, which can be interpreted by unskilled counsellors as linguistic *errors*, and become prone to misrepresentation in the same way that they are in other kinds of professional–client relationships. Teachers, for example, may not only overlook the effects of stress on expression but may fail to see 'Deaf English', PSE or SSE, for example, as legitimate means of communication because the emphasis is on the teaching and learning of *standard language forms*. This view can be transferred to the counselling relationship.

Limited language competence tends to be associated with mental disturbance or stagnation, but counsellors need to be wary of making assumptions especially when they are unfamiliar with language nuances. Steinberg (1991) points out, for example, that abstract expression using non-verbal stimuli is complex and difficult to comprehend in the absence of familiarity with sign language:

> 'For example, a deaf patient chose to stop communicating during therapy with the statement, "Church – Stop." For this man, who had a bipolar disorder, church was a place in which he felt safe and nurtured. "Stop" referred to the cessation of racing thoughts that were intrusive and disturbing. "Church – Stop" was, in fact, a poetic, abstract expression of an affective experience.'

> (Steinberg, 1991, p.383)

Whereas there are undoubtedly deaf people who have *additional* learning difficulties because of particular kinds of mental disturbance, most deaf people have a restricted language because of restricted learning opportunities. Both groups, however, may make use of linguistic nuances in particular ways. If counsellors allow assumptions and expectations about language competence to invade the counselling relationship, the client will recognise these as a symbol of their past oppression and succumb to the power of the counsellor.

LANGUAGE FOR GROWTH

Truax and Carkhuff (1967) emphasise that counsellors of all theoretical and practical persuasions must be accurately empathic if they are to be able to enter the inner world of their clients and plant the seeds of growth. They cite the counsellor's ability to communicate empathic understanding and unconditional warmth as being necessary for beneficial change. However, some counsellors, most especially those who, in other roles, are used to viewing the *how* of communication skills rather than the *what* or the *why* as central to the tasks of that role, risk over-identifying counselling process with a restricted understanding of the communication skills that serve it:

> 'Being good at communication skills is not the same as being good at helping. Moreover, an overemphasis on communication skills can make helping a great deal of talk and very little action. Technique can replace substance. Communication skills are essential, of course, but they still must serve the outcomes of the helping process... Empathy that is

trotted out, as it were, for helping encounters is likely to have a hollow ring. These skills cannot be gimmicks. They must become part of your everyday communication style.'

(Egan, 1990, pp. 147–8)

d'Ardenne and Mahtani (1989) point out that all counsellors choose and change their communicative expression to match what they perceive as the client's intellectual, social and emotional level. As we have seen, assumptions made by hearing people about deaf people can be seriously flawed, and counsellors may fail to make the same kind of cultural and communicative adjustments when working with deaf clients. In their everyday lives, most deaf people will be used to hearing people who talk...at...them...like...this... by...slow...ing...down...and...sim...pli...fy...ing...every...thing...they... say, or who *SHOUT BECAUSE THEY BELIEVE THAT DEAF PEOPLE WILL BE ABLE TO HEAR THEM BETTER!* These modes of expression are usually based on uncertainty and lack of knowledge of how we can communicate with a variety of deaf people, but they can also be a direct expression of oppressive attitudes towards deaf people. Just as the language choices and skills of the counsellor can determine the degree of empathy they can establish with the deaf client, so too can the way in which they express themselves. So, though hearing counsellors might well express themselves appropriately and in different ways if their client was a child or an adult, the tendency of unskilled counsellors to express themselves to *all* deaf clients as if they were children works against accurate empathy and leads to the client questioning the counsellor's attitudes and genuineness. A deaf university graduate will not respond favourably to such ways of communicating on the basis of feeling intellectually insulted, but a deaf person who has not been to university may well become disenchanted very quickly with patronising ways of communicating. Whereas an overemphasis on *methods* of communication can work against counselling process, the *effectiveness* of communication does assume greater importance when working with deaf clients:

> 'The major problem was not the so-called characteristics and limitations of deaf individuals. Rather, it was the limited number of qualified therapists competent to work with deaf clients and to communicate with them according to the mode of communication they prefer and are most comfortable with, and through which they best understand and are understood.'

(Sussman, 1988, p.5)

It is only when the counsellor takes a number of positive steps towards finding a common language with their client that the core values of counselling can be sustained. When we, as counsellors, demonstrate to our deaf clients that we are prepared to take these steps and learn from them, our clients feel a greater sense of contact and safety and there is a correspondingly greater chance of a growth-producing climate being enhanced by the counselling relationship.

BOX 4.6 CATHERINE AND ROBERT

Catherine is aware that although Robert is experiencing difficulties in functioning within various environments, these may or may not be a direct result of his disability. She senses that there is another piece of the puzzle which remains hidden. In the fourth session, a significant development occurs which paves the way for exploring an alternative scenario. Robert has in previous sessions referred to members of his family as if they were abstract entities. Catherine has noticed that the expression on his face is either angry or sullen and subdued when he makes these references. However, when she attempts to draw him out, he retreats quickly into his protective foetal shape, curled up on himself. Initially this happens accompanied by an angry outburst, as in the first session, but gradually, as the relationship with Catherine becomes stronger, Robert becomes dismissive rather than angry. It is at this point that Catherine feels it might be appropriate to probe a little deeper. She begins this session, as before, by asking Robert to reflect on his written 'reflections'. His response is direct and simple:

R:'I feel washed up. I can't say or do any more of that. They are all asking too many questions. I'm scared.'

C:'What are you scared of, Robert?'

Silence.

C:'It feels as if we've got stuck somewhere. How can we move out of that place together?'

R:'I don't understand. What you mean? Got stuck?'

C:*(pauses)* 'It means that the feelings have got stuck inside somewhere and you can't express them easily. I'm trying to understand your feelings and I'm a bit stuck too, my feelings are stuck too. Does that make it clearer for you?'

Robert nods but remains silent for a few minutes. Catherine allows him to be, attending to him carefully.

R:'Will you help me? Will you help me to stop hating them all so much? I can't do it by myself.'

C:'You are not alone Robert. Hate is a difficult thing to feel. Sometimes it feels overwhelming… like it takes over.'

R:'That's why I'm scared… I'm scared it will make things worse, and they're bad already, very bad. It's just that… why do I have to be all these things? Why do I have to do all these things? Why do they make me? Why do they hate me so much?'

BEGINNINGS

It is a common myth that *all* deaf people are more used to and expect didactic advice. In reality, this will depend on their past experience and whether they have had the opportunity to develop communication and negotiation skills, for example. It is however a feature of many deaf people's experience that hearing people will 'tell' them something as opposed to 'explain' something because it is usually quicker (Callow, 1991). This can create a need for both counsellors and their deaf clients to clarify the difference between advice and counselling at the start of the counselling relationship in 'preparation' (see Chapter 9). For counsellors, this may involve encouraging the deaf client to think for themselves, which necessitates a shift from thinking in the short term to long-term thinking. This can be a difficult task when counsellors are faced with a deaf client's history of restricted and inappropriate education and its effect on their ability to receive and understand knowledge and to make life decisions, particularly so if the counsellor works with deaf people in other professional roles which commonly utilise short-term thinking. But 'preparation' also involves clear explanations of counselling terminology and why particular values held by counsellors, such as confidentiality, are vital to the counselling process whatever the cultural origin of the deaf client and however culturally inconsistent these concepts may be, and to the exploration of the deaf person's view of themselves, their language choices and their cultural and social affiliations. The emphasis must be on explanation *and* exploration, and if simplification is necessary, this must be accompanied by expansion so that as much information as possible is given. For example, Catherine uses a term which is commonly referred to in counselling when attempting to draw Robert out a little more.

Counsellors must not underestimate the importance of information and its links to feelings of 'control' for deaf clients, and should be prepared to view counselling as an on-going opportunity for their client's social-emotional reeducation, which challenges society's tendency to close the doors on deaf people for fear of the floodgates opening and the liberation of deaf consciousness:

> 'Stressing the relationship itself is especially important when helping is seen as a forum for social-emotional reeducation. The kind of social-emotional reeducation that takes place through the interactions between helpers and their clients is sometimes the most significant outcome of the counselling process. Clients begin to care for themselves, trust themselves and challenge themselves more because of what they learn through their interactions with helpers'.

(Egan, 1990, pp. 58 – 59)

Most deaf people, to some degree, are deprived of information through everyday channels of communication being deficit or blocked completely. For example, I am unable to use a voice telephone. I have both a minicom and a fax machine, the latter having been obtained specifically so that I can write enquiries over the phone instead of phoning them through on voice and so I see this as a necessity rather than a luxury. I am dependent on newspapers, which may give me biased information or information with a particular political emphasis, books which may expand my knowledge but not necessarily answer the questions I have, edited and simplified television subtitles, flashing lights to tell me that someone is at the door or the phone is ringing, and my partner or friends remembering to tell me things they have heard on the radio or through the grapevine, for example. I feel angry when hearing people leave voice messages instead of faxes, or when I cannot understand the person at the door without an interpreter, or when the editing of subtitles insults my intelligence, censors the language to what society thinks I *ought* to have access to, and dictates to me what I can and cannot watch. It takes me longer to read and paraphrase the information I do have, and I have difficulty remembering things unless I have seen them written down. I have to be constantly alert to visual signals, read lips which convey very little meaningful information accurately (most is guesswork, and I get it wrong sometimes), and try not to get upset about the fact that most of my significant others do not sign and feel nervous about speaking to me on the telephone through a third party. Immediately a new acquaintance opens their mouth, I know whether we are going to be able to bridge the communication gap by the shape of their lip patterns and the quality of their facial expression, because I home in on the face as the centre of communicative space, *and not the words that they are speaking*. An open, expressive face with a 'mobile mouth', and direct, unflinching eye-contact are essential. Even when the most fluent, graceful signing is present, a bland, detached face with a tight mouth makes me feel nervous and distracts me from the clues provided by the signs, because the face is the centre of signing space and not the hands. Likewise, there are certain qualities of character or behaviour which I have come to recognise produce particular feelings in me. A person who is clear, unhurried and creative in their presentation, who does not mince words and who gives me time to think and to translate allows me to open up and begin a dialogue; a person who is perpetually in a rush, unpredictable, changeable and full of rhetoric brings a glaze over my eyes which interferes with my receptive skills because I get tired with having to concentrate to understand. What counsellors need to be aware of is that for most deaf people, there is no such thing as passive listening in the sense that hearing people use the term. Counsellors know the level of concentration and attending required for one hour of active listening or advanced empathy. It should therefore not be too difficult to imagine what a lifetime of forced active listening is like especially when deaf people are constantly told that they have 'got it wrong', have 'misunderstood', or 'take things too seriously'.

All of the life situations described above represent stressors of which deaf people are rarely free, and the glut of information produced and feelings of anxiety, frustration and anger will be brought to counselling. If, as counsellors, we are not prepared to facilitate the exploration of grey areas and educate where necessary, it is unlikely that we will enable deaf clients to discover their personal power, and they will continue to do the things which make life difficult for them. This is why experienced practitioners such as Egan view helping activities including counselling as an education process the aim of which is self-learning through self-control:

'We must confirm the ways in which the client is not undirected but misdirected; not weak, but inept in how he is using his strengths; not adrift in life, but paddling crosswise and backwards against the current.'

(Driscoll, 1984, p.113)

WHAT IS COMMUNICATED AND WHY IT IS COMMUNICATED

Preoccupations with methods of communicating with deaf people can encourage failure to pay attention to *what* and *why* we communicate. If we look at standard 'how to' textbooks on counselling, we will note that the focus of the counselling task is listening to the 'problem-based' information that clients give and using this information by modifying it, emphasising it, exploring it and encouraging the client to see the opportunities it presents by developing options and alternatives. The counsellor's choice of language in achieving this task sends messages to the client about the counsellor's values and their attitudes towards deaf people and the deaf community. We saw some examples in the previous chapter of how different counselling styles might produce different counsellor language, and we can speculate on what the outcomes will be for the client who is faced with these very different counsellor messages:

BOX 4.7 THE LANGUAGE OF COUNSELLORS

THE DEAF CLIENT ASKS FOR HELP:

My friend really hurt me when they said I was only interested in myself. It's all their fault anyway because I tell them and tell them how to help me and they just keep on forgetting. I'm fed up with hearing people.

THE COUNSELLORS RESPOND:

The Benevolent Humanitarian	Oh but that is *terrible*. It must be absolutely awful for you. I don't know how you can *bear* it, especially when it happens all the time.
The Expert	I was reading something very interesting the other day – I think I've got the book on the shelf over there somewhere, remind me to show it to you, but it's about hearing people being deeply frightened of what you represent and so the reason they reject you is because your deafness is seen as…
The Power Broker	What do you expect? People haven't got time to spend their lives thinking about your needs. It is very egocentric to think otherwise.

The CAN	I'm afraid that is what happens when you waste your time with trying to establish relationships with hearing people. Life's a pain, but why worry about it? There's a whole new world waiting out there in the Deaf culture. Why not learn to sign?
The Stockbroker	I expect your reaction stems from your childhood… I remember you told me that your mother behaved in exactly the same way towards you. Maybe if we explore your relationship with her we can solve your problems in communication.
The Panic Broker	Erm…why did your friend say that? *Thinks: But I'm hearing…maybe she's fed up with me too? How on earth do I get around that one? I mean how do I get her to trust me if she's fed up with me?…*
The Empowerer	It sounds as if your friend doesn't listen to you, but I wonder why she feels bad about you being interested in yourself? It feels to me as if you care very much about your friend or it wouldn't hurt so much when she behaves in this way. Do you feel that all hearing people hurt you in the same way?

In many instances, the language used by the counsellor will reinforce a particular message for the client, and in some cases, this can be vital to the outcome of the counselling relationship for the client. Consider the following dialogue between Ruth and her counsellor, Sarah:

BOX 4.8 SARAH AND RUTH

S:(*signs*) 'Sex signs…you know many. Learn where?'

R:'Don't know…'

S:'Mother your explain?'

R:(*dismissively*) '…Mother can't sign; talk, no; listen, no.'

S:(*pauses*) 'Tell more me, you want? Talk more, you want?'

R:'No talk…only fuck, only blow-job, want stop – no, fuck more, say won't tell. Why? love no more. Hurt, love, why? Understand me? no.'

S:'Must be secret you think?'

R:'Must, must. Mother, no love, he no love. School stay forever… He say me bad, must fuck, no love, must…' *Describes very rapidly and in great detail all the things she was forced to do, becoming more and more agitated.*

S:'What happen… You have such pain… Maybe you scared feel; maybe you hurt feel. You brave me tell…(*pauses*) This happen where?'

R:(*with emphasis*) 'There…'

S:'There?'

R:'Can't tell. Me bad tell. Me no love tell…'

S:(*with emphasis*) 'No! Fault your? No! Bad you? No! Other children, happen what? Same. He behave how? Wrong. Must tell. Hurt, no more. Pain, no more. He wrong.'

Sarah is attempting to remove guilt and responsibility from Ruth, which is the vital first step in listening to and supporting disclosures of abuse victims. The messages 'It's not your fault', 'You're not to blame', 'You weren't responsible' and 'You're not alone, this has happened to others' must be conveyed (Milner and Blyth, 1988; Kennedy, 1990). Sarah also avoids the four major problem areas suggested by Robinson and Falconer (1982), in the messages that she conveys:

1. Assumptions that the abuse was a terrible experience – if the client has mixed feelings this can multiply guilt. Sarah waits until Ruth has said what she feels.

2. Criticising the offender as a person – she criticises the offender's behaviour and acknowledges that love is or may be an issue for Ruth.

3. Projecting her own reactions onto Ruth – Sarah feels very threatened and shocked by Ruth's language but resists disclosing this.

4. Using leading terms which might cause alarm such as 'rape' or 'incest'.

The need to avoid these areas has, however, been balanced against Ruth's cultural need as a deaf person with BSL as a primary language for direct communication which explains clearly what is meant.

If *what* counsellors say can be construed by the client as audist, oppressive or insincere, it will influence the entire counselling process and, in the end, will betray the counsellor. To avoid this, the counsellor must focus on using language which is acceptable and accessible to the client, which can often be determined by consulting the client and listening or watching carefully to their responses to the use of particular terms. Counsellors must also develop an awareness that language changes its meaning and connotation over time and, above all, communicate their *respect* for their clients' seeing *skills* and linguistic *abilities*, whatever their language preference or competence.

For example, there are many references in history to deaf people as 'the deaf and dumb' or 'deaf mutes', and these labels are still used by lay people and the media in their ignorance or denial of deaf people's difference. In professional circles, these terms were eventually superseded by terms such as 'hearing impaired' or 'deaf and hard-of-hearing', but these too caused a problem for some deaf people because they defined deaf people as impaired hearing people or because they created artificial divisions between deaf and hard-of-hearing people on the basis of the degree of their hearing loss, which again implies a deficit relationship to hearing people. Then the term Deaf was developed to distinguish that group of deaf people who formed a linguistic and cultural minority apart from the rest, who were called deaf. This has also proved problematic, because some deaf people have objected to the lower-case 'd' on the grounds that it symbolises that they are inferior to and have fewer problems than Deaf people, who are ascribed an upper-case 'D'. Certainly this view has tended to be enshrined in special service provision, where BSL users or 'Deaf without speech' are often given priority over 'oral' deaf people and seen to be in greater need. The present dilemmas are over the use of the term 'disabled' in relation to deaf/Deaf people, and the desire of deafened people to be considered as a discrete group in order that they can begin to move away from the negative connotations ascribed to them by both Deaf and hearing people.

I have run many training workshops on language and labelling because it is my belief that the language used by the different cultures of society reinforces oppresssion. When asked to think of labels which may be ascribed to deaf people, workshop participants always produce long lists of labels which actually describe deaf*ness* and not deaf *people*, and, for the most part, are negative or technical descriptions. The lists produced by professionals are usually very much longer that those of lay people, and often confined to professional jargon. Meanwhile, psychology textbooks are littered with negative terminology in relation to deaf people (Lane, 1992), and those outside of an awareness of deaf issues, including some counsellors, continue to use terms which are inappropriate and, in some cases, offensive to deaf people. For example, Nelson-Jones (1988, p.271) in his 'Glossary of helping terms' uses *tunnel vision* as meaning 'a narrowing of perception under threat so that the individual focuses only on certain factors in a situation and excludes others which might be important'. This may well be the counsellor's meaning, but *tunnel vision* is one of the common terms used to describe people with Usher's syndrome, and is the literal translation of the sign USHERS, which can be an extremely distressing experience as it may involve a deaf person losing their sight gradually to different degrees. The definition of *tunnel vision* given is clearly not appropriate in relation to these people and is in any case reminiscent of the old denotative meaning of 'deaf'. Thomas Mahan (1993) in an article on counselling people with disabilities, uses the phrase 'how many *ears* must a man have before he can *hear* people cry?' together with phrases such as '*blind* others to the whole person' and 'would inevitably *cripple* her in this regard', which use the disabling meanings of these words. Even Mearns and Thorne (1988, p. 24) use the phrase 'turn a deaf ear and a blind eye' in the context of complacency, the use of which some deaf people would regard as complacent in itself.

Another dimension to the use of oppressive language is that we often use language in general to deny or distort the particular experiences of another person because perhaps we are unable to comprehend their perception of a particular situation. For example, Dorothy Stiefel gives us a flavour of this situation as encountered by a deaf person with Usher's syndrome who has been absorbed in listening to the accessible sounds around her and becomes disorientated by what she believes initially is a dog being run over:

"'Did you see what happened?'"

"No, but it sounded like the car went over a bunch of twigs and debris and it made enough racket to make the dog move," I surmised.

"No. What happened was that it was a police car, and the driver turned on the siren momentarily, just enough to scare the dog out of the middle of the street."

"It sure didn't sound like any siren I've ever heard," I said, chastising myself out loud for making still *another* error in what had taken place.

"But I *saw* it and I *heard* it at the same time, you didn't."

I thought about that. In fact, I stopped, turned around, and said to her, "I still can't believe how I am confused so much about what I think is happening with what actually is taking place. I never used to do this!" (Or maybe I have and no one has ever corrected me. But then again not many other people know about the debilitating effects of having a dual disability.'"

(Stiefel, 1991, p.52)

Language like this is generally to be avoided when counselling deaf people, and we should remember that some deaf clients will also be Black, physically challenged or disabled in some other way. Oppressive language in general has no place in counselling.

When working with Deaf people using sign language, a particular difficulty is that there are no standard signs for counselling concepts, and some of the existing signs do not accurately convey what the concept means in *visual–spatial* terms. For example some varieties of the sign COUNSELLING are quite directional in movement and do not convey the idea of a counselling *relationship* or of sharing. This may be a result of Deaf people's unfamiliarity with counselling, but it creates a misleading impression of the complexity of the activity. I have also seen signed translations of the concept 'active listening' which use the sign LISTEN in its hearing connotation (a cupped hand placed behind the ear). This is clearly not the meaning of 'listening' that many Deaf people will have, and is culturally and experientially inappropriate in working with Deaf people. Further, because BSL is a youthful language in comparison to English or other spoken languages, Deaf people are only beginning to see the influence of issues which were addressed in the English language and hearing society years ago. There are still many sexist, racist, disablist and homophobic signs in use, and it is only recently that Deaf people have begun to see challenges from Black Deaf people and disabled Deaf people, for example, which have resulted in the development of new and more appropriate signs (see Figure 4.2). Counsellors *and interpreters* must be aware of these changes and find the signs which are appropriate for individual clients. It is also worth using 'politically correct' signs and explaining why they may be more acceptable if the Deaf client does not know the signs, for it is exactly this kind of awareness and consciousness raising that many Deaf people are isolated from, and this can lead them into difficult situations both within their own community and in the hearing world.

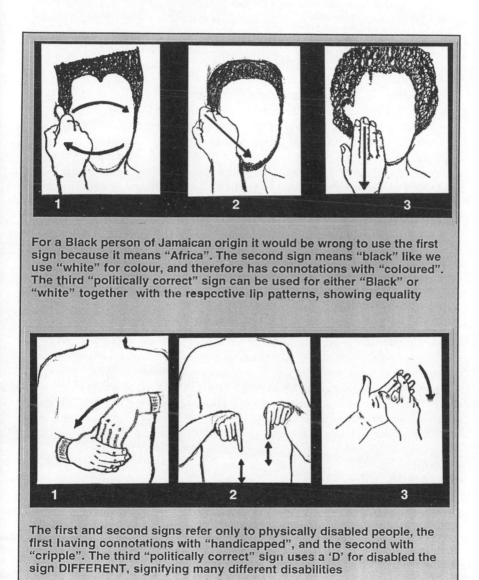

For a Black person of Jamaican origin it would be wrong to use the first sign because it means "Africa". The second sign means "black" like we use "white" for colour, and therefore has connotations with "coloured". The third "politically correct" sign can be used for either "Black" or "white" together with the respective lip patterns, showing equality

The first and second signs refer only to physically disabled people, the first having connotations with "handicapped", and the second with "cripple". The third "politically correct" sign uses a 'D' for disabled the sign DIFFERENT, signifying many different disabilities

Figure 4.2 Examples of 'Politically Correct' Signs

Counsellors are often advised to use language in counselling which is *clear, simple, direct* and *concrete*. When working with deaf clients, this advice needs to be modified to include avoiding oversimplification wherever possible, because this can be construed as paternalistic, and avoiding, in particular, language which has a double or multiple meaning or an interpretation which might be regarded by some deaf people as oppressive. We saw some possible terms above, but it is particularly important to understand that if a term has both a familiar and an obscure meaning, a deaf client who has had restricted education which has resulted in a limited understanding of the world is likely to understand or home in on the familiar meaning of the term. 'Concrete' is a case in point. The familiar interpretation of the term is 'the hard stuff that buildings and pavements, for example, are made of'. A deaf client in this position will possibly not know of the meaning of 'concrete' as in the opposite of 'abstract', and use of this word may therefore cause confusion because it appears to be placed in the 'wrong' context by the client. Other simple examples which may occur in counselling are, with unfamiliar and familiar meanings in brackets: '*draw* out' (facilitate expression *or* sketching), 'free' (liberated *or* no charge), 'key' (very important *or* an object which locks a door), 'measures' (steps which can be taken *or* measurements), 'play a *part*' (help *or* part of something and playing), 'two *parties*' (two people *or* celebrations), 'relative' (compared to *or* a family relation), 'right' (human rights *or* right as the opposite of wrong and right as the opposite of left), 'sound' (firm and strong *or* a noise), 'terms' (words, names and conditions *or* school terms) and 'type' (a sort *or* kind or office work) (Nickerson, Zannetou and Sutton, 1986). These are over and above words which can be mislipread and the confusion which may be created by the counsellor signing a word literally, as in 'feed-back', for example, where the signs FEED and BACK are combined to convey a totally inappropriate and nonsensical meaning. Counsellors must be doubly certain of using signs in the correct context, and aim to develop as wide a vocabulary as possible, in addition to being alert for client responses which seem odd or bear no relation to the counsellor's question. A strategy for more effective communication with deaf clients – a 'language for growth' – is summarised in Box 4.9.

THE USE OF INTERPRETERS IN COUNSELLING

The paucity of deaf people who are trained counsellors and hearing counsellors who are able to communicate fluently with deaf people through spoken or sign language means that if deaf people are to obtain access of any kind to counselling and their right to be understood is respected, counsellors must be prepared to consider using interpreters to translate the content of counselling dialogues. A hearing client could ask to be referred to another counsellor if they were unhappy with their present one, but if a deaf person were to have the same options, using interpreters is often the only solution. However, this is easier said than done. Just as deaf people have a wide variety of communication preferences and competences, counsellors and deaf people vary in the skill with which they can work with an interpreter and in their ability to select an appropriate interpreter, and interpreters themselves are not uniform in

BOX 4.9 FINDING A COMMON LANGUAGE

COUNSELLORS WORKING WITH DEAF CLIENTS MUST:

- TAKE RESPONSIBILITY for learning the client's language and for learning about the difficulties that deaf clients face in communicating in an alien or unfamiliar language
- BE CONSTANTLY ALERT to any visual clues they may be giving, and also to those coming from the client such as a tendency on the part of the client to answer in monosyllables or with a signed YES or NO
- ALLOW MORE TIME for the exploration of the client's significant feelings and experiences, for example by approaching a particular topic in a number of different ways in order to help the client to elaborate more clearly
- CHECK OUT INCONGRUENCIES in the client which may indicate they have misunderstood and ascertain that the client's meaning has been correctly understood
- NOT MAKE ASSUMPTIONS about language preferences and aim to find the deaf client's 'most comfortable' language
- USE THE CLIENT'S LANGUAGE changes and adjustments constructively within the counselling relationship to explore the client's feelings
- RESPECT the deaf client's 'seeing skills'
- AIM TO DEVELOP a level of non-verbal skill which is at least equal through advanced empathy
- BE PREPARED TO USE art and body work to enable expression of communication blocks or difficult feelings (see Chapter 5)
- KEEP THEIR LANGUAGE clear, simple, direct and concrete whilst ensuring that their expression is not patronising
- AVOID TERMS including counselling terms, which are unclear or have both a concrete and an abstract meaning, have a double or multiple meaning or have an interpretation or association for deaf people which might be regarded as oppressive
- RECOGNISE that their attitudes are part of their cultural inheritance and be aware of the many subtle forms in which this inheritance is revealed
- BE AWARE of the content of their own language and avoid language which is audist, sexist, racist, homophobic or oppressive in any other way
- PAY ATTENTION to the information content of their communication, explaining and clarifying wherever possible, in addition to educating the client when asked to do so
- INTEGRATE REGULARLY with deaf people and become familiar with the range of deaf people's language preferences and language nuances
- BE WILLING AND ABLE to make use of an interpreter when necessary, and to monitor the resulting communication

their skills or their understanding of the counsellor's task. There is still some confusion in the way in which 'interpreters' are defined, and although the Council for Advancement for Communication with Deaf People (CACDP) have attempted to clarify matters, the debate continues and is as fierce as ever. We have seen that the term 'counsellor' is often used erroneously to describe ad hoc or informal helpers, advice workers, providers of guidance services and so on. The same is true of the term 'interpreter', which is often used as a blanket term to describe registered sign language interpreters, communicators, trainee interpreters, lipspeakers, deaf–blind communicators and family members or friends who provide 'communication support'. As in other settings, the 'interpreter' selected may be selected because they happen to be available, and although registered sign language interpreters are bound by their code of practice not to accept work which is beyond their level of skill, many informal translators, trainee interpreters or communicators do this in practice because they do not want deaf people to miss out, because they do not understand the ethical or legal considerations of failing to carry out the job effectively, or simply because they need the work to pay their bills. This introduces an element of risk for the client, quite apart from the fact that they may not feel so free to open up about deeply personal matters in the presence of a third party, especially when that third party is known to them. The chances of this happening are quite high within the deaf community, as we shall see in Chapters 8 and 9. But there is also an element of risk for the counsellor who could be sued by a deaf client as a result of an interpreter's misdemeanour. Counsellors, therefore, must be particularly aware of the threats posed by using the most available or unofficial source. Shackman (1985) has suggested that these threats include innacurate translation, bias and distortion particularly as a result of over identification with the counsellor's agency, lack of client confidentiality, lack of understanding of their role in the counselling process, failure to explain cultural differences between client and counsellor, personal unsuitability, and exploitation of the client. However, even with a registered sign language interpreter, there are advantages and disadvantages to the client–counsellor–interpreter triumvirate, which are summarised in Box 4.10.

BOX 4.10 THE PROS AND CONS OF USING INTERPRETERS IN COUNSELLING

WITH INTERPRETER	WITHOUT INTERPRETER
Linguistic input is indirect	Linguistic input is direct
Temporal distortion due to delay in translation	Temporal distortion due to counsellor misunderstanding or the need to decipher
Content distortion due to:	Content distortion due to:
• Lack of interpreter listening skills	• Innacurate counsellor communication skills

- Innacurate interpreter perceptions or understanding

- Projection or transference of interpreter feelings, thoughts and attitudes

- Interpreter simplification of counsellor and client messages

- Blocking of client's seeing skills due to focus on interpreter

- Interpreter lacking full or relevant vocabulary

- Lack of linguistic matching between interpreter and client

In group therapy, all linguistic activity in counselling is accessible, leaving counsellor free to focus on the relationship

Interpreter–client alliance possible

Client may not trust interpreter

May be difficult to work with the same interpreter throughout the counselling relationship – lack of consistency

- Client's failure to understand concepts

- Counsellor's failure to make full use of client's language nuances

- Counsellor simplifying by focusing on client's deafness

- Client's focus on their seeing skills

- Counsellor oversimplifying what is communicated because of client's deafness

- Cultural mismatch between client and counsellor which blurs cultural distinctions

In group therapy, counsellor may have to act as interpreter for other group members, which may cause boundary difficulties

Counsellor–client alliance possible

Development of trust may be slow

Consistency for relationship building

Many of the disadvantages of using an interpreter can be overcome if the counsellor is prepared to take responsibility for the triumvirate of counsellor, client and interpreter. To ensure that risks to the client are minimised, there are positive practical steps that the counsellor can take (see Box 4.11), but some of these steps may appear controversial from the interpreter's perspective. For example, a registered sign language interpreter's Code of Practice specifies that they should not counsel, advise or interject personal opinions. Whereas we would sometimes find 'interpreters' with lesser qualifications doing all of these things, it is obviously in the interests of the client that an interpreter is used in counselling who has a very high level of skill. In Britain, this means a registered interpreter. It is extremely important for interpreter and counsellor to mutually clarify roles in advance of working with a deaf client, particularly in respect of communication with each other in the counselling relationship:

> 'Smiles exchanged between the…counsellor and the interpreter, joking asides, a shake of the head – any of a number of events, when unexplained to the deaf client, may lead to a breakdown of trust and a

nurturing of suspicion. From the deaf person's perspective, communication is occurring of which the client has no knowledge, and the client by rights should be apprised of everything the interpreter hears. There should be no conversation without the deaf client's involvement, just as there would be none in the client were...hearing.'

(Roe and Roe, 1991, p. 101)

There are differing views about how this should be done, and whether the client should be involved from the outset. My view is that counselling sessions are the client's time and this valuable time, which is often extremely difficult for the deaf client to find at all, should not be taken up with discussion about issues which relate solely to the relationship between the interpreter and the counsellor. However, such meetings should not happen *before* the client has indicated that they are happy to work with a particular interpreter in the counselling situation. If the two professionals fail to clarify such issues and mistakes are made, any later suggestion of separate meetings will simply confirm for the client that his or her worst fears are true. The counsellor and the interpreter are seen to be in collusion with each other against the client, and the meetings they have with each other may be seen to trespass on the confidentiality of which the deaf client has been assured, and may send confusing messages about the interpreter's role.

The client must be informed that the counsellor and the interpreter will need to establish in a separate meeting how they are going to work together but also be reassured that this discussion will not involve any exchange of information about the client. Thereafter, any particular issues relating to communication or, in the case of Deaf clients, culture, must be built in to the counselling sessions, or the client may feel that their trust is being abused. Stansfield (1987) emphasises that the counselling process depends greatly on the quality of the relationship established and, because they are present, the interpreter becomes part of that process whatever their code of practice, and counselling greatly alters the circumstances of interpreting. Further, because the counselling relationship determines client growth, interaction between the counsellor and the interpreter will have a direct impact on process. Thus the two professionals must operate within clearly defined roles, and both must be prepared to 'give' a little in order to facilitate the client's growth.

However, because the interpreter is part of what can be a very stressful and difficult journey, the counsellor must remain aware of the interpreter's feelings. For example, trust and confidentiality are two issues that repeatedly occur in the lives of interpreters, in part because some unscrupulous or unskilled practitioners have damaged the reputation of the interpreting profession in the eyes of some Deaf people. It can be very hard for a 'good' interpreter to accept that a Deaf person does not trust them sufficiently to use them in the counselling situation, but many of the reasons for the lack of trust are to do with the uniqueness of the counselling situation as opposed to perceived deficiencies in the personal or professional qualities of the interpreter on the part of the client. Some clients, for example, view interpreters as yet another barrier to independence (Crammatte, 1983), and are resentful of having to be dependent on the skills of an interpreter for basic communication. In the counselling situation, this resentment may contribute to feelings of mistrust which become centred on the interactions between the interpreter and the counsellor (Stansfield, 1981). It is important for interpreters and counsellors in this situation to remember that many of the problem situations that deaf clients bring to counselling have happened because of blocked or

---

BOX 4.11 WORKING EFFECTIVELY WITH INTERPRETERS

WHEN USING AN INTERPRETER, COUNSELLORS SHOULD:

- Take responsibility for the triumvirate relationship
- Ascertain whether there is linguistic matching between interpreter and client, and that the matching is on the basis of the client's *most comfortable* means of expression as opposed to the interpreter's linguistic bias, for example
- Establish a professional relationship with the interpreter *before* accepting work with deaf clients to determine boundaries relative to particular codes of practice, clarify counselling terminology and explain counselling style, and try to work with the same interpreter
- Ensure that the interpreter is acceptable to and trusted by the client
- Recommend that the interpreter is trained at least in basic counselling skills. If this is not possible, explain clearly the counselling process, core values and particular issues such as transference, and what kinds of client information or communication are important or significant for counselling
- Ensure that there are no personal or cultural differences which might intrude upon the counsellor's or the interpreter's effectiveness
- Encourage the interpreter to be part of the counselling relationship and to convey, for example, when they feel that the client is blocked or failing to understand
- Use straightforward language
- Actively listen to both the interpreter and the client, observe their body language and maintain eye contact with both
- Allow more time for the counselling session to enable full explanation and clarification
- Check constantly whether the client has understood
- When the session is over, allow a short time for the client to ask questions or raise points, but make it clear what this time is for
- Be aware of the pressures on interpreters, and be prepared to have a post-session interview with the interpreter to assess communication during the session, their feelings, and any difficult issues which need referral
- Be prepared to include the interpreter in supervision activities

(after Shackman, 1985)

damaged communication. As a result of these situations having been attributed to the client's *deafness*, rather than to the inability of others to communicate with them, the client will feel sensitive about needing help with communication when they are exploring problems with communication.

In some cases, there will be a need for the interpreter to leave the relationship and the reasons for doing so must be discussed with the client. However, in most cases, difficulties that arise can be solved by the interpreter have access to qualified counselling supervision, preferably alongside the counsellor, or by winding-down sessions between the interpreter and the counsellor. If this occurs, it must be understood that being honest with the deaf client about the existence of a supervisor or of meetings where the client is not present may present a challenge to the client's understanding of confidentiality and initiate a setback in their ability to trust. That is why both counsellors and interpreters must have a great deal of patience, trust in each other, and respect for the client.

SUMMARY

The philosopher Ludwig Wittgenstein (1967) suggests that language is related to the shared activities of living, which he calls 'forms of life'. He stresses that it is the *use* of language which gives it its power, and therefore we need to constantly examine what language is doing or achieving in a particular situation. Wittgenstein (1967, p.5) uses the term 'language-game' to describe language and the actions into which it is interlaced. The counsellor is the artisan who lives by weaving language. She listens to her client's messages and weaves them into a pattern, sometimes, like the *Empowerer*, altering a few threads here and there to strengthen the weave of the client's inner self, or, like the *Power Broker*, binding the threads together so tightly with destructive language-games that they keep the client trapped in the web of their own misery:

> 'They are playing a game. They are playing at not playing a game. If I show them I see they are, I shall break the rules, and they will punish me. I must play their game, of not seeing I see the game.'

> (Laing, 1970, p.1)

Deaf people have for the most part been taught that their predicament lies in their language 'impoverishment' and that the 'disturbances' that they experience in personal relationships are a result of their inability to use language or certain types of language fully. Some would say, that on the basis of this assessment, they are prime candidates for counselling *per se*, but because this belief is based on assumptions and lack of knowledge about the ways in which deaf people actually *use* language, counselling risks becoming another form of straight jacketing which, like many elements of deaf education restricts the client's world of meaning to the judgements of others, and they risk accepting these judgements as if they were their own truth:

> 'Unless the words a deaf child is taught relate to life, that child is being taught a dead language. In such vocabulary-orientated teaching, men-

tal hungers are fed with an assortment of memorised word meanings instead of the semantics of experience and concepts; and communicative drive withers under drill, repetition and correction.'

(Levine, 1981, p.73)

We all know that words or signs, by themselves, are meaningless, and we all underestimate the power of the activities which impart meaning. Perhaps the real difficulty with deaf people is that somehow they have tapped a part of this power and they have built it into their communicative infrastructures in ways which threaten complacency and provoke secrets from their hiding places. In having this skill, a deaf client poses a constant challenge to the counsellor's genuineness and demands more of the counsellor's skills than a hearing client might. In addition, deaf language, though it should be familiar to counsellors as a partial reflection of their non-verbal listening and attending skills, becomes a potent probing device for the client which deprives the counsellor of some of their personal power in the counselling relationship. The counsellor may feel that they are forced on the defensive, struggling in their search for a common language and the keys which will open doors for social-emotional reeducation, whilst feeling deprived of the one tool of their trade which is regarded as the root of their effectiveness, and is therefore indispensable. This is perhaps why the seeing skills of deaf clients are difficult for counsellors to acknowledge as *skills*; but the irony is that seeing skills are *the* keys to meeting *The Deaf Challenge* in counselling, and the foundations on which a language for growth, deaf people's sense of being-in-the-world, is built.

'From that first meeting I was sharply aware of the differences in the cultures that had spawned up. I was certainly responding to something more basic than our contrasting means of expressing ourselves. And yet the differences in our gestures seemed to hold the key to our widely different heritages and the ways in which we learned to see our relation to the world.'

(Kopp, 1972)

CHAPTER 5

THE METHODOLOGICAL CHALLENGE –
MOVING BEYOND A 'TALKING THROUGH'

with contributions from Paul Redfern

'There is a continual need to think about what is happening at any time and to consider what might best help. This requires a therapist to be open to the validity and value of a wide range of theoretical stances, and to have sufficient knowledge of their potential application. Clinicians who are comfortably rooted in one therapeutic model should not become so securely settled in it that they are unable or unwilling to consider what others have to offer.'

(Walker, 1992, p.174)

In the previous chapters, we have looked in detail at many of the fundamental issues which challenge counsellors when they begin to work with deaf clients. If counsellors are able to take these issues on board and deal with them unconsciously and consciously there is a chance that the Island of Growth will come within their sights, and the *real* journey, the task of counselling, can commence. There is however one remaining obstacle to client growth, which might best be described as the *methodological challenge*. This is not, and never was intended to be a 'how to counsel deaf people' book, since counsellors and deaf clients will constantly be discovering or rediscovering different ways of working which serve the task of counselling. It is, however, a book about issues which are relevant to counselling deaf people. We have, throughout the preceding pages, spent much time exploring the inappropriateness of some existing 'counselling' practice for working with deaf people in general, whatever social affiliations they make, whatever the nature of their problem situations, and whatever the landscapes of their inner worlds. In previous chapters, we worked through what is probably the most fundamental issue of all – the deaf client's right to understand and be understood, and how this is directly linked to access to appropriate counselling services. Yet getting the attitude, language and communication right is of limited use if it is not placed within a responsive methodological framework or way of working; without such a framework, the *Benevolent Humanitarians*, The *Experts*, The *Power Brokers*, The *Panic Brokers* and The *Stockbrokers* of the counselling profession will continue to wield their power over deaf people and flourish their weapons of self-esteem and identity destruction. This chapter is largely an account

of how I developed my own particular framework of working, both theoreti-
cally and from a practical perspective. This framework is not proposed as a
definitive one, nor as *the* way to work with deaf clients, for I am constantly in
a state of redefining my experience and my understanding, as are deaf clients:

> 'In the flow of experiencing, the past is taken up as an experience which
> is immediately present. If I weep for a rejection of twenty years ago, it
> is happening now. But (and this is important) it is guided by the future.
> My experience, now, is shaped by my anticipations, what I envisage:
> what shall be, what might be, what I hope for. Experiencing is not static.
> There is movement. If I can stay awhile with raw experiencing, if I can
> wait attentively; then perhaps, with luck or grace, a new possibility
> might emerge: a movement, a carrying forward.'

> (Hobson, 1985, p.33)

I believe that this framework incorporates most of the features of theory and
practice which will be needed by counsellors working with the vast majority
of Deaf or deaf clients, whether the counsellor is themself deaf or hearing,
because it presents a possibility for movement and change.

INTRODUCTION

Before we begin to develop this framework, it may be useful to bring together
all the threads and issues raised in previous chapters through the eyes of a
Deaf client, for the framework must grow from such experiences if it is to be
a responsive one. Paul Redfern has spent many years trying to educate
non-deaf people about being deaf through training and writing. He writes
here about his need for counselling to be a place where he 'can escape his
oppression'.

ESCAPING OPPRESSION – ONE DEAF PERSON'S SEARCH FOR SAFETY

Counsellors or therapists who have deaf clients are faced with issues encom-
passing culture, power, oppression, communication and linguistics. As a Deaf
consumer of counselling services, I have chosen a non-deaf counsellor who is
a member of a minority group and I am now receiving counselling based on
humanist principles. Previously I was in psychotherapy, but would not again
chose this mode of work unless very strongly convinced that the therapist was
not him- or herself oppressive in a hearist way. I have made this decision after
many years of grappling with some of the more difficult issues in my life and
do not want to place myself in the hands of someone who lacks an understanding of the issues of oppression.

The most important issue for me in choosing a counsellor is for them to
actually support me in my belief that there is nothing intrinsically wrong with
me in terms of my deafness. So, when I am angry about situations, I am
supported in believing that I have a right to my anger because those situations
are a result and a symptom of the oppressive society in which I live. Should
the counsellor in any way indicate that I am unreasonably angry because I

have a basic problem with being Deaf, or that I have problems because I am Deaf, then I would lose trust and probably would terminate the relationship. I state this for, as a result of many years of trying to be as 'hearing' as hearing people, I have come to the conclusion that this is akin to chasing rainbows. I am not hearing nor will I ever be. I am Deaf. To wear or even pretend to wear hearing people's clothes is to be dishonest about who or what I am. Being dishonest means that I have no personal integrity as a Deaf person. I behave and think as a Deaf person. I perceive things differently. I am different. But that does not mean that I am disabled. I identify as a member of a cultural minority. Many disabled people are vociferous in stating their rights and I support that. What I cannot accept is their insistence that since I am Deaf I am also disabled because I have a hearing loss. I do not have a hearing loss. I do not have a hearing disability. I do not have hearing difficulties. 'But you can't hear the birds sing!' is a constant refrain. And neither can many hearing people use sign language is my riposte. 'Ah but we are capable of learning!' Really? As a BSL tutor I suspect otherwise; if this were true, where are our counsellors?

Oppression works in several different ways. Deviation from everyday acts of communication is incredibly difficult for many to handle. The number of times I have been confronted with a giggle on the face opposite bears testimony to that. Non-deaf counsellors are not immune to this so it can be very easy to end up feeling that once again I am engaged in a battle within the therapy simply to be understood and to understand. If I am crying, I cannot see the face of the counsellor, so in effect, I cannot see any words or hear any murmurings or comfort should there be any. If I am angry, my voice can become distorted and the counsellor may not understand, so I have to be controlled until such time as I am confident enough in the counsellor's ability to understand me, whatever my mood. Sometimes the counsellor can be difficult to lipread – some words do not lend themselves to ease of understanding. This latter phrase could easily look like 'someone does not like themselves to years of understanding', which of course is nonsensical. The act of communication also leads to a great defensiveness on the part of many non-deaf people. If I get angry in telling a story of some idiotic ticket collector who could or would not understand that it was the Leicester train and not the Leeds train that I wanted, there are plenty of non-deaf people who rush to the defence of the hapless unknown hearing person. Very rarely do non-deaf people empathise in everyday life. They often recount their own tales of meeting someone equally idiotic which often doesn't make me feel any better since it ignores the everyday frustrations that I have to live with. Sometimes it is of some comfort – If they can't manage it how can we? But, more hurtfully, there is a tendency to explain away the behaviour in terms of ignorance, lack of knowledge, poor training or gross over-expectation on my part:

> 'The therapist is a person-in-relationship. He is what he has made of his experiences. What counts is not what has happened to him but what he has created from what has happened to him. All too often, the pronouncement 'In my experience...' is a justification for repeating our mistakes. To share in a dialogue which carries forward, means that the therapist is open to immediate experiencing in relation to (the client), ready to reassess and revalue past experiences, to scrutinise them, let

them go, and to have the 'immense patience' to wait until they are turned to blood...'

(Hobson, 1985, p. 36)

For many non-deaf people, the physical environment is not an impediment to the process of enabling. For a Deaf person, it may add to the oppressive features of the agency. Standing outside waiting for someone to come to the door because I cannot hear the entry phone system ping is not conducive to the feeling of empowerment. As a point of fact, I generally place my hand on the door and when I feel the ping, it gives way. Occasionally I have been taken by surprise when someone has opened it and I do not lean too hard in case I tumble over. Counsellors need to think about the physical environment and at least make this as non-oppressive as possible. They should also spend time reading and learning about deafness and clarifying their own perspectives, and think very carefully about the language they use. I, for example, do not want to be called 'hearing-impaired' since that presupposes that I am impaired in some way. Nor do I want to have a 'sensory handicap' or any of the other official terms with which I routinely get labelled. I just want to be called Deaf. I recognise that other deaf people may be different. For example, I would also venture to say that having a strong understanding of oppression may not be terribly helpful for those people who have lost their hearing. Because many have spent a large portion of their lives as hearing people, they may carry baggage which sees being deaf as a tragedy, and if they encounter a counsellor who focuses only on oppression, then it could be difficult to achieve meaningful communication. The partial solution is for any counsellor to rigorously examine their own standpoint, and to be clear whether they may be allowing their own ideological baggage, of whatever variety, to prevent their client from determining their needs and their own solutions.

But, returning to *me*, I am able to make judgements about *my counselling needs*. Questions such as 'How long have you been deaf?' should be eschewed as well since they reaffirm the medicalisation of deafness. The proper question is 'How do you want to communicate?'. The degree or aetiology of my hearing loss is immaterial to my need to communicate and to be understood. The chasm in culture and perspective affects our language and counsellors need to understand this and beware of falling into the trap of medicalising my 'problem'. Because I am Deaf, it does not actually mean that I know nothing of how the hearing world functions. I spend a great deal of time in the hearing world, absorbing its values and procedures. Granted, I am marginalised in many ways by the lack of access to services, but this does not mean that I cannot understand. Nor does it mean that my reality becomes invalid simply because it is different. It is all too easy for people, including counsellors, to dispute my version of reality, as John McKnight sums up aptly:

'While it is clearly disabling to be told you can't decide whether you have a problem and how it can be dealt with, the professional imperative compounds the dilemma by demonstrating that you couldn't understand the problem or the solution anyway. The language of modernised professional services mystifies both problem and solution so that citizen evaluation becomes impossible. The only people "competent" to decide whether the servicing process has any merit are professional peers, each affirming the basic assumptions of the other.'

(McKnight, 1981)

WHERE DO WE START?

McKnight's concluding remark about the competence of professional peers in assessing the merit of servicing processes, 'each affirming the basic assumptions of the other', is an interesting starting point in itself. As we saw in Chapter 1, there is probably no one definition of counselling that will satisfy every counsellor or every client. This, in part, is due to the proliferation of counselling activity, as it has extended its influence to many other fields including education, management, cross-cultural communication and international peace work (Mearns and Thorne, 1988), and to the proliferation of counselling theory, as it has become necessary to inform counselling practices further and develop new ways of working (for example, Nelson-Jones, 1982; Dryden, 1984; Patterson, 1986). That being said, we will recall that the British Association for Counselling (1977) has defined 'counselling' as:

'When a person, occupying regularly or temporarily the role of counsellor, offers and agrees explicitly to give time, attention and respect to another person, or persons, who will be temporarily in the role of client. The task of counselling is to give the client an opportunity to explore, discover and clarify ways of living more resourcefully and towards greater well-being. The counsellor provides a secure and facilitating atmosphere for this to occur.'

This definition defines 'the task of counselling' in a way which parallels Paul Redfern's expectations of counselling and yet it is clear from his account that not all counsellors approach this task in a way which allows him to be himself or to develop a trusting and genuine relationship with his counsellor. This implies that he feels that *being able to choose* is important in his pursuit of 'the ideal counsellor', and as Gough (1990) suggests, 'it seems only practical to *increase* the number of options available' within the professional service of counselling. However, the previous chapter suggests that the options from which clients like Paul *are able* to choose within the present climate are already limited and his access to appropriate counselling restricted, because, in identifying what it is that he is searching for, he has found the system lacking in its response. What is important about this is that Paul is able to articulate what he wants and is also clear about who he is as a Deaf person, so he knows when his expectations of counselling are not met. Most people instinctively know what makes them feel good, indeed, most people inherently want to feel good about themselves, behave in constructive ways, and are striving for 'self-actualisation' as a basic human need (Bozarth and Temaner Brodley, 1986); but there are different reasons why particular things make them feel good or bad and they have different ways of expressing why they feel good or bad. However, some people do not understand that they *have the option* of feeling good when they feel bad, and this is exactly the kind of situation Paul may initially have found himself in when he had psychotherapy, or that Rachel discovered when she saw a male counsellor (see Chapter 6). Paul's feelings of oppression were magnified because his first counsellor could not see that there was the option of abandoning an oppressive stance, and he saw counselling as *an opportunity to escape his oppression.* If counselling is to be responsive to the expectations of deaf clients, this dichotomy must be recognised and resolved. For example, Paul says that it is better to ask a Deaf client how they want to communicate as opposed to asking them when they went deaf. But if there is no common language or a language dissonance between counsellor and client, how can we ask in a way which is meaningful to the client? We may, for example, learn sign language if we wish to work with a Deaf client and we are hearing, but it may take years for us to become fully proficient and we may not, as Paul suggests, have the appropriate characteristics to learn effectively, however skilled we are as counsellors. Do we meanwhile ask the client to wait patiently as we muddle our way through communication blocks or do we refer them to a counsellor who does sign but who may not be their natural choice of counsellor because they are known to them within the Deaf community? Do we continue our search for a common language into the realm of our shared experience? Or do we, as Melanie Klein did with autistic children (Mitchell, 1986) try to find a language where there is none, at least none that we as counsellors can comprehend? These are all questions which have implications for methodology. They are all questions that counsellors must be asking themselves when they consider whether they can work with deaf people and they begin to search for a methodological or ideological framework. Not asking them implies a preparedness to abandon deaf people to their problem situations.

PROFESSIONAL PROTECTIONISM

Since we have indicated that existing counselling services are at best patchy, we have to consider ways in which we might expand these services in a way which allows potential clients such as Paul to have a *real* choice. I feel that expansion has *three* sides because the deaf community is diverse both culturally and linguistically, and different deaf people have different counselling needs and expectations. First, and most importantly, more deaf people should be facilitated in their desire to train as counsellors. We will look at some deaf perspectives on training issues in Chapter 10. Second, we must encourage more existing counsellors, particularly those who work within methodological frameworks and philosophies which are accessible and acceptable to deaf people, to develop an awareness of deaf people or continue to explore alternative ways of working which open up opportunities for deaf people. And third, we must identify skilled communicators who have appropriate personal qualities to train as counsellors. If we do not pursue all three approaches, we will continue to turn needy deaf people away, because we must at all times remember that the deaf community is small and if we limit ourselves to that community in our search for the 'right' people, we restrict client choices and increase the possibility of role overload or role confusion in existing professionals. Further, just as there is a move within the hearing community to open up the white, middle class foundations of the counselling profession to members of different minority groups, so too is this needed in the deaf community. If Paul were Black as well as Deaf, and he wished to work with a Black counsellor or a Black Deaf counsellor, his choices would be even more restricted. It might also be said that the vast majority of professionals working with deaf people in a variety of roles are women, and if Paul wished to see a male counsellor, he might have an even longer search. Despite the knowledge that there are many hearing people who use their 'caring' as a means of having power over deaf people, it is clearly important to embrace the view that it *is* appropriate for *some* hearing people to counsel *some* deaf people. Within our broad definition of 'deaf', this seems acceptable from the methodological perspective as long as fluent communication is achieved, counsellors can address their oppressive unconscious, or more non-verbal ways of working are explored. But it also incorporates acceptance that a counsellor who is hearing may not be acceptable to a client who is Deaf.

However, returning to McKnight's comment about people 'affirming the basic assumptions of the other', we may find the first methodological obstacle is the *professional protectionism* of the counselling profession, as it relates to the emphasis on counselling as a 'talking through', and to the tendency of the profession to marginalise 'alternative' approaches to counselling which place less emphasis on 'hearing' and 'listening' in the usual sense of the words. Counsellors, like most professionals, are not immune to defensiveness when they are challenged about the validity of their own particular way of working for a particular client group, and some approaches have a built in view that it is difficult or impossible to pay due regard to the client's experience of these approaches, because 'it threatens some of the most fundamental assumptions held by counsellors about the nature of their craft':

> 'Another significant factor in the neglect of the client's experience has been the influence of psychoanalytic theory on both researchers and practitioners. From a psychoanalytic point of view, what the client says about his or her experience will often be interpreted as evidence of defensiveness, fantasy or transference... Further, even though their theoretical model is very different, behavioural theorists and researchers are similarly sceptical about the usefulness of what clients have to say about their experience. For behaviourists, it has traditionally been more important to focus on client *behaviour* and how it can be changed, than to be concerned with vague internal events such as experiences.'
>
> (McLeod, 1990, p.2)

Further, research that has been done (for example, Mayer and Timms, 1970) on the experiences of *hearing* clients in counselling has often demonstrated a wide division between client and counsellor expectations and assumptions. Given that many counsellors are nervous about working with deaf people, and, as we have seen, harbour attitudes and assumptions which mean that they can pose a direct challenge to Paul's way of viewing himself, for example, we might anticipate this division to be wider when clients are deaf. An *oppressive* behaviourist might focus on Paul's view of himself and how he 'behaves in a Deaf way' as being in need of change, and ignore the role of non-deaf people in determining this behaviour or Paul's deep-felt experience of being Deaf. We see examples of this all the time in informal helping situations, where the helper beams when the deaf person shows a 'hearing characteristic', in particular when they apparently 'hear', but criticises or ignores any evidence of a 'deaf characteristic', or dismisses deaf people's anger as being indicative that they have 'a chip on the shoulder'. Views like this can 'affirm the basic assumptions' made by the members of a particular counselling discipline to the point where these views may become entrenched and resistant to change, but they can also 'affirm the basic assumption' made by the profession as a whole that 'hearing', 'listening', 'language games' and 'talking' underpin counselling activity, *and counselling cannot occur without it*.

Counsellors may also be protective of their craft in other ways which are of relevance to deaf people. For example, we explored the use of interpreters in the previous chapter. A counsellor may have difficulty in working with an interpreter because the presence of the interpreter might make them feel disempowered and de-skilled. There can be doubts about the interpreter's ability to transcribe the counselling dialogue when the interpreter conveys in a few signs something that has taken the counsellor several minutes to say:

> 'Counsellors may feel uneasy about having an outsider watch their therapy techniques or may be unaccustomed to having others present in individual sessions. Feelings of being left out, mistrust of the interpreter, and resistance to the "intruder" all lead to the possibility of dysfunction in the therapy setting. In addition, the counsellor may need to turn over a degree of control to the interpreter, even though it is the counsellor who directs the course of the therapy.'
>
> (Roe and Roe, 1991, p.98)

We have the view given by Moira Walker at the beginning of this chapter that there is a need to remain open to different theoretical stances if we are to be able, as counsellors, to maintain our relationships with deaf clients. She also says of abuse survivors as clients:

> 'Therapy with each individual follows a unique path. Different therapists and counsellors have their own favoured methods and theories, but effective counselling and therapy with abuse survivors essentially requires flexibility. Those who adhere rigidly to a particular model, and who are unable to incorporate and integrate other ways of thinking, may not be best suited to work in this field.'
>
> (Walker, 1992, p.174)

This view is also expressed by Ellis in relation to counselling methodology in general:

> 'Like the scientific method itself, efficient therapy remains flexible, curious, empirically-orientated, critical of poor theories and results, and devoted to effective change. It is not one-sided or dogmatic. It is ready to give up the most time-honoured and revered methods if new evidence contradicts them. It constantly grows and develops; and it sacridizes no theory and no methodology.'
>
> (Ellis, 1984, p.33)

It is possible to use some of the preceding discussion in identifying those approaches to counselling which might *not* be applicable to working with deaf clients in Britain, *given the present climate*. I would be wary of dismissing these approaches without a second thought, however, because this climate may change in the future, but I do not believe that linguistic mismatching or oppressive attitudes and assumptions bode well for constructive counselling relationships in *any* climate.

THERAPEUTIC LIMITATIONS

Therapeutic limitations are issues raised by particular aspects of methodology and ideology in respect of particular clients which are seen to represent blocks to effective therapy and, possibly, to impede client growth. It could be said that the three greatest limitations to the effectiveness of different counselling methodologies in working with deaf people lie in the *fundamental assumptions* behind the approach, the degree to which the approach is *dependent on verbal dialogues*, and the *identity of the counsellor*, as might be illustrated in Box 5.1, with respect to a variety of approaches.

Dryden (1984) has analysed the behaviour of counsellors from different disciplines in terms of eight 'expressive/evocative' dimensions. His results seem to suggest that transactional analysis, rational emotive therapy (RET) and behavioural therapy are all *highly expressive and/or evocative*, and therefore require fluent communication and a common language to be functional from a methodological perspective, whereas Jungian and Freudian psychoanalysis, Gestalt, and person centred counselling are *low* on these aspects. We have already suggested that behavioural therapy may not be appropriate for working with deaf clients because of the assumptions underlying it make its practice more open to abuse by oppressive counsellors. RET has been used with Deaf clients in the USA (Gough, 1990) on the basis that:

> 'RET has an active, energetic style of therapy, calling upon the creativity, spontaneity, humor and courage of both therapist and client – attributes certain to be found among many deaf individuals… The most effective RET therapists tend to be those who have developed an understanding of and sensitivity to the nuances of their clients' language styles and non-verbal communications.'

(Gough, 1990, pp. 97–98)

But we must remember that there are several factors which enable this to happen which would not necessarily be present in Britain. The first is that the path to achieving a common language is less rocky in the USA, and that the therapists in question first ascertained that there was indeed a common language and fluent communication. The second relates to legislation, in particular the Americans with Disabilities Act, which guarantees the right of access to public services and has resulted in a greater determination on the part of counsellors to provide a service which is responsive to a variety of deaf people's experience. RET may be culturally appropriate for Deaf people, but

BOX 5.1 LIMITATIONS WHICH THERAPEUTIC APPROACHES MAY HAVE FOR SOME DEAF CLIENTS

THERAPEUTIC APPROACH	POSSIBLE LIMITATIONS
Freudian Psychodynamic Therapy	Not appropriate for clients who want the therapist to take responsibility for the management of problems; cannot look beyond their deafness as a symptom of all their problems; have difficulty with relating to therapist or with expression of thoughts and feelings; are reluctant to engage in therapy because they have come under pressure from others (Jacobs, 1984)
Kleinian Psychodynamic Therapy	Holds the view that external factors are not of primary importance and cannot encompass the broad sweep of extraneous human factors (Cooper, 1984)
Jungian Psychodynamic Therapy	May not be suitable for those whose early dependency needs have been almost entirely unmet, or whose 'ego-consciousness' is insufficiently developed (Lambert, 1984)
Person-Centred Therapy	The human limitations of the counsellor; the extreme demands on the practitioner and the attitudinal climate established between client and counsellor; the limited changes in behaviour that can be effected (Thorne, 1984)
Personal Construct Therapy	Counsellor being threatened by giving over total control to the client at some stage; when a common language cannot be found for interaction and communication (Fransella, 1984)
Existential Therapy	The verbal nature of the approach (van Deurzen-Smith, 1984)
Gestalt Therapy	The client's attitude towards therapy, and the increased dissatisfaction with convention, hypocrisy, pretence and the pain of seeing the destructiveness of many social and cultural forces and institutions that the therapy creates which may make the client more unfit for or unadjusted to contemporary society (Page, 1984)
Transactional Analysis	Can be used by unscrupulous therapists to manipulate their relationship with the client; the colloquial language of the TA concepts (Collinson, 1984)

if there is any doubt at all about linguistic matching between the client and the therapist, it may not be appropriate.

Another way of viewing counselling methodology is to look at the level at which the therapy operates in the client. Rodda and Grove (1987), for example, have illustrated how cognition, language and emotional development might interact with each other in deaf people. They point out that different counselling approaches input into the emotional, cognitive and language systems of deaf (and hearing) people at different points and therefore invoke different frameworks for change. It is clear from their work that many approaches to counselling are heavily based in the emotional (orectic) and mediating components of language, and this may be difficult for that group of deaf clients whom we identified in the previous chapter as tending to experience language dissonance, or with deaf clients where the deficiency on the part of the counsellor is in respect of understanding the complexity of their own and the client's feeling world:

> 'In this structure, language becomes a key variable in the development of social coping skills and emotional stability. It is very important to remember that when deaf people are linguistically deprived, they miss out on language, not only as a vehicle for thinking, but also in emotional development. They cannot think out problems, and they are also deprived of developmentally important social and emotional experiences.'

> (Rodda and Grove, 1987, p. 328)

Most of the limitations described above are limitations *to practice* which have been proposed by experienced practitioners themselves without specific reference to deaf people. All will acknowledge that there are some members of their discipline who have attempted to remedy some of the limitations with particular groups of clients who pose a challenge. That is to say, most approaches to counselling develop over time as new challenges present themselves. It might, for example, be possible for person-centred counsellors to overcome attitudinal or cultural divides by developing an awareness of themselves and of their clients. Exponents of existential therapy point out that even where an approach to counselling is highly verbal, it is possible to modify the approach to accommodate clients who are discrepant from the counsellor in their verbal expression and reflection:

> 'Because the existential approach favours the use of vocabulary that is as close to the client's inner frame of reference as possible, this makes it feasible to communicate symbolically. Gestures, neologisms, pieces of music, drawings and dream symbols may all be used as long as the client initiates this process and providing their underlying meaning is explored and comprehended. It is therefore possible to work existentially wherever meaning is expressed in some way.'

> (van Deurzen-Smith in Dryden, 1984, p.324)

Gestalt is an approach which emphasises right-hemispheric, non-linear thinking, not at the expense of other ways of knowing but as a complement to these

(Clarkson, 1989). Thinking with the right side of the brain implies the kind of intuition which can, for example, lead people to sense the affective climate of a school or college as a whole from the atmosphere in one classroom, or the deepest feelings of an individual from a minute and fleeting change in their facial expression. The Gestalt approach uses metaphor, fantasy and imagery, and involves working with body posture and movement, enactment and visualisation, time distortion and the full expression of feelings involving the whole body in action. It therefore incorporates many non-verbal features and may make good use of a deaf client's seeing skills. A Gestaltist would always work within the matrix of the person with needs in a socio-cultural context and therefore the Gestalt approach incorporates a systems perspective on human problem situations. Likewise, some limitations of the Gestalt approach may be difficult to overcome, in part because of the nature of individual clients and counsellors. Many deaf clients will seek counselling because they are already going through the pain of seeing the destructiveness, hypocrisy and pretence of an oppressive and culturally divided society. They are unlikely to feel comfortable with a therapy which heightens their awareness of this pain, however self-aware, and able to get in touch with feelings they become. It is often an expectation on the part of deaf clients that their pain will be eased, and sometimes, because they may come from a tradition of not being allowed to take responsibility for themselves and their own agency, they may also expect their counsellors to give them advice or to provide solutions to their problem situations. These expectations must be respected because they are legitimately based on the client's experience, but the opportunity must be grasped within the counselling relationship to explore how dependency on others can also be destructive in some circumstances.

I have also found that some of the *theoretical bases* of these approaches may be useful in informing awareness of some deaf people's life situations, even when practice may not be feasible. For example, we might say that the appropriateness of Gestalt for working with some deaf people is supported by the work of Poizner, Klima and Bellugi, (1987) who looked at the effects of damage to the right hemisphere of the brain in a Deaf artist who experienced a stroke and a subsequent loss in her ability to draw, particularly in terms of 'overall spatial organisation' (p.174). From this study, the authors were able to draw conclusions about the location of visio-spatial behaviour in the brain, and this has informed thinking about sign language. This work is also highly relevant to contemporary discussions within the counselling profession about 'right- and left-brained activities', which are at the root of Gestaltist thinking. Likewise, the deaf–hearing dichotomy and individual deaf people's battle for a coherent identity can be described in terms of or informed by Jungian theory. This is considered to be one of the most complex psychoanalytical theories in existence, and whereas on this basis it may not be appropriate for work with some deaf people on a practical level, it may be useful from the theoretical standpoint. For example, Jung (1971) suggested that the inner world of the psyche operates by means of four functions. He called these sensation, thinking, feeling and intuition. Thinking and feeling are opposites, one conscious and the other unconscious. The same is true of sensation and intuition. Jung noted that any one of these functions could be predominant in an individual's way of dealing with experience. For example, if sensation predominates, the perception of actual facts is most important, whereas if the accent is on thinking, the significance of the facts is to the fore. Jung suggested that it is not healthy for a function which constitutionally should have occupied second or third place to be pushed to the fore by compulsion or training, so that it takes the place of the main function. Deaf people may not develop the left hemisphere dominance for verbal materials usual for hearing people. They have after all been through an education system which focuses on 'intellectual development', and in their attempts to promote experientially irrelevant intellectual development in deaf people, many educationalists have ignored the natural tendency of deaf people towards right-brained activities, of which this book has given many examples. This may have implications for deaf people who are constantly forced to concentrate on the function, or part of the function (hearing) at the expense of those functions which would usually be more dominant (Corker, 1990a), and must therefore inform the counselling process. Similarly, Jung (1971) wrote at great length on the subjects of self, shadow and archetypes, some of which we explored in Chapter 2. We may perhaps recall that the archetypes are theoretical entities which represent predispositions to experience aspects of life in more or less stereotypical ways. They are like the people of the inner world of the individual. When the archetypal stereotype meets or projects itself upon objects or people corresponding to it in the real world, there is nearly always a clash between the stereotypic aspects of the archetype and the object or the person as they actually are. So, for example, if a deaf person has hearing parents who have not met his or her needs in childhood, he or she may develop an archetypal 'bad' parent or an archetypal 'bad' deaf person which is presented to the psyche in terms of imagery. The 'bad' parent may be the 'bad hearing' parent, in which counselling relationships with *any* hearing person may be problematic; the 'bad' deaf shadow may encourage a (false) dependency on an acquired hearing self or identity (which is 'good'). These ideas inform the counselling process from the theoretical standpoint as they contribute to our understanding of the mechanisms whereby problem situations can arise in some deaf people, and they represent yet another way where, with a little thought, therapy can be used to encourage these clients to discover their own resources in achieving growth.

METHODOLOGICAL APPROACHES TO OPTIMISING THE VISUAL, NON-VERBAL EXPERIENCE

Together with the need for counsellors to tackle oppressive attitudes and assumptions and to aid them in their search for a common language, it seems that a positive response to the methodological challenge posed by deaf people to counselling is to find ways of emphasising the visual, non-verbal experience of deaf people, valuing their seeing skills, and developing their ability to feel a sense of achievement and agency. Some of the approaches outlined above explore increasing the accessibility of the approach by using art and drama, for example, but we must not forget that art and drama, in themselves, are at the centre of quite discrete approaches to counselling – art therapy, psychodrama and dramatherapy, which the counselling profession has tended to marginalise as 'fringe activities'. It is heartening to see the recent upsurge in counselling texts related to these approaches, which is resulting in a long overdue rise in their profile within the profession. But I have always been surprised, and somewhat frustrated, that though these approaches have been used with people with learning difficulties (Kuczaj, 1990) and with dyslexic children (Feilden, 1990), for example, the profession has not yet embraced the value that these approaches – in their use of storytelling, image making, body movement, music and writing – have for working with deaf people in counselling. This value lies particularly in the emphasis on such features as the distancing of difficult feelings arising from linguistic or expe-riential mismatching between counsellor and client by enhancing expression through another more comfortable channel, and in the accessibility and visibility of these kinds of therapy for deaf people, though it should be stressed that these techniques have many more uses. For Deaf people, their value lies also in the fact that these approaches are culturally relevant, as we will see below.

Deaf Images

Jane McIntosh, who writes in Chapter 6 of a counselling relationship in which she encouraged her client to use images, once impressed upon me that 'the client doesn't need to be an artist to engage in person-centred art therapy', whereas art therapists from other schools of thought suggest that 'an artistic therapist needs to be an artist in their own right' (Jennings and Minde, 1993, p.12). Many people adopt the general view that art is 'therapeutic' in the sense that it is a relaxing and creative leisure activity which does not require a great deal of thought and therefore allows people to switch off from the stressors of everyday living. Doubtless this view will be challenged vociferously by professional artists and arts educationalists, and rightly so because it has created a false impression of both art and therapy, and the boundaries between the two. The use of art in art therapy is not generally speaking a casual activity and it requires a great deal of thought if it is to be used effectively by both counsellor and client.

Art therapy is not intended to replace verbal approaches to therapy, rather to supplement them in recognising that language and communication are multi-layered:

'Some might assume that arts therapists do not believe in traditional verbal therapy, or that they believe that language is not important. I do not want to be a carrier for such an assumption because I find language extremely important. However, art often helps people to experience the world in different ways and therefore helps to give more substance to words, which makes the words more *alive*... I have seen how art has helped me to look at language in a different way. It has helped me to listen more to the ways in which things are expressed, the sub-text of what is said rather than in what dialect they are spoken.'

(Minde in Jennings and Minde, 1993, p.36)

In using art in a therapeutic way, clients:

'meet the landscapes, ideas or inner visions they want to create. While creating, they become absorbed into the landscapes and become part of the art-work, but at the same time, they come out of it and try to see it from different perspectives.'

(Minde, in Jennings and Minde, 1993, p.37)

There are documented examples of art therapy being used with deaf people, but these are generally hard to find in the way of explicit accounts. For example, Eldredge and Carrigan (1992) write a moving account of how they used the strong storytelling and visual symbolism traditions of American Indian culture in a short-term art therapy project for young deaf American Indian adults who were in the process of transition from secondary school to a community placement. They describe their client group's situation as follows:

'For centuries American Indians have recited ancient chants evoking the Spirit presence. These chants and other ritual poems, stories, dances and visual symbols are all part of the elaborate structure in which American Indians recall and transmit their traditions, beliefs and social norms… Indian children who are deaf frequently are isolated from their cultures and heritages. In many cases they have not heard the history, have not sung the songs, have not learned the traditions of their people. And because of their minority status, they also may not be fully accepted and acculturated into the Deaf culture either.'

(Eldredge and Carrigan, 1992, pp.29–30)

We may perhaps recall from Chapter 1, the situation of deaf people who regard themselves as 'disabled' and also that of CODAs, as being like having 'a passport without a country'. The above situation is similar. Through providing an opportunity for their clients to create a story or myth about art pieces which they produced, the authors recognised practices such as storytelling and folklore which, although not equivalent, are respected in both Indian and Deaf communities (Padden, 1989; Rutherford, 1993). In Indian culture, an individual is only seen to be disabled if they cannot contribute to society in any way, and the term 'disabled' does not imply impairment of any kind. Deaf American Indians 'become disabled only in a social context such as within a residential school' (p.37). Because the clients in this study worked as a group with two therapists who had Indian ancestry, the issue of deafness was not to the fore and their common ground 'evoked a sense of wonder and pride, which may have served to establish a basis for trust and disclosure by creating a sense of group unity and identity' (p.30) which later facilitated individuation of the separate identities of the men. The most important expression in their art was perhaps consequentially related to their need for connection to their

Indian cultural heritage, rather than integration within the dominant society. We can also observe this reduction in emphasis on deafness in other Deaf therapy groups (see Chapter 8) and within communities of Black–Deaf people where focus on Black cultural history may happen, as opposed to Deaf cultural history (Aramburo, 1989; RAD, 1991). In an American study on identity, 87% of the Black–Deaf people questioned about their 'double immersion' in the Black and the Deaf communities identified as Black first and Deaf second, with those identifying as Deaf first coming largely from Deaf families and residential school background. The larger group expressed ongoing concerns about the isolation of the Black–Deaf community within both the Black community and the Deaf community (Aramburo, 1989). Information like this is useful when considering any counselling practice.

Certainly, when I view my fellow deaf, I am constantly surprised and on occasions stunned by their natural artistry and this suggests to me that there is a place for art therapy in counselling deaf people from the perspective of communication. Perhaps I should not be surprised. It may yet be that the lack of reference to the fact that deaf young people achieve their potential in arts related subjects in secondary school, when compared to so-called 'academic subjects' (Powers, 1990), is more a reflection of our tendency to devalue the arts and to place literacy and numeracy above agency and practical creativity in overlooking the skills of deaf students in these areas, than the accessibility of these subjects. If this is so, then perhaps art therapy is a natural tool in the counsellor's search for a common language.

I have found the use of images invaluable in the exploration of difficult feelings, or feelings for which words or signs cannot easily be found, both personally and with clients, with and without accompanying language. Images can also help when I get a sense that I am failing to fully understand something that my client has expressed, and can be used in training to explore the non-verbal. However, I must stress that I do not aim to interpret the resulting images, preferring to encourage clients to explore the image with me and use the image as a kind of springboard for their feelings. This is important because of the distinctiveness of Deaf art, as cultural expression:

> 'Deaf art is a very important tool for Deaf people because Deaf people can't hear and they use sign language. It is about our feelings, what we feel inside ourselves, the fact that we use visual and facial expression and movement and the way we think. Deaf art is very different from hearing art, which is often narrative and really not relevant to Deaf people. Many Deaf people get no pleasure from it. I feel I have to demonstrate Deaf art in general terms. My paintings, designs and prints use sign language and body movement to encapsulate a lot of expression. It's a bit like a drama, it's about communication and awareness. It's about the positive aspects of sign language, just as hearing people use their own representation of the world.'

(Landell, 1991, interpreted from BSL)

Over the years, I have come across many examples of deaf people using images for self-exploration, and self-therapy, sometimes as a substitute for poor communication, the failure of significant others to meet human needs,

Figure 5.1 Usher's View

or the lack of facility for being listened to, and sometimes because as a visual expression it is of enormous cultural relevance. I believe that this needs to be encouraged more, especially within education if the kind of frustrations that many mainstreamed deaf people experience are to have a safety valve, and where there is a great need for a more in-depth understanding of Deaf culture. We do, however, have to make a distinction between art work which is therapeutic and images which are made within the context of the counselling relationship and can be explored in detail in that context. Both are valuable, the first because as well as granting the deaf person expression, it can provide the observer with more information about the individual deaf person, and the second because the images can help to gel the counselling relationship and act as a bridge between the inner and outer worlds of the client. It must also be emphasised that counsellors can work with their own images as part of their journey to self-knowledge, and I will explore some examples from my own experience below.

Like writing, images are an expression of self, but images can also become a way in which the self makes sense of the world around them. Stiefel writes about the additional importance that images may have, in her case, in helping her make sense of the 'madness of Usher's':

> 'A glimmer of light working through a malfunctioning "camera" still delivers a picture of something. I suspect that some sense of validity is attempted by the cognitive information-gathering system. I have caught myself shaking my head, denying what I have seen. On the other hand, I have been caught up with the imaginative illusion, bought into it, and then been shamefully embarrassed at the craziness the situation has caused… Looking away and back again or changing the viewing distance helps the eyes regroup and locate a different focal point. Lately I have employed this method to draw meaning from pictures, snap-shots, paintings and any stationary objects around me. I can no longer trust that what I am seeing is the true reality.'

(Stiefel, 1991, pp.53–54)

Figure 5.1 shows an image created by a young woman who had just discovered that she had Usher's syndrome, having only comparatively recently adjusted to being Deaf and developing strong affiliations with the Deaf community. The discovery had sent the entire family into turmoil with cycles of blame and guilt repeating themselves with renewed force. She describes the history of the image poignantly through poetry, where she places her experience in the context of the two diverging and contrasting paths taken by most deaf people, respecting though pleading with those who go the disabling way to join with Deaf people so that they can more easily come to terms with trauma through belonging:

BOX 5.2 'WHEN THEY DOLED OUT THE DECIBELS'

When they doled out the decibels
We were short-changed.
I found the silence enchanting
You did not

I joined the Deaf legions
You soldiered on alone

My army always fought for
recognition
You wanted anonymity

We rejoiced with our eyes
You revelled bravely in sound

We danced in our language
You sang in yours

Side by side we grew
I found my freedom
I sacrified the normality.
But you soldiered on.

Mutilated and war wounded
You fought for justice
But you lie alone in the poppy fields
As your hearing comrades wander
effortlessly on

You pick yourself up.
You always were a marching Heroine
You didn't ever want acclaim

I am conquered, beaten by sound
You pretend to be infallible
Your triumph only lies on the horizon.
It perches on the eternal skyline,
Forever waiting to be claimed.

Deafness never got you.

Now genetic hooligans are on our tail
A new strategic attack,
In a shell blast
They dropped a Hiroshima
On your eyeballs.
Tear gas muted your emotions
Stifled by heated explosion
Still you soldier on alone

I beg you to overlook
Military paraphernalia
And join our legions.
Don't try to shoulder your fury.
Eject from your solo fragility
Fall into safety
Let our arms entwine

For then you will never lie
Alone in the poppy fields
While your comrades wander
effortlessly by.

'Communication Through Love' is a textile image which grew out of the intense feelings of a deaf woman when she encountered love for the first time. She had felt bad about the inadequacy of words for describing what she felt about being loved so deeply and for herself, and that when she said them, the words jarred and felt wrong. She describes the point at which the image materialised and gave her the motivation to construct it:

'I saw myself looking outwards through a window of life at my love's hands weaving a web of golden gossamer, holding me safely and gently, giving me a security which I did not believe was possible, whilst at the same time allowing the warmth of the sun to filter through and nurture. The frame of the window is round and whole, a circle never ending and always beginning. Each day is a new day met with joy and anticipation; each day those hands weave a new thread, rebuilding my life with silken care and quicksilver smiles. My hands, in forming love, become a bird who flaps her wings at dawn and flies in search of feathers for her nest. They join the dance of equality which fans the flames of my heart. This is the ultimate communication – communication through love which transcends language and transcends the pain caused by those who try to rubbish or demean its beauty, without understanding its meaning or its depth or its timelessness. The image lingers while words blow away. It is a testament to the strength of my love.'

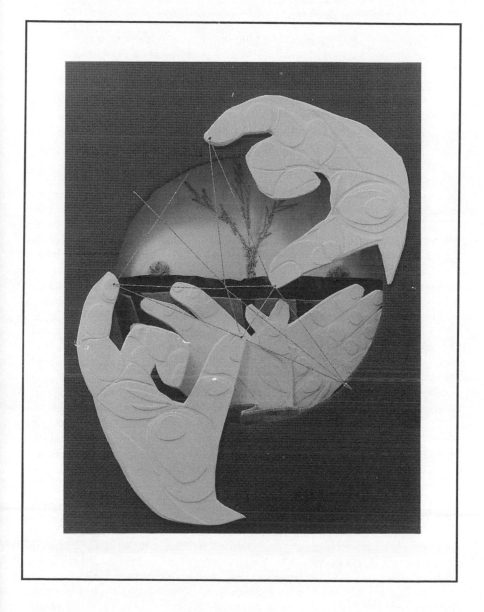

Figure 5.2 Communication Through Love

It is clear from these two vignettes how words or signs and images may marry with each other to enable a deeper expression that might be possible using one channel or the other.

Writing can be another way in which deaf clients can be encouraged to express themselves. Although sign language has no true written form, I choose in this context to describe sign language as 'writing in space', because the creation of sign images through signed poetry, for example, is equivalent to the creation of word images, though the words or signs themselves can appear to remain the primary medium of expression:

> 'The art of creating poetry in BSL, however, is relatively new, the nature of the language demanding that it is performed and not read as it has to be seen in action to be appreciated. The potential for the creation of poetry in BSL is tremendous, since the language itself constantly makes use of imaginative forms and rhythms. Miles has described the elements that are present in BSL poetry, in which there are established conventions which exploit the properties of the language to achieve poetic form.'

> (Gregory, 1993, p.6)

In respect of the written word, it is sometimes assumed that the power of words is lost in their transformation to word images on paper, because, it is suggested, the emotional element of spoken language is conveyed by the sound of the voice. However, it frequently happens that an untrained observer will overlook the tone of the writing or the mood of the writer by failing to read between the lines, and fail to see the emerging patterns or to recognise that the choice of written language can be very revealing. A counsellor can do this with writing in the same way that they can with face-to-face communication, though it is advisable to encourage the client to write as part of the communicative framework of counselling. Haley and Dowd (1988) have shown that Deaf clients indicated a greater willingness to see a hearing counsellor who used some sign language or an interpreter, rather than written communication, but we might imagine that English-dominant monolinguals would be more receptive to writing. I have used written assignments and dialogues with deafened people to assist the expression of feelings.

However, we must not underestimate the power of the image in its own right. Shapiro, Foster and Powell, (1968) found that judgements of counsellor empathy can reliably be made by both trained and untrained raters from photographs, with facial cues being particularly important. I have long been an enthusiastic amateur photographer even enjoying a brief spell as a professional and I know that photographic images are important to me in terms of their memory value and their ability to pick up details that otherwise might go unnoticed. Frequently, my holidays become photographic expeditions – a search for the patterns that make order out of chaos which I described in the Preface to this book. People who look at my photographs are puzzled because 'they are not really holiday photographs', meaning that they are not pictures of other holidaymakers, hotels, nightclubs and beauty spots! They are more likely to be photographs of waves, waterfalls, rock formations, ruins or a bird's feathers at different times of day and in different weather conditions, because it is these coloured subtleties of nature which I wish to capture or they seem too fleeting to be tangible. It is interesting how only a few people who are close to me see what I see and understand what I feel about those photographs, which perhaps is because they are a reflection of the deepest core of my individuality. But I am aware that images can harbour surprises, sometimes unpleasant ones. I recall once looking at a friend's old family photographs with her, and there was one image in particular which stood out, but I could not quite put my finger on why. She was talking in some detail about the family members who were portrayed in the photograph – her mother, her brother and herself, and all the time she was talking, I kept being drawn back to the image, trying to understand what is was that bothered me. My eyes somehow kept travelling towards an area of shadow in the photograph, and slowly I realised that it was the shadow of the photographer which, in part fell over my friend, who was then a young girl. This shadow had a sense of menace about it – it loomed over her. I asked her who had taken the photo-graph, because I could see the shadow of the photographer and she suddenly realised what she was looking at. She became extremely agitated, and even-tually the story came out that the photographer was her father, who had systematically abused her when she was a child. Something in the photograph had acted as a trigger for the release of the many feelings that she had about this, though at the time it happened, it proved to be a very profound experi-ence for both of us.

Figure 5.3 'Layers of Meaning'

I have since used photographs like the one in Figure 5.3 to enable counselling trainees to develop a more finely-tuned perception of non-verbal language, and an awareness of visual symbols which are often overlooked. This particular photograph seems to me to raise questions about the relationship between the child on the left, who is deaf, and the two on the right, who are hearing, and although much of the imagery is very subtle, for some reason the photograph disturbs me in its reminder of a past life. It is interesting to see what happens when the relationship begins to unfold – it is quite enlightening to discover the many different layers of meaning which one photograph has for different people.

Berman (1993) has looked at the therapeutic use of the photograph, highlighting the hidden messages behind the images and attempting to develop a therapeutic framework within which photographs can be used constructively:

> 'Photographs can be seen as a powerful form of language: what is the nature of this language? How do photographs communicate their message? In what intricate ways can these soundless images speak to us? What are the limits of this language?... If we begin to consider these questions closely in relation to photographs, we may discover in them many new and interesting features. The pictures may soothe or shock, amuse or frighten, disgust, repel, or attract us. They also ask questions that make us think or ponder. They give us a specifically descriptive kind of information, showing us more about the world in which we live. Exploring photographs with an open mind, using our powers of imagination, deduction and identification, we can receive strong and irrefutable messages from the visual images that remain uncluttered by the verbal.'

(Berman, 1993, pp.9–10)

In Chapter 8, Margaret Kennedy brings together some of these threads in her use of 'art-in-therapy' with deaf young people and adults who are survivors of childhood sexual abuse.

The Drama of Being Deaf

Within the deaf community, drama, that is music, dance and art, has enormous cultural significance and is increasingly being used as a way of transmitting Deaf culture and of educating the hearing community about deaf people, the two activities being quite distinct (Gregory, 1993). Most people will have seen the play or the film 'Children of a Lesser God' by Mark Medoff, but few will recognise that this is set apart from the Deaf dramatic tradition (Ruane, 1993), and has no connection with the art forms of the Deaf community. Certainly, sign language is often dramatic in its own right, and this provides a core of Deaf drama, with plays on signs and signed metaphors conveying the spirit of the Deaf community past, present and future, and we have now begun to see evidence of other cultural influences such as Black culture and Jewish culture in the work of Deaf theatre companies and Deaf dramatists. These activities do not constitute psychodrama or dramatherapy, but they represent a potential for the use of these activities with deaf clients which merits development because it makes use of the natural skills of many deaf people. Sue Jennings defines the difference between psychodrama and dramatherapy:

> 'Psychodrama...builds on human beings' capacity to dramatise through the use of role play, role reversal and other psychodramatic methods. Psychodrama is a form of group psychotherapy, which makes use of dramatic techniques and emphasises the importance of catharsis. Dramatherapy shares many methods with psychodrama, but emphasises the art form of drama and theatre as its central focus...there are many other therapists who incorporate a dramatherapeutic approach to the way they work.'

> (Jennings, 1992, p.11)

As with art therapy, counsellors who work within the discipline of dramatherapy vary in their emphasis on the non-verbal, and they all hold in common the view that people can experience the world in different ways and have different ways of expressing or bringing to life these experiences. There is not always a clear dividing line between art therapy and dramatherapy. Art therapists and dramatherapists are constantly looking at ways of making language more alive through a distancing from the experience and for example through both literal and metaphorical use of space (Jennings and Minde, 1993). The dividing line will be even narrower for Deaf people, as Landell (1991) suggests when he describes his images as using 'sign language and body movement to encapsulate a lot of expression'.

It is commonly construed that dramatherapy is a group activity, and indeed, it can be of use when working with groups of deaf people, or on occasions and with teams of deaf and hearing facilitators, with mixed groups of deaf and hearing people. However, we need a great deal more detailed information about how deaf people construct and use their 'life stage' before we can consistently and reliably develop established techniques and enable deaf people to write the scripts of the plays. It is useful, however to explore ways in which the methods of psychodrama and dramatherapy can be used within an integrated counselling framework which is responsive to deaf people. In Chapter 10, I mention, for example, that I used *body sculpts* in my counselling training. Body sculpts are where people mould themselves into a dramatic stance which aims to paint a picture of a feeling or a set of feelings held by the individual. It can be a spontaneous activity where people enact parts in a drama or one individual can be given the task of moulding the group in order to demonstrate relationships. We could describe the photographic image 'Layers of Meaning' presented earlier as a sculpt in the sense that it is an image frozen in time by the photographer. But if these children were in the room before us, the effect may be very different and perhaps more complex because we may notice more of the subtleties of facial expression and body posture for example, but if I direct a group of people to play particular roles, another layer is introduced into the drama:

'The process we are engaged with is both expanding the frame of the scene (like using a wide angle lens) and focussing the element(s) (like using a zoom lens). It is the process of the dramatic imagination which both expands and focusses the scenario. It is a process that we continually need to practice in order to develop our own imagination.'

(Jennings, 1992, p.66)

Figure 5.4 Deaf Children work with Masks

This is exactly what happened in my counselling group. We were discussing family relationships and I was becoming a little frustrated with rambling narratives, so when it came to my turn to volunteer, I felt I needed to *show* the family scenario, as opposed to talk about it. I chose people from the group and sculpted them to represent members of my family, leaving the remainder of the group as the audience. It soon transpired that not only were the audience able to gauge the scenario, but the 'actors' began to develop individual feelings about their roles in relation to 'me' and to the others in the scene which included an experiencing of acute empathy or a feeling of stepping directly into the shoes of the person through the enactment of the role. This proved to be a powerful experience, because it felt as if the members of the family became real, and though they were physically off stage, their *feelings* were immediate. However, I did not realise until later that the exercise was not finished properly and some people had felt that they were left hanging in mid-air together with all the feelings they had taken on board. This emphasised for me the importance of clearly structured dramatherapy where people are given the opportunity to disengage from their roles, as opposed to this kind of spontaneous exercise which is plucked out of the air in an attempt to work in a more experientially relevant way. Nowhere is this more important than with the use of masks, especially when we remember that masks, because they cover or partially cover the face, may be quite threatening to deaf clients, and may actually interfere with communication rather than assist it. When used with care, masks are one way of helping a greater concentration on a theme, an image or a character:

> 'A mask also enables a transformation from a person's everyday self into that character. It is a paradox of the mask that it both conceals and reveals: it conceals individual identity and reveals either hidden aspects of the individual or a collective representation of a class, profession or deity.'

> (Jennings, 1992, p.110–111)

The facility of drama to show feelings and relationships, although commonly associated with group work, is also useful in individual work:

> 'Many dramatherapists have an in-built response that one-to-one work must necessarily be verbal, or that drama is not possible unless there are several people present. There is a wide spectrum of dramatherapeutic methods appropriate for one-to-one sessions, including embodiment, projection and role techniques. However, clients usually need longer to habituate to this active method of work. An invitation to "show me how your family looks" (instead of telling me about it) is a useful way in to the use of sculpting.'

> (Jennings, 1992, p.94)

Clients can either make their own representational images, choosing from a wealth of materials, or they can for example, use models such as toy animals or dolls, living objects such as plants, or even different shapes and sizes of building bricks to demonstrate simple and complex scenarios which can then be explored with the counsellor. These ways of working, in part because they are a throwback to the early development of human beings – all these techniques are used naturally and spontaneously by children as they grow and learn about the world around them and their significant others – must be considered in assisting the counsellor's development of a growth-producing climate.

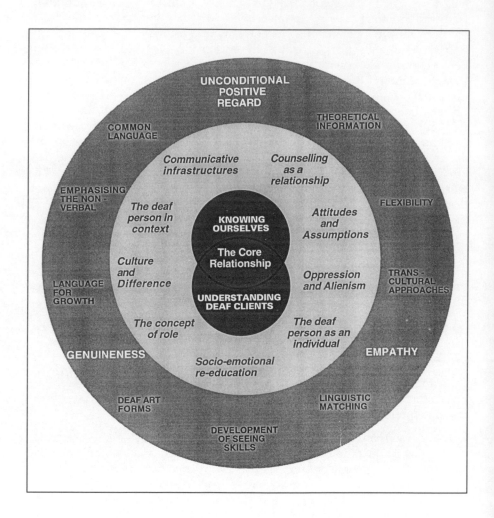

Figure 5.5 The Deaf Client's Right to be Understood – Frameworks for Growth

BUILDING THE FRAMEWORK – INCORPORATING DIFFERENT PERSPECTIVES

The above discussion can be regarded as an exploration of the methodological building bricks of a responsive, experientially and culturally relevant framework for working with deaf people where the counsellor's core values can function effectively and a *level* of common language can be found when there is linguistic mismatching or dissonance, which can encourage and inform the path that communication takes within the counselling relationship. This framework might be described as shown in Figure 5.5, which comprises three layers:

1. The core relationship, or *what is* (the inner layer).

2. Issues to be brought to conscious awareness, or *what needs to be* (the mediating layer).

3. Process and practice, or *what achieves what needs to be* (the outer layer).

If all factors are considered together, it seems that the particular characteristics of deaf people plus the need for counsellors to be flexible, suggests that we are looking for foundations to our framework which incorporate a broad-based humanistic core such as the person-centred philosophy of Carl Rogers (1951) or the framework of Gerard Egan (1990).

The majority of genuine counsellors who are working with deaf people would have a large measure of agreement with the core values of Rogers' philosophy, because without them, for the reasons that we have explored in great depth, counselling can become a strong preserver of an unhealthy status quo through the disclosure of alienistic values laden with assumptions, instead of being a force for social and attitudinal change. Humanistic approaches to counselling incorporate a positive awareness of transcultural issues, coupled with an implicit demand that counsellors know themselves if they are to work effectively within and across cultures:

> 'Clients in a transcultural setting must make transitions in a number of different ways. Not only are they dealing with the changes that face us all in personal growth, but they may, in addition, have to deal with an alienating and often hostile environment…we assume at present that *the majority culture is hostile* to people from other cultures, at a number of different levels. In counselling, this ranges from counsellors blaming their clients' cultures for their problems, to being ignorant of and patronising towards clients…in order for all members of society to have equal access to counselling, majority counsellors will need to acknowledge their own *ethnocentricity*… Counsellors at present remain "culturally encapsulated" when they are unable to see issues from the perspective of another culture.'

(d'Ardenne and Mahtani,1989, p.7 and pp. 12–13)

Talking about disabled people, Lenny gives us another extension to this awareness:

> 'In recent years, counselling has become an important mechanism for addressing, if not resolving, the paradox between the individual and

society. Therefore it is not surprising that disabled people should see counselling as a way of dealing with the relationship between their individual impairments and their disabling society. The crucial question posed (is)...can counselling do it? Do disabled people need counselling? As I have demonstrated, not *all* counselling can, but I believe that person-centred counselling has a substantial contribution to make because, by its very nature, it does not make judgments about how people adjust to their disabilities. It does not impose its own meaning on situations, does not make judgments in advance or put labels on people. It is not about someone's impairment or their disability, but about helping them to make sense of the relationship between the two.'

(Lenny, in Swain *et al.* 1993, p.239)

Person-centred practitioners provide us with one final compelling reason why the person-centred approach may be an appropriate foundation for counselling deaf people in the context of the issues explored in this book:

'The distrust of experts runs deep among person-centred practitioners. In some ways it is fair to state that the person-centred counsellor must learn to wear her expertise as an invisible garment if she is to become an effective counsellor. Experts are expected to dispense their expertise, to recommend what should be done, to offer authoritative guidance or even to issue orders. Clearly there are some areas of human experience where such expertise is essential and appropriate. Unfortunately, all too many of those who seek the help of counsellors have spent much of their lives surrounded by people who, with devastating inappropriateness, have appointed themselves experts in the conduct of other people's lives. As a result, such clients are in despair at their inability to fulfil the expectations of others, whether parents, teachers, colleagues or so-called friends, and have no sense of self-respect or personal worth.'

(Mearns and Thorne, 1988, p.6)

Experts are, after all, the bane of deaf people's lives and the bearers of the prevailing winds of 'expertise'. They can and do suffer from 'expertosis' (Andrews, 1992). Whereas I would claim to be an expert in my own inner landscape, my boat holds no assumptions about the lives of other deaf people, or about the counsellors who work with them. Every relationship is different. In counselling, the key lies in acknowledging the particular quality of the difference and allowing this to blow the winds of change. That is the core relationship.

PAUL CONCLUDES

Counsellors are faced with a myriad of issues in working with deaf people that perhaps they have never thought about. That is not to say they should be avoided. They have been avoided for far too long. Many deaf people have for example experienced abuse as children but have no-one to turn to. Many need someone to discuss their human issues with, but have difficulty in communicating with people with appropriate skills. Counselling is a branch of the helping professions which has woefully neglected to make provision for deaf people. It is high time that it stopped adding to the oppressive features of our society and offered equity to deaf people by challenging their oppression. The counselling situation may actually be the only place where I can concentrate on being myself, without all the struggles to communicate or manage the oppression. It is therefore vital that it does not add to the oppression since, if it does, *I have no place to focus on my identity as me*, as a Deaf person, not as an oppressed person.

As Sheldon Kopp (1977) says:

> 'These are not *the* ways to work. They are simply *my* ways of working. They need not be yours, though some may suit your own path. I offer it to encourage you to become ever clearer about the fundamentals of your own style of work. To free oneself from the bondage of attachments to its results, it is necessary to be clear about the Work. When we do not concentrate one-pointedly on the basic work, we pay attention instead to the patient's "progress" or to our own ego-bound "Look how well (or badly) I'm doing" trip. Neither path benefits the patient or the therapist. At the point of impasse, the only thing that helps is to go *back to one*. But to find your way back, you first must know what "one" is for you. Clarity about what you do, and about how you run the therapy is absolutely necessary. It is sometimes useful, creative, and fun to vary from the basic parameters of your work. But first you must know the personal baseline from which you are varying. Otherwise how can you know when to return home, and how to find your way back?'

SECTION 2

DEAF EXPERIENCES OF COUNSELLING PROCESS AND COUNSELLING TRAINING

This section brings together the experiences of a variety of deaf people, all of whom are working or have worked with deaf clients in the counselling role, and have been through discrete or mainstream counselling training using a sign language interpreter. In Chapter 6, a deaf client, together with her counsellor (who is hearing and uses the person-centred approach) explore their own experiences of counselling process from the deaf client's and the hearing counsellor's perspective, and attempt to identify key counselling issues for working across the deaf–hearing boundary. In Chapter 7, the situation is reversed, addressing the practical issues which arise for a deaf counsellor working with a hearing client, in particular exploring examples of working with a parent of a deaf child. The concept of 'the-client-in-absence' is explored, which, in the case of a deaf child or parent who is present but does not contribute to the counselling process, gives rise to complicated transference and countertransference phenomena. The role expectations and language challenges presented in face-to-face counselling and telephone counselling using an interpreter or a TDD communication device are pinpointed. Chapter 8 relates the experiences of a deaf counsellor who uses art-in-therapy to overcome language barriers, assist the release of deep and difficult feelings, and complement the natural iconicity of sign language users in the therapeutic environment. In Chapter 9, a deaf counsellor focuses on the 'Deaf Alliance', where both the counsellor and the client are deaf, highlighting the cultural issues that must be taken into account when working with Deaf clients and exploring how these can be used in the constructive development of counselling style. Chapter 10 addresses issues of training deaf people as counsellors, using experiences of discrete training or counselling training aimed specifically at deaf people, and experiences of mainstream or integrated training with hearing people through the use of an interpreter, from both the trainee and the trainer's perspective.

CHAPTER 6

WORKING ACROSS WORLDS I
DEAF CLIENT – HEARING COUNSELLOR

Jane McIntosh and Rachel Wood[1]

This is an account of the key stages in a four-year counselling relationship between a deaf client and her hearing counsellor, written from both the counsellor's and the client's perspectives. For the counsellor, the experience of working with a deaf client was a first, but, as it happened, it was also her first experience of working long-term with someone who, at the time, was experiencing a great deal of intense pain and trauma which had built up over a long period of time. For the client, this was the fourth attempt at a satisfying counselling relationship with a hearing counsellor. Both the client and the counsellor kept a record throughout the counselling relationship, though interestingly, neither knew that this was the case until the opportunity presented itself to write about their experiences. In this chapter, they have tried to focus on key themes and stages of the counselling process to illustrate both the profundities and the difficulties in 'working across deaf–hearing boundaries'.

JANE

I remember my first meeting with Rachel clearly.[2] I had already outlined initial arrangements as with all clients, but had done so by letter in order to preserve confidentiality. I was both curious and apprehensive about meeting with my first private client who was also deaf. I didn't know what to expect but unexpected situations have always seemed to attract me so I presented myself at the place where she both worked and lived, ready to face anything.

I remember a rather dim room which had little tangible evidence of Rachel living in it and which did nothing to comfort the misery she felt: this she quite quickly conveyed to me with an outline of her life at that time. The necessity of good communication arose straightaway – on two levels: the superficial but essential one of the two of us being able to converse with one another; and the underlying level of a relationship in which Rachel felt accepted and profoundly understood. The latter was, and remains, an eternal need for her survival in a world that is hearing.

---

1   Rachel Wood is not the client's real name, which has been withheld in the interests of confidentiality.
2   The account presented here is given with Rachel's full agreement.

I also remember having no hesitation about my commitment from the start. I realised I could well have been Rachel because I suppose on reflection, I am perhaps not quite entirely of the hearing world. There was an acute awareness of deafness in my family, my great grandmother and my grandmother having experienced being deaf to different degrees. I also went through a period of deafness as a child. Whether it was physically inherited, or psychologically caused has never been established, but this experience fixed my interest in Rachel and my later dogged determination to endure her struggle alongside her. She impressed upon me early on, how painful it was for her if communication was defective and how she was trapped at that time in unproductive relationships. Her struggle in the first two years of the four in which we worked together was to address her need for meaningful communication with other people, especially in and during close relationships. In the last two years she put into practice what she had discovered and used her counselling to monitor her progress.

My approach is person-centred and so I spent several early sessions listening to Rachel's story. She had been in a long counselling relationship already which meant she was very well aware of what she was feeling, especially anger, low self-esteem, loss and isolation and as a skilled client, she was more ready than I expected to 'open up'. As I knew she was lipreading me, my reflections and responses felt at first much more deliberate than with a hearing person, and so I think this cannot have helped her feeling of isolation. I was also being more careful and less spontaneous than I became subsequently. I did wonder, however, if the physical dynamic of my speech, which was precise, measured and more strongly emphasised than usual, encouraged the more dramatic and quicker disclosure of deep feeling from Rachel than I had experienced with hearing clients, for my manner and Rachel's disclosure seemed to match each other in intensity. I later learnt that the isolation Rachel felt within the hearing world created these powerfully intense feelings because Rachel felt no-one really listened to her pain, but by then our method of communicating had become natural to me and matched the mutual understanding and flow that had developed between us. I am therefore confused as to how much Rachel's deafness caused initial differences between her and other clients and feel there's a chicken and egg situation here to which I shall refer later on.

In fact this was the first time I'd counselled an adult with such intense long-term pain and I found it very stressful at times. However, I had time during the week to recover having given up my full-time work and I had the support of skilled supervision. I remember feeling almost pinned to the wall by the power of Rachel's outrage at her treatment by the world (although she never expressed any anger directly at me). I felt strangely honoured to be facing all this anger directed against the rest of humanity, though it was more difficult to deal with because of the sense of inequality in the deaf–hearing relationships. I felt it was very important for all humanity I took the pain, and also important for Rachel that I did not get sucked in by it. I resisted being sucked in fiercely. Like Rachel I have a Scots legacy of endurance against all odds, something which gave me a sense of kinship with her, and I used it.

Rachel's sense of herself was extremely negative. I found this scarcely surprising once she had told me more of her life story. Her feeling she had been criticised all her life came from the attitude of her family and those she encountered in her education that she was 'sick'. Rachel felt that her mother held this 'sickness' responsible for her father's terminal illness (which was, in fact, of physical origin) and was devastated by her mother's inability to comfort her in her grief over the subsequent loss of the one person in the family whom Rachel felt understood her. Rachel felt deeply unloved by her mother, whom she believed would have preferred her death instead of her father's. Then Rachel's marital relationship later left her feeling completely misunderstood and sexually used. She felt empty and afraid of being alone; that she could give no warmth; that she sabotaged relationships with her own dislike of herself; that she could not communicate with people as part of a group and was wary about being patronised and insensitively singled out. She felt she would only be somebody in a close relationship with someone else and yet she had no confidence in her ability to establish such closeness. A deep hopelessness would ensue when yet another attempt to be close to someone failed, and she would be very critical of and disgusted with herself. She would become swamped by negative feelings and despair which she sensed was too much for others to take. The lack of physical warmth in her life meant she longed to be touched and held.

I felt I needed to be straight and clear in 'holding' Rachel and her pain. I needed to be strong in accepting her emptiness, loneliness, numbness, despair beyond words. I didn't want to offer physical contact (although I was prepared to revise that later) because I felt it would alter the counselling process and transgress our boundaries. I did not feel experienced enough to experiment beyond the process I knew to be effective and did not trust myself to cope with being flexible. I do wonder however, if my refusal to give physical contact was damaging to Rachel or not. It may well have been (and I think it is important to explore the physical dimension in working with deaf people) but I am inclined to think also that my refusal helped her realisation that she might not get everything from one relationship. I felt that building up her self-image by trying to express her feelings within the counselling process would strengthen her ability to take the ups and downs of relationships with others. Later on she did express how closely attached to me she felt and was able to sustain that feeling within the boundaries of our relationship. I had had that same experience within my own counselling and it had altered my perspective constructively. I think it had a similar effect on Rachel. She began to show slight signs of recovery after long periods of pain and as her counsellor it felt like a miracle the day she said she was beginning to feel calmer at the end of some of our sessions.

This acknowledgement only came, however, after deeply painful work on the bereavement she had suffered, the frightening, overpoweringly evil feelings she had about herself as a result of not being able to share her feelings in the past and her awful isolation. Her panic after a fortnight's break in counselling and the great pressure I felt to rescue her come through even today from the notes I made at the time. I relied heavily on my supervision however, and doggedly stuck to our contract. She then exposed the conflict she felt within, between her deaf and her hearing self. Which was she? She liked the directness of culturally Deaf people but wanted confirmation of acceptance as a deaf person in the hearing world. She did not want to be treated as a victim but to be accepted as 'equal but different'. I responded to her statement as a challenge. This took courage but mirrored the courage she had shown in raising the issue, and feeling I was speaking on behalf of the hearing world first checked out whether we had now achieved effective communication. She said we had – it had been difficult at first but was now very good. I then said how much I wanted to understand her on a deep level and how easy it could be to dismiss her difficulties as a deaf person because her communication with me, a hearing person, was so good. I wanted to make this observation and recognise the situation between us.

This highlighting of the relationship between us within our sessions seemed in retrospect to have precipitated a period of extreme panic and crisis in which Rachel feared a complete breakdown. Again, in retrospect, it was scarcely surprising. The very core of her identity was being questioned and the only answer we had reached was that for the moment Rachel had to accept that the 'see-sawing' uncertainty between deaf and hearing was, in the meantime, her identity. I felt at the time, however, that the impending explosion was beyond our control and we had no option but to wait for it to happen. (I later found reassurance in Winnicot's view (1986) that the fear of breakdown is in itself evidence that the breakdown has already taken place in early life when the individual had no means to make sense of it. Working with the fear would enable the healing the mature individual could achieve). This was a key moment and very dramatic for me.

I sensed Rachel's utter isolation within our relationship. She appeared to find me cold and unfriendly. It was after I observed, however, that the panic she had been through was over an expected breakdown that had not now happened, she disclosed that she was beginning to have happy feelings, strange and disorientating though they were. What now ensued was a testing period in which I felt she was doubting my ability to help her. Did we have to stop our sessions after an hour? I said I could not manage more than an hour and a half. Was working with her difficult? Was it a relief to leave her? The answer was 'No' to both. I knew I would get too involved, and would have difficulty with keeping the boundaries between us if our sessions were longer and would begin to collude with her. This was juxtaposed with the revelation that she had turned down a job in another county because she felt our counselling had just got established. Her unwillingness to make the move plunged her into another period of uncertainty because she loved her work, but she felt that she needed to come full circle. We reached the compromise of working twice weekly for a limited period.

Now Rachel was strong enough to take full advantage of my increased support and expressed her grief over losses in her life. She began to use art to express her feelings, finding she could then represent every nuance and detail faithfully in her own time. We worked on her images in a person-centred way, enabling her to touch on very deep feelings. She realised her pain within was only matched by her hatred of her mother. In a particular image about perceptions of herself in relation to other women, she used the unseen but

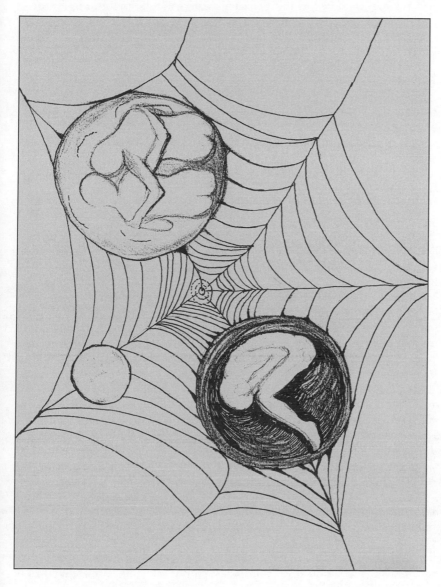

Figure 6.1 'Spider'

tangible presence of a spider to represent the very great fear within her, caused by her experience of her sexuality and also by her feelings about her mother. She said that if she expressed this fear, she was very scared of what would emerge. She did not allude to that image again, but her later increased confidence in expressing her sexuality suggested to me that the image work itself helped to exorcise her fear.

Rachel cried a lot privately, did not see anyone else in the evenings and continued to feel very angry, isolated and lonely. She acknowledged in sessions that she felt extremely vulnerable but that she saw her willingness to stay with her fragile feelings as positive. She was afraid, though, and asked if she could contact me at home if everything became too unbearable. I said no, because this would have infringed the agreed boundaries of our relationship, but suggested instead we extended the twice weekly period and that I felt that not only was she able now to delve into deep feelings but through expressing them, could lift herself out of them too. Then came a blow that knocked both of us, for different reasons...

Rachel had wanted to be part of a therapeutic group for some time, a decision we had discussed and felt would complement our counselling. It would perhaps help her to feel less isolated and would give her a chance of trying out communicating with a group of people. She had followed up various ideas for groups she could join but the reasons given for her rejection this particular time were what threw us. She was very angry to be told that her main problem was she was not accepting that she was deaf. (After all, what had her recent traumas been about?) She was also told she needed individual psychotherapy in order to 'experience her feelings' rather than counselling in which she was only 'exploring them'. This last reason also made me angry. I kept it to myself, however, as I did my mounting doubt that I had been wrong for Rachel and that she *would* have been better with 'deeper' therapy. I suggested I ask my supervisor what she thought about these reasons and her positive response reassured me considerably. She commented that psychotherapy and counselling may use very different methods although they may not be incompatible. Of course she confirmed that clients do experience their feelings as a result of person-centred counselling but perhaps by a different process than in psychotherapy. In the end, much to our surprise, however, Rachel was accepted as a member of the therapeutic group after all with no apparent explanation, and this heralded a new phase in our counselling.

Rachel's life now opened up more. She coped with being a member of the group, though she found it horrendously painful at times. She moved to a rented flat which she could furnish herself. She was now able to test out the strength of her self-image. Her work, which was so vital for her independence, was going well in spite of anxieties about the future, and she was meeting new friends. She did repeat her old ways of relating, but could check this out with me, and had an increased awareness of whereabouts in her body her feelings came from. She began to be able to arrest the 'downward spiral' within her of depression she'd felt in the past. She said she felt me to be a nurturing wise parent. I found the 'parent' image difficult to identify with although I did feel nurturing and wise at times. I for my part was testing my ways of relating with a deaf client as a hearing counsellor and so I was aware of a kind of equality between us.

I felt there were some ways in which I very much identified with Rachel, for example in her experience of victimisation. Maybe this was because I too had once been deaf and had a real sense of the confusion caused by being treated in a way that was not explicit but assumed by a group of other people. Rachel had to struggle with the label and accusation of 'victim' in her new relationships. I think I did understand how important it was to give Rachel all the space she needed to express her frustrations at the real victimisation that was taking place.

Just as Rachel was taking more responsibility for herself in the counselling process, for example telling me how she found some of my interventions I was feeling more confident and relaxed about checking out my understanding of her feelings and speaking more directly to her about her experience of being deaf. A more balanced relationship of taking things as they came and being able to say what we wanted began to develop and this was reflected in Rachel's relationships with other people. She was still, of course, very scared at times of the unknown and of losing control. The image she drew at this stage was related to her fear of letting go of old behaviour patterns because she was still uncertain of where she would fall and what that place would hold for her. She perceived that place as being something of great warmth, light and expanse, but it still scared her as she knew she had to make the journey alone. She could not imagine a time when she could do without her dependence on me as her counsellor, and she still saw me at times as Pegasus who was free to leave her, Bellepheron, lonely and floundering at the end of a session. I remember responding that I feel I can leave the responsibility of a client for their life with them when a session is over and I think Rachel increasingly took that statement on board through the last two years of our working together.

By this time we were now meeting in the room I used for counselling in my house. We were still able to sit either end of a sofa which we were accustomed to doing and I felt a great ease and closeness in our relationship for much of the time. I could often sense how Rachel was feeling and felt I now genuinely understood many of the issues she brought. Her suggestion to come once a fortnight tested the strength of that understanding and I had to begin to accept that Rachel was now experiencing much of her life independently of the support I gave her. The success of her progress made this acceptance possible and here I realise I did feel like a 'parent', letting go, but with the satisfaction of seeing that Rachel could now cope. She handled disappointment and success in relationships, changing her job and buying her own property. She found that if she got depressed or doubted herself she could experience those feelings for herself, let them go through her and then stand back from them. She began to envisage the idea of loving herself more and was more in touch with a positive image of being deaf. She felt increasingly self-confident and six months before we finished she said she was ready to wind down our sessions. She felt sad at finishing but felt she could sort out her problems for herself. She had felt no 'downward spiral' for some time.

I was sad too. Rachel confirmed the mutual trust we had in each other and said she appreciated my attentiveness to her throughout our counselling time. I felt sombred by my experience with her. Being deaf in a hearing world is a truly horrific experience. There had been nothing unstable or disturbed in Rachel that was not of the hearing world's making in its treatment of her. The counselling process, however, had enabled her to get in touch more fully with her inner strength, and that strength she has needed to pull herself out of depression and face up to the gross injustice she has experienced as a deaf person in this world.

My journey with Rachel has left me with a profound sense of that injustice. I feel shamed that those of us who are hearing are so little prepared to take the risk of changing our own attitudes and of opening ourselves up to new ideas suggested by the deaf world that would provide the bridge of new understanding on a basis of equality. The injustice of inequality is one of the many and different gaps between us of which I became aware throughout my counselling relationship with Rachel. I also realised that some gaps were gaping holes, some were chasms and some were bottomless pits. This awareness became increasingly difficult to convey to my supervisor who had little experience of working with deaf people and although her support of me was most expert in person-centred work, consistent and indeed in the end effective, I felt I was exploring the hearing counsellor with deaf client dynamic alone.

This exploration was therefore experiential, experimental and a journey into the unknown. The first gap between Rachel and me that became apparent was the superficial one of communication: that one was bridged, but it belonged still to the hearing way of relating and I became more aware of a gaping hole between us which concerned how we related culturally, or in the different way that we used language to communicate with each other. It was as though the way of relating I was used to with hearing people was too one-dimensional with Rachel and I needed to pick up other signals that made me relate more fully in trying to fill the hole between us. Rachel told me she could read my facial expressions before I spoke. I made a deliberate decision not to think of this or I would have become wooden and self-conscious. In return, I learnt to read her feelings through her body position and movements, of which I was particularly conscious because we sat at each end of a sofa. After a time I could tell by the way she was sitting what her mood was, particularly if we were silent and I think this development helped us out of a long stuck period in which I felt Rachel was cataloguing her depression but not moving on. I think it also made up for the inevitable lack of eye-contact between us.

Then there was the 'chicken and egg' situation I referred to earlier – a situation that was and is, difficult to fathom. My guess is that more communication and research between hearing counsellors with deaf clients would help to unravel my confusion. Were Rachel's feelings a direct result of being deaf or would she have felt the same as a hearing person undergoing similar life experiences? On the other hand, her life experiences would have been different had she been hearing; hence the 'chicken and egg' situation – and another gap. Not a big gap, however, because through the person-centred process we worked on Rachel's feelings, wherever they originated. Thus the person-centred approach may indeed have been more effective than others would have been.

The greatest chasm that opened up between us was caused by the strength of pain and outrage Rachel rightly felt about her treatment by the hearing world. I felt her intense anger and felt responsible for it as a hearing person. The chasm was only bridged when I took the courage to acknowledge to Rachel my responsibility, and the difference between us, and then was able in honesty to stay with her through her crisis of identity. Then we began to relate increasingly more easily and the chasm began to close. Finally, however, I was always aware of a bottomless pit between us when Rachel was particularly depressed. It mirrored her 'downward spiral', was very much about the oppressive feelings of being deaf, and I daresay could have swallowed us both up. It was certainly the unfathomable measure of feeling and experience I could not understand, although its presence I most certainly acknowledged and accepted. After four years, however, Rachel had developed other aspects of her inner self which established her independence, not only from me as her counsellor, but as a person in her own right.

RACHEL

When I referred myself to Jane on the recommendation of a friend, I was in a state of complete despair. I was so desperate for help, for someone to care, for someone to listen, even for someone to do something about my situation, that I was verging on being suicidal. I had never found it that difficult to express myself, but I had enormous difficulty in stopping the floodgates opening when I got on the emotional roller coaster that had become part of my life. Prior to beginning my counselling relationship with Jane, I had experienced many kinds of 'help', all of which had made me very angry in one way or another. I knew for example that I did not feel comfortable with talking to a man, but when I first tried counselling, I was allocated a male counsellor. I had also tried talking to 'friends' and, because they couldn't cope with me, I had made a habit of attempting to share my feelings with anyone who would listen, always trying to trust them and hoping that they would keep things to themselves. But I was always betrayed by someone in such a way that my private life, or at least a somewhat distorted version of it, suddenly appeared to become public property and I had experienced frequent back-stabbing, not always understanding why it was happening. Far from feeling angry at the breaches of trust and the selective listening, I was furiously angry with myself for having expressed anything at all. But such was the intensity of my pain and self-denigration that I could not stop the expression, and the roller coaster got faster and faster.

With hindsight, I realise that I was desperately lonely, and grieving for a number of recent and significant losses in my life. I had experienced a gradual loss of hearing, being close to death in early adolescence, my father's terminal illness over a period of six years during which he physically abused me, and a broken marriage with a hearing man which resulted in the loss of my home and children. One thing continuously screamed out at me through these long years – 'It's all my fault, everything is my fault'. Generally speaking, those around me didn't try to change my mind. All these things had come together to make me feel as if I had lost myself, but, at the same time, I had always been uncertain and scared of who I was, and too worried about what others thought of me. Throughout my adolescence, I had become increasingly attracted to women, forming deep emotional attachments and experiencing painful rejections. These somehow always reminded me of my relationship with my mother. I had always longed for a close relationship with her, but it seemed as if I had been replaced in her affections by my siblings, who were hearing, and that none of them took the trouble to learn how to communicate with me or understand me. I think I had borne a massive chip on my shoulder about the fact that my mother was prepared to spend a great deal of money on technical aids, hearing aids and so on, but she couldn't express feelings which said she loved me. I know I felt unloved.

As a young adult, I had friendships with men, but as soon as they became sexual, I was conscious of a sick feeling in the pit of my stomach. The pressures of my family and convention forced me into marriage, and despite having children, I continued to feel that deep physical revulsion. I felt as if I was being driven to make decisions which precipitated further loss. I just wanted to run away and hide with the subsequent pain of the separation, whilst my significant others, especially my mother, were reinforcing the blame. At this time, my deafness didn't seem to be a part of all this, in fact I think I blocked it out because I had had it drilled into me over the years that I had to cope or I wouldn't be worthy of loving. Besides which, I think my emerging sexuality was a far bigger issue for me. It brought with it numbing fear of double rejections wherever I turned, and more promises of taunts and harassment – rejection of my deafness and political naivete by the lesbian community and rejection of my sexuality by the deaf community. This was, in the end, my experience. Because I had to have reasons, I wanted so desperately to understand what was happening to me and why, and because of the two pressing issues, I felt my sexuality would carry with it a life of fear, lies and secrets, I put all my eggs in one basket so that my deafness began to thrust itself forward to the extent that it took over and hid all the things I was so scared of.

I do remember that at the start of my counselling relationship with Jane, I was totally preoccupied with failed relationships and my wish to maintain a 'cool' professional veneer in the face of these inner onslaughts, but I could not talk about my sexuality or about sex without cringing inside. I avoided *all* the important issues, despite Jane's hesitant attempts to probe and explore with me. Eventually, the *only* way I could talk about these things was through images. The spider's web was an early one that stands out in my mind. My professional life was my only source of self-esteem at the time, and it felt as if even that foundation was being shaken to the core by the unconscious discoveries I was making about my identity and the cruelty of the hearing world. My initial reaction to Jane was particularly representative of all that was wrong with my personal relationships, and I can remember feeling very embarrassed by it, to the extent that it only appeared to be a kind of guarded uneasiness. Because I had come to see myself as a rather bland and uninteresting person, I was inextricably attracted to popular, larger-than-life, vibrant, and most especially fun-loving personalities who paid attention to me. I found that, in their company, I suddenly became more extrovert, to the extent that the adrenalin flowed so fast that I experienced a very strong reaction – trembling and profuse sweating. I thought this reaction was about feeling good, and therefore managed to ignore the uncomfortable feelings that went with it. It took me the full four years of my counselling relationship to recognise that the feelings of physical revulsion experienced earlier and *this* feeling came from the same place, in part because Jane helped me to become aware of my bodily feelings and to understand where feelings were coming from. This particular 'gut feeling' came to mean for me that I was deeply afraid of being something that I was not, *but which everyone else seemed to expect me to be*. At the start of our counselling relationship, the notion of not wanting to lose what I thought was a 'good feeling' was so strong within that I was disappointed when I met Jane, and this was in addition to the sense of powerlessness that I felt about her being hearing. I felt she was and is a quietly humorous, considered, highly intelligent woman, careful with her feelings and not easily given to strong, overt expression, but with a wonderful clarity in what she says. I am certain that I had expectations of her and was given to comparing her with the three counsellors I had seen before, the last of whom *was* the vibrant personality I craved. At first, I wondered if what I was seeing was Jane's counselling persona – I don't think that I had any way of determining whether it was or wasn't, and that irritated me, because I had a great need to know and understand her, to get straight to the point by the most direct route possible.

I felt that I wanted to explain the powerlessness and the disappointment to her. *I wanted so desperately to feel powerful and sure*. It had always felt odd that I preferred to work with a hearing counsellor, something which I knew would shock many of my deaf colleagues for it *was* a conscious preference. Professionally, I felt a great deal of pressure to be 'politically correct' and to affiliate myself with deaf people, but there had come a point in my life where this became a burden to me, in part because of the expectations placed on me by the deaf community to be Deaf, and in part because I could at least acknowledge that the difficulties I was facing in my personal life, in particular in relationships, were not confined to my relationships with hearing people, though it is possible that they may have been rooted in my treatment at the hands of the hearing world. It is true, though I found it very hard to admit to myself or to Jane for some time, that I felt very guilty about the fact that I had spoken English as a first language, and consequently, it was very difficult for me to feel good about things that others recognised as my 'achievements' because they were linked to my ability to use this language. I found I was always apologising for my speech quality or having to justify my deafness and I got fed up with being a paradox. I wanted to be able to express myself better in sign language, and to join with Deaf people, but I felt clumsy with physical expression and embarrassed at my clumsiness and my nervousness at communicating in what was, for me, a foreign language, and, at the time, could not allow me to communicate the things which were at the core of my beliefs and existence. I always felt trapped in this situation, and it was at this time that the spider materialised.

In counselling, I became obsessed with the dichotomy. How could I reconcile that on the one hand, I hated the fact that Jane was hearing and envied her in her hearingness, and on the other, I needed the challenge of hearingness and to learn how to deal with it in a safe place? It sounds simple when I write it here, but it wasn't simple at the beginning when my self-esteem was so fragile. I am not so cruel and unfeeling that I cannot appreciate another person's feelings, even if they are my counsellor and I am paying them for a service (something I told Jane that I resented). But I think also that I was desperately scared that she would reject me if I said what I felt, as all the other people had done before her.

So, instead of trying to rationalise and reconcile, I hid my more immediate anger in the mess of more generalised anger at the world and the quality of the people I shared it with. In part this generalised anger was very real and genuine, but I felt that I was using it to avoid direct communication with Jane, lest I tell her about my disappointment with her. I was also conscious of a very great need to keep the ball in my court all the time in case there was a communication problem. I had always found it very difficult to deal with communication blocks because they always seemed to be tinged with the jarring tones of that inner voice which said 'It's my fault because I'm the one who's deaf', and I hated conflict. I had no alternative after all, and lacked the assertiveness which would be required to find one and stick with it. Through-out all of this, I worried incessantly between sessions that I was too overpow-ering, which again was typical of my approach to relationships in general, and Jane did not show what she felt about my behaviour in any overt way. I wondered if she felt powerless, and that would give me an excuse for terminating the relationship before she had a chance to challenge me and expose my vulnerability. Unconsciously, that *is* what I wanted to do with this relationship. If I worried enough this desire would become all-consuming, and, in the end, I would get what I unconsciously had learned was all that I was good for.

Eventually, this happened through an event which turned out to be a crucial point in the early part of our relationship. I was able to express my very intense desire for Jane to say something that would make me angry – really angry as opposed to indirectly angry. I think I wanted her to say something incredibly cruel, something that would prove my expectations of failure! When she responded in her usual considered, calm way with what even now seems to me the very brave self-disclosure that she found such ways of expression difficult, I felt something snap inside. I think that it was from that point on that I trusted Jane enough to begin to express myself more directly. She *had* made me angry, but not in the way I had expected. I realise now that she had also used her counselling skills to demonstrate to me that she was totally with me and would not be swayed from that fundamental baseline by any game-playing on my part. I began to feel safe with Jane; she had somehow passed the test I had set for her, though I didn't know that it was a test at the time.

At first, it felt as if I abused the safety. I became very skilled at talking my way into problems and reinventing the wheel because, as I later realised, I was terrified by the silences which happened when I could not express anything. It is difficult to unravel that fear even now. I am deaf and yet I fear the silence which, though not total, I have grown accustomed to. It may have been that much of the content of my sessions at this time was linked to exploration of my identity – whether I was deaf or hearing, or even a mixture of the two. It became clear that I was living in a kind of half-way house with no clear aim as to which direction felt right for moving on from there. I used to run through the positive and negative agendas for each route in my head and it seemed as if for every positive, there was always a negative which cancelled it out, however compelling the positives were, and I was always more prepared to put the feelings of others first than to listen to my own gut feelings about what I wanted. I was getting fed up with the see-saw, but I couldn't break the vicious circles, and began to wish that Jane would say something that would solve the problem for me. Instead, she reflected back my position as I was seeing it, which had the effect of making me see it for what it was. She could see my affinity with the deaf community *and* the hearing persona that I was born with, and she did not encourage me to take sides. I think that must have been quite a difficult position for her to arrive at, let alone maintain, but I grew to respect her for allowing me to find my own way, and I feel certain that I would not have arrived at where I did if I had felt pressured one way or the other. There were nevertheless ways in which she instinctively related to my deaf characteristics which surprised me.

As is often the case with persistent reinvention of the wheel, I ran out of oil to keep it turning. It felt rusty and grated against my internal need to 'make progress' or move forward. In one session, I transferred this frustration onto Jane in the form of a direct question: 'Do you get fed up with me going round and round in circles?'. She waited before replying: 'I find it quite difficult and frustrating', which was such a mirror of what I was feeling inside that I was taken aback. When I left after this session, Jane did not see me off in her usual way. I noticed an expression on her face which I could not read, and physically, it felt as if I was walking away and leaving a part of myself behind. I was frightened by this feeling, and worried about it between sessions.

In the following session, I checked out these feelings with Jane with a directness that I was unaccustomed to within our relationship, and received appropriate and honest reassurance about the meaning of her expression. This removed one block, in that it enabled me to start talking about feeling uncomfortable with talking, about words never sounding right leading into more words which sounded even worse. I began, after two and a half years, to feel trust. In her suggestion that we returned to pictures instead, Jane provided me with a solution which not only invented a new wheel, but also reawakened a sense of more positive aspects of my past which I had long since buried and forgotten. I realised for the first time why the pictures were important. As a teenager, which was one of the most difficult periods I had to go through, I threw myself into making images, painting, sculpting, anything that my hands could weave and my eyes could nurture. I discovered that I had a talent, but I don't think I recognised at the time the relationship between creativity and pain – the role of creativity in easing or moulding pain into something more manageable. My previous therapist had suggested punching pillows as a form of creativity – creative aggression, but it made me feel stupid.

I used images within counselling more often after that, and I found that I was filling my time more and more outside of counselling sessions with painting and sculpting, sometimes bringing these activities into my work. I began to notice how much I 'felt good' about this activity, but I also recognised that this quality of 'feeling good', *and the place it came from*, was different from that that I had experienced before. Within sessions, I found I was not content with sketches, nor did I always want to bring the fruits of my labour into sessions. I could work on a piece for hours in my own time in an attempt to portray all the different aspects of a particular feeling or issue. This seemed to be more important than talking about it and building it up with words. Though I did not bring all of the images I developed to counselling, they became important to self-expression, self-understanding and a focus for my feelings. There was a very strong sense of feeling 'at home' when we worked with images, but it took me quite a long time to feel comfortable or spontaneous with words.

Another related issue for me was the question of physical contact. There was a time when I felt as if words were not capable of providing me with the kind of 'holding' that I wanted. From the journal that I have kept erratically over the years, I discovered that I began to want the reassurance of physical contact with Jane at a time when I was deeply depressed. I remember the agony I went through asking Jane to hold me after a long bout of crying. I cried a lot and easily, but when I was crying, I felt so alone, as if the feelings were spilling over and there was nowhere for them to go and no-one to catch them. I couldn't see or hear Jane's presence – she felt so distant. It was another of those occasions where I was wanting something and not wanting it at the same time. I did ask, and Jane responded, but I think that *both* of us felt very uncomfortable with it. I was not used to physical warmth outside of an intimate sexual relationship; indeed I found it hard to separate physical warmth from the sexual element. At the same time, touch was important to me and I liked to feel different textures, and I wanted to feel easy about human contact. My instinctive reaction when Jane held me provoked a great deal of internalised thought about my nervousness, and once again, this had repercussions outside of counselling. I began to have aromatherapy on a regular basis and this helped me a great deal in feeling secure about my physical reactions, and also about getting in touch with my inner feelings. I never wore my hearing aids while being massaged, and always kept my eyes closed. It was like crying, though less traumatic because I could feel the presence of another person. I have since gained a great deal from non-sexual physical contact, and have begun to value and enjoy friendship and emotional bonding more, almost to the point where sex is unimportant in comparison. Again, there was a sense of going back to my roots, of recapturing the past, or at least, the parts of the past which were positive.

As my trust in her grew, I learnt that Jane's persona had other dimensions. For example, she showed a kind of firmness as opposed to the roughness I thought I wanted. She could show this quality to great effect when it became important for her to provide affirmation for my feelings. There was one session in the final year of our counselling relationship which I wrote about in some depth. I had, over a period of six months or so, been beginning to feel a glimmer of self-confidence and to discover aspects of myself that I liked.

This discovery was made through the somewhat astonishing revelation that I was beginning to enjoy working with Jane because it felt as if there was a lot of common ground between us and *she was more in tune with how I perceived myself to be*, without the complications of relationships. In Jane's mirroring of me (or was I mirroring her because something in me recognised that it felt right?), I began to get a sense of the light at the end of the tunnel – that what I was looking for was a feeling of belonging to others who were like me, and not who were different from me, but this was the me in entirety, not just the deaf me. I wanted commonality, common ground, not the conflicts that difference brought. In this particular session, these feelings began to surface.

My renewed and better feelings about myself had led me to attempt another relationship with someone who, at first sight, was very different from the partners I had had before. This person had expressed a willingness to learn sign language and shared some of my deeper interests. As time went on, I had begun to realise that the relationship was not working, not for the usual reasons, but because I acknowledged to myself that I was in danger of treading the same path of self-denial that I had trod in previous relationships *before* it actually happened in this one. I then took steps toward self-preservation and attempted to assert myself and my needs, which received an angry reaction, followed by an abrupt and somewhat nasty parting. In this session with Jane, I talked through all my feelings about having made my first real attempt to be myself and look after myself within a relationship, and the feelings that I had about the subsequent rejection. Jane listened for a long time, and when I was spent, exhausted, she made eye-contact with me and said 'It's *not* fair! It's *not* your fault!' with great emphasis. I do believe I saw a flash of anger in her eyes.

I can remember falling into a quiet silence. There was something in those simple words that I had been waiting to recognise in somebody else for what seemed like my entire life. The affirmation came from the directness of the eye-contact (which was unusual because I was a very talkative client and Jane a cautious counsellor and, as I had a tendency to look at anything in the room other than her whilst I was talking we rarely made eye-contact), and the noticeable shift in her body posture towards me, in addition to the forceful precision of her lip-patterns. I burst into tears with sheer relief.

Because I had so much respect for Jane, and because it seemed to me that she was the only person in my life who was capable of understanding my feelings in a non-judgemental way, I was increasingly tempted to ask her about her life and find out more about who she was, but I felt this interfered with our counselling as I was tempted away from the here and now of *my* feelings. The same was true when I made a very unwise excursion into group work in an attempt to address my nervousness in group situations which had a damaging effect on me and I felt set back the progress I had made in individual counselling because it changed the focus. I still found it quite difficult to put my own feelings first, much preferring to campaign on behalf of others, and I think joining this group was more about setting another precedent and the pursuit of perfection than about what *I* really wanted. The times when I was put on the spot about my deafness were acutely difficult, but I hope that I have learned from the experience of counselling. My work with Jane on the difficult issues emphasised that I didn't feel comfortable with any challenge which placed me in a vulnerable position. That was why the images helped – they were more gentle challenges, and more powerful in what they revealed.

Before my counselling relationship with Jane, I had terminated counselling on the pretext that I was feeling okay, or because I hadn't felt comfortable with the counsellor. There was no recognition that the feeling was temporary and the result of having started a relationship outside of counselling. Then, when things went wrong, I went back into counselling or to the doctor for anti-depressants! The decision to end counselling with Jane did not stem from the same source. It is true that I finally found a satisfying relationship – one that I had very good reason to feel sure about, towards the end of my four years with Jane. But the start of this relationship did not precipitate my desire to finish counselling on this occasion. Something about Jane had become a part of me, and as opposed to the earlier situation I described where I was afraid of leaving a part of me behind, I now felt at the end of every session that a part of her went with me in a place where it felt safe and secure and where there was no risk of loss. When I arrived for sessions, I didn't feel I wanted to talk any more. I just wanted to be…to sit back and reflect. It felt as if I was entering a period of consolidation, having learnt so much about myself, my feelings and my responses to others that I needed to take time out to decide what it all meant for me and, more importantly, how I could use it. For me, the parting felt calm. There was no regret, only hope for the future.

Have I ever felt I wanted to go back? Yes, once, when a major trauma happened in my professional life which ran so deep that it threatened everything I had built up over the years. Indeed I did see Jane twice during this period – I think for affirmation of my feelings and because she was an outsider to the situation who was also very much a part of me. I survived that trauma, but I have no doubt whatsoever that it was a result of the four years that we spent together and the support that a change of self-perspective had brought into my life, rather than those two isolated sessions in themselves. I have also no doubt that, at some stage in my life, I will go into deeper therapy, because I can now see the value of self-exploration for self-growth and the setting of boundaries, and no longer view counselling as something to be afraid of or as a place for solutions to problems. The place for that is within me, and the roots are beginning to grow.

JANE AND RACHEL REFLECT

Jane: I acknowledge now that it was very difficult for Rachel to express her anger directly at me. Apart from the inevitable inequality between counsellor and client there was the extra dimension of my being hearing which gave me yet more power. I did try to redress this imbalance between us but resisted feeling powerless in the face of Rachel's desire to be powerful. Had I been strong enough to risk being powerless, Rachel might have been able to be more directly angry with me. Rachel has highlighted for me in her account how cut off from me she felt when she cried in our sessions. This has come as a shock to me. She cried a lot and I made the assumption that she felt comfortable doing so. I thought I understood her to quite an extent through her body language but I obviously misread one of the most vital expressions of feeling. In the later stages of our counselling, I feel that I should have checked out my assumptions with Rachel much more. Then, when she cried, I would have found it natural and appropriate to offer her physical comfort.

Rachel: I have continued to grow since leaving my counselling relationship with Jane. The relationship that I started before counselling finished has lasted and has become one of the most loving, warm and rewarding experiences I have ever known. It goes from strength to strength every day – I found the closeness that Jane talked about, and it is something I feel very protective about. I have often thought about Jane and felt her voice talking inside me when times got bad, as well as when they were good. Two things stand out for me in what she has written. She recognised my need to feel powerful and she allowed me to become powerful, to feel a sense of my own power. But because she also kept her position clear and consistent, I never became so powerful that it was destructive or damaging to our relationship, and I learnt to handle my power through expression of my feelings. The second thing leaves me with a sense of shock. Jane's sense of anger and outrage that she is somehow part of an oppressive culture surprised me in its intensity because she rarely showed this within counselling. I feel certain now that this was the hinge which held the door to our relationship open: she acknowledged that she oppressed me and she worked with it quietly and carefully in counselling. *She did not deny the oppression.*

CHAPTER 7

WORKING ACROSS WORLDS II
THE DEAF COUNSELLOR AND THE HEARING FAMILY –
FACING THE EXPERIENCE OF FAILURE

'Family life is something like an iceberg: most people are aware of only about one-tenth of what is going on – the tenth that they can see and hear. Some suspect there may be more, but they don't know what and have no idea how to find out. Not knowing can set the family on a dangerous course. Just as a sailor's fate depends on knowing that the bulk of the iceberg is under the water, so a family's fate depends on understanding the feelings and needs that lie beneath everyday family events.'

(Virginia Satir, 1988, p.2)

This chapter is something of a contrast to the previous chapter for a number of reasons. First, it may be interpreted by some as an account of failure, if counselling is to be interpreted in terms of success or failure. It is of course a fallacy to assume that counselling relationships always result in client growth or that the counsellor never encounters clients that they cannot work with. Most counsellors, including those with years of counselling practice behind them, live with such experiences. Some of these experiences can be extremely painful or frustrating for both them and their clients, and can result in the counsellor feeling de-skilled and disempowered to the point where the counselling relationship cannot continue. Second, it looks at a particular situation where the statutory system has failed miserably in its provision of helping services for those in need, in part because perceptions of *who* is in need at a particular point in time have been displaced and helping services have therefore been misdirected and poorly planned. And finally, it is about the failure of organisational structures and management to understand or respond to the supervision needs of counsellors working within organisations, particularly when counsellors are implicitly required to be some kind of professional 'role model' for the organisation and therefore, indirectly, for their clients.

GENERAL ISSUES

It is difficult to accurately estimate the numbers of deaf children in Britain today. Existing surveys have a tendency to concentrate on a particular situational context such as the education system. Thus, we have figures which suggest that there are 65,000 deaf children in full-time and further education who are said to be 'educationally disadvantaged by their hearing impairment' (British Association of Teachers of the Deaf, 1986), but we do not know how many of these children are educationally disadvantaged *by the education system*, perhaps because they have been placed in inappropriate schooling, nor how many are experiencing or have experienced what may loosely be defined as socio-emotional and psychological problem situations at home or in school. There are three possible reasons for this, apart from the more general reason that, as we saw in the opening quotation, family life can be like an iceberg with a large portion of family dynamics hidden from view. First, such surveys tend to employ a pathological approach to deafness which suggests that the 'problem' is located in the deaf child. It is therefore *assumed* that if a child is deaf, they are educationally disadvantaged, and so these figures actually represent the numbers of deaf children and young people within a particular classification of 'hearing loss' in full-time and further education. Using this approach, those with 'mild or moderate hearing losses' may not be classified as presenting educational 'problems', though this may be far from true. Second, although non-statutory guidance suggests that Local Education Authorities might like, *wherever possible*, to take into account the feelings and perceptions of the child when deciding on educational matters, this is not backed up by legislation. This means that there is widespread adultism within the special education system which can mitigate against the socio-emotional and psychological well-being of deaf children. Third, and on a more political level, education is seen by some to be moving backwards in its teaching of the value systems which underpin a healthy affective climate in today's diverse and multi-cultural society, to the point where the existence and quality of diversity is in danger of being ignored or denied. It is rare to find within the school curriculum occasions where stereotypes of deaf or disabled people are challenged, despite the existence of excellent curriculum materials aimed at doing this (for example, Reiser and Mason, 1992), and so the myths persist and are reinforced from a very early age.

The vast majority of deaf children are born to parents who are hearing – Sharon Ridgeway quotes ninety per cent in Chapter 9. This means that they will initially be part of a family dynamic which is woven around hearing cultural norms, which may embrace alienism and which allows them to integrate with the family with varying degrees of success. It must be emphasised once more that this dynamic operates largely through the *unconscious*, and, from the parent's perspective, there is a trend towards archetypal responses to the presence of a deaf child in the family being reinforced by many of the professional systems and individuals that they encounter from the time of their deaf child's birth. The possible professional contacts which might be made by parents in this position could potentially be seen to exist at some point between the two extremes illustrated in Figure 7.1 (Corker, 1992b). The right hand side of the figure represents those professionals which are acces-

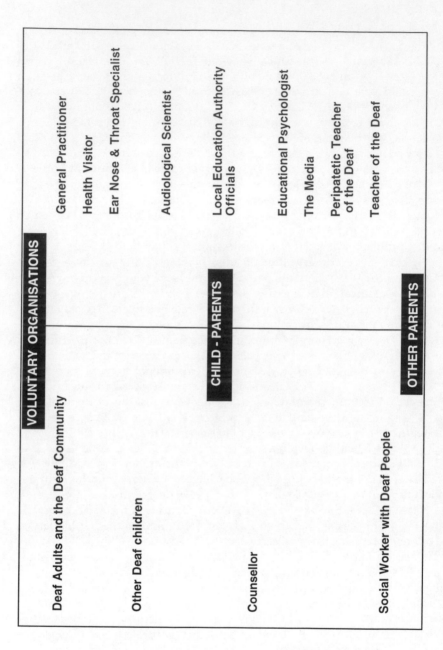

Figure 7.1 Families with Deaf Children – Contact Networks

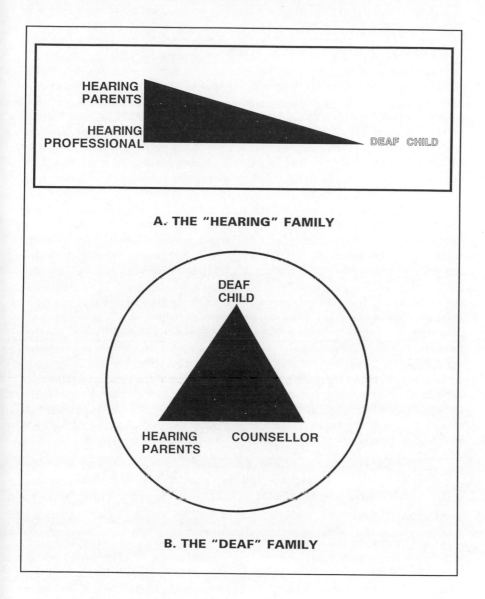

A. THE "HEARING" FAMILY

B. THE "DEAF" FAMILY

Figure 7.2 'Professional Roles in Shaping Family Dynamics'

sible to most deaf children and their families, and the left hand side, a system which is rarely available and, as we can see, includes counselling.

Most of the services provided by the professionals on the right hand side of the figure are statutory services, and the vast majority of the professionals involved are hearing and without even a basic knowledge of counselling skills. This means that the counsellor qualities of empathy, unconditional positive regard and genuineness will rarely be observable unless they are instinctively provided. It could be said then that the two systems may lead to a set of relationships between hearing parents, deaf child and professionals which may be represented as shown figure 7.2, though obviously, there will be families who exist in a kind of half-way house between the two through compromise of some sort, and families who move between two extremes at different times in the child's life.

In the top half of this figure, the deaf child is distanced from the other members of the triad and the closeness of the parents and professionals suggests a conscious or unconscious collusion. In reality the collusion is often reinforced by the ease with which professionals can communicate with hearing parents when compared with deaf children – professionals and parents have a *common language*, and the power which is inherent in the *expertise* of the professional from the parent's perspective which indicates that the professionals must be 'right'. The triangle, however, is also sharply angular, which suggests tension in the relationships formed. This triad may lead to the formation of a 'hearing family', where hearing norms and values are encouraged to persist, and unconscious alienism risks becoming conscious oppression. In the situation represented in the bottom half of the figure, the triangle is equilateral which suggests a shared relationship with all parties contributing equally and with the deaf child at the peak of the triangle providing the focus for the relationships. The latter situation is one that Luterman describes as 'the deaf family':

> 'We must keep in mind the notion of the family as a system in which all the parts are intimately and inextricably linked; deafness in one member means that everyone in the family is to some degree deaf.'

> (Luterman, 1987, p.99)

The 'deaf family' aims to embrace this notion and may be viewed as one way in which a healthy equilibrium between hearing parents and their deaf child can be established through the strengthening of child–parent bonds and the acknowledgement that, for many hearing parents, the birth of a deaf child can set into motion a sequence of feelings which is not unlike that experienced following bereavement. However, this is only one view. Oliver (1978) advocates a more dynamic view, which focuses on limitations resulting from disability as a consequence of socially constructed meanings and social restrictions. If there is loss, it is seen to derive from such restrictions, rather than from any innate feeling of emotional loss. 'Loss' becomes a social product. Probably, there are elements of both, for undoubtedly we get a sense of very deep emotional loss when working with hearing families in the counselling situation. It does not seem appropriate in this arena to make judgements about the source of that loss. All parents dream of the perfect child and many have high expectations of that child. A deaf child may be seen to challenge that dream and so they can become a natural target for their parent's unconscious alienism. Reactions to the shattering of the image of the perfect family range from the need to talk to tears and anger, which are all part of the mourning process. If the parents are not allowed to go through this process, alienism can become conscious oppression of the child, which is especially true if parents become stuck in denial of the reality with which they are faced and view it only from a negative perspective (Corker, 1992a).

This chapter now attempts to explore the situation where a deaf counsellor becomes part of the family dynamics of three 'hearing families'. When reading the accounts below, it is important to remember that this is a somewhat unique situation in Britain, and there are therefore few comparisons which can be made. Deaf counsellors can feel extremely isolated in working with this client group for a variety of reasons. As we shall see, there are occasions when working with a 'hearing family' cannot be distinguished from counselling a deaf child *by proxy*.

CLIENT-CENTRED ISSUES

Family Dynamics[1]

When observing 'hearing families' there are a number of key concepts which I have found useful in looking at family dynamics, and which help in the exploration of the part of the iceberg which is below the surface. These are *family myths, family transference distortions and countertransference, and interlocking pathology*. Byng-Hall (1973, p.239) describes the family myth as a defence mechanism, whereby a pattern of mutually agreed, but distorted roles are adopted by each of the family members. Because the myth represents a compromise between the individuals in the family, any threats to the myth threaten the individual's defences and, likewise, any changes in individual roles threaten the family myth. The family myth allows family members and others to remain unaware of the 'avoided theme', which is usually something deeply unconscious. Fear of being deaf, and desire for the deaf child to be replaced by a hearing child are two examples. Using the notion of the family myth enables the counsellor to conceptualise the functioning of unconscious processes in the family system. The success with which the family myth can be maintained depends on the roles assigned to the individuals in the family and the way in which these individuals communicate with each other. Ackerman (1966) and Satir (1988) have both attempted to provide a structure for these role assignments which have a communicative infrastructure. The former suggests three primary family roles (*attacker, healer* and *victim*) whereas Satir, as we saw in Chapter 3, identifies four – *placator, blamer, computer* and *distractor*. In 'hearing families', the absence of a healer is common and can lead to extreme polarisation of the roles of the attacker and the victim, as we shall see below.

---

1   Much of this section is taken from some of my earlier work on *Deaf Perspectives on Psychology, Language and Communications*. Part 6: Systems (1990d, pp. 5–10), reprinted here with permission from the publishers.

On an unconscious level, members of the family transfer on to each other the 'child' and 'parent' positions, which stem from their own past relationships as they attempt to deal with their own unacceptable, frightening and hostile feelings. This transference is reciprocated by the countertransference of any newcomer to the family, or existing members of the family who are on the receiving end of the transference.

The concept of interlocking pathology contains several different aspects involving the reciprocal and interrelated nature of unconscious processes operating within the system. It has been identified by a number of authors (e.g. Wynne, 1965; Jordan, 1970). The 'symptom bearer' is seen as undertaking a particular emotional task for one or more family members and will often express a certain attribute symbolically on behalf of the family member(s). It is my experience that the symptom bearer in 'hearing families' is commonly the mother, and she performs the emotional tasks of all the family members.

These issues arise because communication within the family system has been displaced or damaged. In *displaced* communication the deaf family member may express frustration, anger, paranoia or extreme suspiciousness and these are identified as the symptom of 'impairment' rather than any expression which is appropriate to the circumstances. The reality of the situation is often that the hearing family members cannot accept the deaf member or integrate them fully into the family. In *damaged* communication, there are often two conflicting levels of communication occurring at the same time. For example, the hearing mother may say to their young deaf child who has removed his or her hearing aid for the umpteenth time in a fit of temper, 'Poor darling, you know it really is so important that you keep your hearing aid in' in a sympathetic voice whilst looking angry and impatient. Here, the two conflicting levels are verbal and non-verbal and, as we have seen, the non-verbal is often more real and relevant for deaf people, whereas the verbal features figure in the experiential landscape of hearing people. The deaf child's continuing anger may be a countertransference of the transference of the mother's anger through non-verbal cues. In the child's view, the mother is not listening to his or her non-verbal message which is 'I don't want to wear my hearing aid!'.

BOX 7.1 SATIR'S FOUR ASPECTS OF FAMILY LIFE

SELF-WORTH	The feelings or ideas we have about ourselves
COMMUNICATION	The ways we use to work out meaning with one another
THE RULES OF THE FAMILY SYSTEM	The ways families determine how they should feel and act
THE LINK TO SOCIETY	The way we relate to other people and institutions outside the family

These key concepts are useful for looking at inner psychological functioning and how it affects the roles and relationships with the 'hearing family'. They can be contextualised more generally using Satir's four aspects of family life (1988, pp 3–4) (Box 10.1).

These processes and patterns of communication are readily observable when counselling hearing families in a number of ways which could be illustrated by the following three case descriptions.[2] I would not wish to imply that this is some kind of definitive framework. These case descriptions are examples of a number of trends which I have seen over several years of working with 'hearing families', and they are intended to provide examples of how a pathologising scenario can be created within a 'hearing family', and the issues that this scenario may create for the deaf counsellor.

The Frightened and Confused Family

This is Sandra Murphy's (edited) account of the early months of her deaf daughter's life. It is a story which I heard many times in the three and a half years I worked with 'hearing families' – a story of parents struggling to find their feelings against a background of a richly varied professional intervention:

> I knew something was wrong right from the start. I didn't feel the same way about her as I did about her sister when she was a baby. There was just something wrong. But no-one seemed to take my worries seriously – they all said that I was imagining things. My doctor said it was post-natal depression! When I finally found out when she was fourteen months old that she was deaf I was absolutely devastated. I thought my life had fallen into pieces. I thought – What did I do wrong? Why me? I'd had one perfect child, why couldn't I have another? But in the end I know that didn't help; it just made things worse. All the time I used to watch her wondering if I could ever have a proper relationship with her, wondering if I should have another child who might end up the same. And every time I heard a voice on the radio or the fire alarm go off in the factory, this feeling came up that I wanted her to hear, to hear the birds, to hear a baby cry. I felt she was missing life, and I felt sorry for her. I didn't want to let her out of my sight in case something happened to her, but I didn't want to be with her either.

> My husband didn't help. He'd always been out a lot, but after she was born, he never seemed to be there. When he was there was this stony silence, and he couldn't even look at her. His mother went on and on at me about getting something done about her (but what?), and her sister screamed at me for not giving her enough attention, and expecting her to help all the time. Watching those deaf people on television didn't help. They all seemed so angry and all that miming and gesturing – I couldn't use my hands like that. I'm even frightened of touching my friends who I've known for years. And so it was absolutely wonderful when this specialist told me about hearing aids and that

---

2   The names of the individual family members have been changed to preserve confidentiality.

Natalie would hear and speak normally…that she would be normal. I stopped feeling alone then.

When a deaf child is born into a hearing family, family relationships begin to alter with the growing awareness that something is wrong. This awareness, which, as in this case study, usually begins with the mother, can commence very early, especially when the family already has a hearing child. However, because the uneasiness cannot obviously be attributed to deafness, it tends to persist as an ill-defined feeling until the child is at the age when parents would expect him or her to start talking. Deaf babies babble like hearing babies for a period of time, and this can further confuse an official diagnosis. There is the added problem that the first professionals encountered by the parents, usually the general practitioner and the health visitor, may lack sufficient awareness to take the parents' worries seriously. This lack of awareness can set into motion a chain of events which seriously affects the parents' self-worth and, as we shall see, that of the child also.

This account has all the classic hallmarks of the pathologising scenario, where a negative view of being deaf is built into family relationships. Sandra sees herself as a victim of fate and this perception escalates into a series of reactions similar to those of the mourning process. Sandra denies Natalie's deafness by emphasising that she wants Natalie to hear and be 'normal' and this denial is reinforced by her mother-in-law's need to 'get something done about' Natalie and her husband's 'stony silence' and repeated absences from home. The sibling rivalry being shown by Natalie's sister increases the intensity of the relationships within the family. Everyone in the family appears to be unconsciously taking on the roles of 'blamer' or 'persecutor', blaming Sandra and pushing her to do something about 'the problem', which props up her feelings of being a victim. It is important to ask where Natalie is in all of this. It appears that she has become something of a shady background figure who is at the centre of this scenario, and yet not apparently present. The growing communication difficulties within the family can isolate Natalie still further.

The first references made by Sandra to the involvement of professionals sound further warning bells. The professional, in this case an ENT specialist, makes a remark which for Sandra is like a God-send, a verification that everything she dreams of *can* be achieved, however shaky the foundations of her beliefs. But wishful thinking and the search for a miracle cure (hearing aids) can form part of the denial process which occurs in the early stages of mourning. The ENT specialist, whilst trying to give Sandra hope, is actually colluding in her denial. And in this respect, the specialist is not alone. Sandra's account continues:

> When she went for her first real hearing test, the person testing was so reassuring. Every time she heard something (yes, she actually heard something!), there were beaming smiles all round. I was quite surprised when, a few days later, a teacher called round to play with her and find out what she could do. The teacher also said what the specialist said – that she would learn to talk normally. She visited me twice a week to start with, but then she only came once a month. By the time this had been going on for about a year, I was bursting

with questions. But the visits were always the same. I know now that it was because they had to put my daughter first, but every time the teacher came, she would sit on the floor with her and help her to do things for two hours, and I sat and watched. No-one ever explained to me exactly what all this play was for. And no-one told me why she still wasn't talking, not real talking anyway, when she was three and a half.

The next piece of information I got was when that psychologist came. He did a lot of tests which he didn't explain to me, and told me not to expect too much from her education. She would only be average for her age, whatever that meant. I started to feel angry then. My mother-in-law said it was because deaf children are too handicapped to learn much anyway.

The professionals' collusion in Sandra's denial continues to such an extent, that when one professional contradicts what has been said before, her response is to be angry, so entrenched is she in denial. Anger can be a healthy emotion, but in this sense, it is destructive of progress. At this stage, the relationship between Sandra, Natalie and the professionals can be described in the terms used for the 'hearing family' above, yet the collusive relationship between parent and professionals is actually mutually supportive of the power imbalance which has been created. The power clearly lies with the professionals because very often they are the holders of knowledge which they then withhold from the parents (the *Experts* of Chapter 3). This can be seen both in the educational psychologist who does not explain the tests he is using and in the peripatetic teacher of deaf children who perpetrates Sandra's feeling of being a 'fly on the wall'. In the above extract, Sandra is a partner in ignorance and her powerlessness in this situation is increased by her own lack of education.

In the above extract, we can also begin to see the power of language in reinforcing the roles and relationships within the triangle. The 'beaming smiles' of the audiology technicians are a very simple example, because they are only elicited when the deaf child 'hears'. For both Sandra and Natalie this is a powerful indictment of hearing being 'good' and deafness being 'bad'. The only knowledge which appears to be lacking by professionals at this most crucial stage in the deaf child's life is a knowledge of psychological functioning and how it affects roles and relationships within a family. For example, the peripatetic teacher of deaf children does not appear to see that Sandra is in need of as much support as Natalie because she is blinkered by what she is *expected* to do. Sandra is very confused and frightened. She desperately needs simple, accurate and unbiased information to ease her confusion; she needs to be listened to because she has so many unvoiced worries and fears; and she needs to know how to involve herself in what is going on. Finally, perhaps most importantly, she needs to know how to forge a relationship with Natalie. These were the expectations she had when she came to see me for counselling, and, in contrast to the following two case studies, I was able to work with Sandra in building her sense of self-esteem in order that she became more able to deal with the confusion by remaining consistent within herself about what she wanted and how she related to Natalie.

The Family in Chronic Denial

Sometimes denial becomes so acute and entrenched, and is allowed to persist over such a long period of time because of the creation of family myths and their reinforcement by professional and societal norms, that it is only when a threat is posed to the uneasy homeostasis that has been created within the family that the parents seek help. The Reids are one such family. Sheila Reid came to see me with her son, James, when James was fourteen years old. This is Sheila's outline of her reasons for coming to see me in our first meeting. I began by introducing myself in speech and sign support (SSE) and attempting to explain about the terms of the contract. Sheila, however, interrupted me before I had a chance to complete the explanation:

> Don't use that stuff in front of him, he doesn't need it and I certainly don't want him picking it up. It will jeopardise his chances of getting into...school, and frankly that's the last thing we want at the moment. He's got to go there. It will do him good to be away from us and then perhaps we can have some time to sort out our own problems. How we can possibly sort out the problems we've got with him around I don't know. His father's being impossible, and it doesn't let up. You've got to get him off our hands. I've tried everything with those people at...and I'm not getting anywhere. Typical teachers – always claiming they know what's best for him, but they can't even have a decent conversation with me, but that's what you might expect isn't it – I mean, how they think the deaf can teach the deaf. They've got no idea of what I want. It's a strain, I'm fed up with him. I just want him to go away!

Throughout this, James sat silently. At the start, when I was signing, he watched me intently, but when I stopped, he rapidly became turned in on himself and stared at the wall. He made no attempt to take part in the exchanges, even when prompted. Sheila took exception if I tried to bring him into the conversation, continuing to refer to him as *him*, and never once using his name. She kept insisting that *he* didn't have a view on anything, when I felt that James *did* have many views. His body language looked tense, possibly even angry. During two periods when his mother became silent (which was rare), his eyes misted over, but when he made eye-contact with me, he looked down, veiling his feelings. Sheila was agitated throughout. She fidgeted constantly and would not look at me when she talked, but at some point just above my left shoulder. She elaborated at great length on the marital problems she was experiencing and how she felt that James was the cause of all their problems. I listened for forty minutes. Throughout this time, if I tried to pick up any points or respond to what she said, she interrupted and continued with her story. When I later expressed that I needed to understand James' feelings also, and confirmed that it was important to work with the whole family, after I had affirmed that I had 'heard' what she had said, she became angry and personally abusive towards me:

> Family? What family? I've just been telling you that we don't have any family to speak of... Well you would want to know what he thought wouldn't you. I mean you deaf are all the same, so proud. It's alright for you – you can speak and he hasn't even got halfway there. How do you suppose he's going to survive

in the outside world? You're just sitting in your ivory tower, you've got it all, so you can be so sorry for him, but I don't suppose for one minute that you care about me, or what I want. I should think you haven't even heard one word I've said. You're no better than the rest of them. I'm telling you that I want him to go away to school and I don't want to discuss it. Do your job, or whatever it is you do.

James had curled into a ball on his seat. He looked as if he was holding years of pent-up feelings inside with tremendous physical effort. Sheila ignored him completely. I was nervous about responding this time, because I felt very angry, but I decided to tell her that I found her remarks offensive and that they made me feel bad. She did pause for a minute on hearing that, but then she got up to go, grabbing James by his sweater and pulling him upright. She retorted that we were obviously getting nowhere and that she had had enough. She wanted to talk to someone else and said that she would get my line manager to recommend somebody. She then left the building. Sheila's expectations were that I should accept her story without judgement or question, and that I should also accept her negative judgement of deaf people (including me). Her failure to refer to James by his name, her references to the deaf teachers in James' school, and her repeated suggestions that I was somehow 'not good enough' were all very clear indications that Sheila had a very deeply rooted difficulty with deaf people. I felt, in fact, that just as she refused to acknowledge James or his feelings, she denied the existence of deaf people in any real sense. Sheila was also 'blaming' James, and later me, for the problems she was experiencing within her relationship with her husband. Sheila was apparently a 'victim' of a situation whereby the family myth of denial had become so entrenched that she could only respond to the 'threat' that I posed by rejecting me outright. My refusal to take on board the blame angered her and her reaction left me hanging in mid-air. My failure to draw James into the exchanges made me feel very impotent and fearful, especially when it was clear that mother and son had existed for years in this situation of complete embargo. I did feel in this case that James had become the focus of the family's breakdown in communication, and although I felt I had made the right decision to challenge Sheila's view of me, it became clear that I had missed an opportunity to work more constructively with this family in a way which would have helped James because of her subsequent rejection of my self-disclosure.

The Abusing Family

It is rare, in my experience, for hearing parents to be openly abusive towards a deaf counsellor, whatever needs and expectations they have of counselling. It is more common for them to shy away from looking at issues of prejudice directly, or to seek the help of a hearing professional whom they see as 'more appropriate' for their needs. This is what happened with Sheila Reid. Sometimes, if the family chooses to remain in counselling, this situation imposes a communication block within the counselling relationship which is subsequently very difficult to break through. However, just as clients can sometimes make assumptions about the deaf counsellor, so can the counsellor totally misread a situation. This can lead to a different kind of 'failure'.

The Wilson family were what might be described as a 'patriarchal' family. Their deaf daughter, Susan, was an only child, who was sixteen years old when the family came to see me. Unusually, the father, Richard, attended the first session with Jean, Susan's mother. I found Richard dominating and sexist. In a similar way to Sheila Reid, he seemed to feel that his job was to give orders and that I was only there to do his bidding. But he was much more aggressive and explicit in his expression of his thoughts and feelings, and within quite a short time, I noticed that he played some kind of cruel game with Jean and Susan, which seemed to have the aim of ridiculing them. He was persistently arrogant and scornful about any contributions they made, and this pattern of behaviour continued over three sessions. In the fourth session, Richard changed the focus of the game. He made numerous unsuccessful attempts to recruit me as a player by invading my personal boundaries in asking intimate questions which included the desire to know the details of my sexual activities. I felt that Jean and Susan found this acutely embarrassing, and were humiliated by his behaviour, but they were not prepared to stand up to him. I felt fear somewhere in the room. Richard made it very clear that he considered his attendance an insult and that he felt counselling was a waste of time. I asked him why he came if he felt that way, because I felt uncertain of how to proceed. His response was:

> My daughter needs to stand on her own two feet and this deaf thing is getting in her way. Personally, I always wanted a son but that's by the way. A wimp is a wimp. She won't go out on her own – scared stiff she is, and I get no privacy with her mother... So I decided things had to be taken in hand. If it's because she's deaf that this is happening, then something can be done about it. I already know that all this is my wife's fault. We had some tests, and she's the one with the bad genes – but it's time Susan got herself a boyfriend, though I dare say my wife will have other ideas. I think she should have one of those operations – what are they called?...cochlear implants. I've read about them – make her ears work like they should then we can stop all this nonsense.

I asked Susan what she felt. She caught me unawares with the clarity of her response:

> I don't want an operation. I want to stay at home. I'm frightened!

Jean tried to support Susan, and was immediately subjected to yet another reference from Richard to the fact that she was useless at making reasonable or sensible decisions that had nothing to do with her anyway. As with James Reid, I had felt drawn into Susan's silence, but this had a different effect now that she had made a positive statement which was striking in its opposition to her father. He deflected any subsequent attempts by me to understand more of Susan's feelings, and I began to feel that it would be more productive if I were able to work with Susan on her own, given her age and the difficulty she had with expression in her father's presence. At the end of this session, I suggested that it might be helpful for me to do this so that we could explore Susan's feelings before any decisions were taken which might not be helpful to her or to the family. Jean indicated her agreement with this but Richard just looked at me with a very unpleasant expression on his face. I found myself remembering that expression for sometime afterwards and wondering what it meant, but because the session was effectively over, I had no opportunity to probe. I did not hear from the family again, despite writing twice (to Jean) to confirm my commitment to working with them and expressing concern that they had not been in touch.

COUNSELLOR-CENTRED ISSUES

The above cases prompted very different internal responses in me as a *deaf* counsellor. What the last two have in common is that the intensity of my responses felt overpowering, and I had great difficulty in keeping the boundaries of the counselling relationship intact. I am aware that I was looking for an escape route and that I wanted to terminate these relationships because I felt out of my depth. When the parents subsequently terminated the sessions, my initial feeling was one of relief, but I became gradually aware of an overpowering feeling of guilt, which made me question my professional credibility as a whole. I did not have the support of a counselling supervisor when I saw these families, in part because it was important for me to work with someone who accepted the oppression which can become part of transcultural counselling relationships. I was not sufficiently experienced to be able to retrieve the relationships, which I wanted to do because of James and Susan, and I feel that this was the source of my guilt. I now have no doubt in my mind that the feelings I experienced were largely linked to the fact that I am deaf, and the effect that this had on the dynamics of these counselling relationships. But I felt that the organisational structure I worked within was not appropriate for developing the skills necessary for listening to and accepting the dynamics of a counselling relationship which is being facilitated by a deaf counsellor. There were some aspects of this dynamic which were potentially very damaging and demoralising for a deaf counsellor to work with in the absence of appropriate support. There are a number of underlying dimensions to this statement which are of relevance to deaf counsellors working with *any* 'hearing family'.

Circumstantial Failure and Client Expectations

Counsellor experiences of 'failure' are an important dimension of the counselling process overall, and it is important that counsellors learn from their experience of 'failure', rather than over-emphasise it to the point where it becomes synonymous with the confessions of a failed counsellor. When I look back at the journal I kept during the time I was working with these families, I recognise that the effects of 'failing' were in danger of causing me to doubt my counselling skills *per se*. Failure with one or even several clients over a period of time *can* be a result of the counsellor's failure to know themselves or a deficiency in counsellor skills, but it can also be linked to counsellor and client expectations of the counselling relationship and to external circumstances influencing the path which a particular kind of counselling relationship may take. Mearns says of *circumstantial failure*:

'Any counsellor, no matter of what persuasion or how skilful, is inevitably going to fail with some clients because of factors beyond both the counsellor's and client's control such as personalities, timing, environmental factors, the intractable nature of so many difficulties and, above all, our limited understanding of the complexities of the human psyche.'

(Mearns, 1990, p. 81)

Perhaps it is possible for counsellors to use their experience of failure within the counselling process, indeed, this is desirable, but there are some circumstances in which even this is denied. As we saw in Chapter 1, there are very few deaf people in senior positions of employment in Britain today, despite numerous campaigns to promote deaf employees as 'good' employees. Of those that we do see, it is probable that the greatest concentrations are employed by the voluntary sector, in particular the so-called 'deaf' organisations, social services and university research departments. In all of these settings, deaf people are responsible to hearing management. We have discussed at length the importance of knowing ourselves for counselling, but it has also been implied on a number of occasions that clients have *expectations* of their counsellors. When these expectations are not met, this is one of the primary sources of the counsellor's 'failure' from the client's perspective. Client expectations can be linked to many factors. Certainly, most clients expect 'help' and many expect the counsellor to give them 'the answers to their problems'. Other clients have expectations linked to the counsellor's personality as we saw in the previous chapter. My experiences of working in the voluntary sector with many 'hearing families' who showed the same characteristics as the families described above suggests that *most hearing parents do not expect the counsellor to be deaf*, and when they make this discovery, the deaf counsellor is immediately subject to deep scrutiny to see if they match up to the parent's expectations of *what a deaf person should be*, or the counsellor is the subject of *unquestioning idealisation*. Employing organisations which have expectations of *the deaf employee as role model* that can be linked to very curious definitions of professionalism or to the organisational *managers' expectations of what a deaf person should be*, reinforce parental expectations if the organisation becomes the setting for counselling or the main source of referrals. Expectations about the deaf counsellor's perception of being deaf may bear no relation at all to the here and now of that deaf person's life situation and, where counselling is concerned, they can work against the counselling process because they place an additional personal burden on the deaf counsellor who may then struggle to remain non-judgemental and develop different and less effective or more directive ways of working in order to compensate for the personal stress incurred. Further, because many of these expectations are linked to some fictional and generalised role model of the 'deaf professional', hearing clients may measure the deaf counsellor against this model and, given certain circumstances, will inevitably find it lacking.

Expectations and Referral

I have had hearing parents referred to me by hearing colleagues who extol my virtues as a lip-reader, and assume that my ability to lip-read them and to speak is an indication that I can manage communication in any situation. Indeed, this was the case with the Reid family. On my first meeting with this family, it became clear quite rapidly that I could *not* lip-read Sheila Reid easily, in part because she talked so rapidly; her avoidance of eye-contact was also disconcerting for me as a deaf person. It is further extremely rare to find a hearing parent of a newly diagnosed deaf child who can sign, and so possible difficulties might be anticipated in communication with the Murphy family. It is additionally the case with hearing parents of younger deaf children or deaf teenagers that the primary reasons for seeking help are the communication difficulties within the family. If hearing parents cannot communicate with their deaf child and vice versa, it seems a very strange assumption to make that communication with a deaf counsellor will be any more fluent. Yet parents may make this assumption as a result of the judgement of other hearing people who base this judgement on their more direct experience of me as a deaf person. In such situations, hearing parents find themselves in a situation which mirrors exactly the difficulties they are experiencing within the family from the commencement of the counselling relationship. Few clients are ready to confront their problem situations in this way so early, and this has often been given implicitly as a reason for terminating counselling. An extension of this example relates to the emphasis which has been wrongly attributed to the deaf counsellor as an exponent of a particular approach to communication. Hearing parents in denial will cling desperately to the hope that their deaf child will achieve fluent spoken language and this hope can become linked to a fierce desire to seek affirmation from a deaf adult. Hearing colleagues, in ignorance of both the parents' inner hopes and fears and of the deaf counsellor's 'oral' stance as a conscious response to the 'role model' demands placed upon them by the organisation, have referred hearing clients to me because they see me as an 'oral' deaf person. However, in my counselling role, I am focused on being genuine as opposed to being neutral, impartial or promoting the aims of the organisation. On meeting these hearing clients for the first time, usually in the absence of any concrete background information, I tended to speak and sign at the same time because this is my natural means of communication and part of my genuineness. I may also fail to achieve fluent communication with many parents in the initial session, because as is often the case, the ease with which I can lip-read increases in direct proportion to the familiarity with the lip-patterns of the person whom I am trying to lip-read. In observing my initial difficulty, hearing parents who have been falsely pump-primed about my skills have felt that they are receiving affirmation of their worst fears in respect of their deaf child. Again has been an implicit reason for termination of counselling, because they feel their expectations have not been met.

Telephone Counselling

One way in which cultural distance can manifest itself is when deaf counsellors have a telephone between themselves and their clients. I use the term 'between' deliberately because it is my view that the telephone does come between a counsellor and their client in the sense that it can produce a distortion in communication. I did not employ telephone counselling with any of the families described above, but the issues raised are relevant ones to the discussion in hand. A deaf person has two ways of using the telephone. One is to use a minicom or similar telecommunications device, the other is to work through a third party such as an SLI, but again, the organisational structure, aims and objectives can be a problem. If the organisation provides a national service, then it is inevitable that many parents will make the initial contact by phone and that some, for economic reasons or because they prefer the anonymity, will continue to access counselling services by telephone. It is unusual for hearing parents to achieve this access by minicom because they do not have a terminal or because they do not know how to type. On the rare occasions when this facility is used there are two very important factors which need to be considered. The first is that in face to face counselling, the contract usually stipulates that sessions are approximately fifty to sixty minutes in duration. There are professional reasons for this, which are linked to boundary setting and to the prevention of counsellor fatigue. Most minicom users know that a minicom conversation takes much longer than a telephone conversation, but when counselling by minicom, more time is needed in order that statements made by clients can be checked out for the client's meaning, and so the counsellor can ascertain how the client is feeling. In minicom conversations, we only see the words, and it is here that we become acutely aware of how little communication is conveyed through words alone. It is not uncommon for minicom counselling to be of two or two and a half hours duration per session and this leads to both counsellor and client fatigue. Moreover, it is not a simple case of the counsellor stopping the conversation after one hour when we consider that the amount of information which can be conveyed in this time by this method is very much reduced for a hearing person.

The alternative is to use an SLI, and again, there are drawbacks. The first is whether to tell the client that a third party is listening in, because some clients will not be happy with this situation or will not feel able to open up so easily. The second is that unless the SLI is familiar with the particular requirements I have for knowing the way in which information is given by clients, mistakes happen. On one occasion for example, an SLI failed to tell me that a client was crying, and I responded completely inappropriately. I would not normally work with an interpreter in face to face counselling, but they can be a necessity for telephone counselling. Given the trend of organisations to use freelance SLIs, it is difficult for the deaf counsellor to establish a trusting professional relationship with a single SLI, and this can intrude on the counsellor's professionalism.

Who Deaf Counsellors are for Hearing Clients

These are examples of situations where the counselling relationship cannot always be established because hearing parents, like many professionals, do not understand the difference between advice and support, and counselling. Having in the past experienced only the former kinds of help, they have expectations of once again being advised or supported by the counsellor. Sometimes they ask for 'a shoulder to cry on' which is not surprising given the complexity of the family situation, but, at the beginning of the counselling relationship it is not easy for them to see that crying is sometimes the first stage in grieving and the real work may yet need to be done. When they realise that, as a counsellor, I am not there to collude with their negative perceptions of having a deaf child (because of my adherence to the core values of counselling rather than because of any political philosophy), their reactions can be very defensive and angry, and in this, they are supported by society's expectations of deaf people. This situation can exist for both deaf and hearing *counsellors*. However, a *deaf* counsellor who is faced with the task of assisting the creation of bonds within a 'hearing family' may be placed in the position of having to receive and contain the displaced anger and defensiveness. Because, ultimately, the parents' feelings are about having a deaf child, I have found myself playing any number of roles or stereotypes for them, some of which are demeaning and offensive to me as a deaf person. Situations like this have lead to feelings of disempowerment and impotence.

There are a number of ways in which the above case studies illustrate this point. One particularly difficult situation, which we saw with both the Reid and the Wilson family, is where the deaf child or young person's existence is being denied despite the fact they are present in the room. Sometimes this is because parents assume that being deaf means that most of what is said will automatically be missed by the deaf child, but with both the Reids and the Wilsons, there seemed to be something more deliberate about their desire to exclude James and Susan. I felt that Sheila and Richard were feeling unconsciously that if James or Susan expressed a view, as Susan did, their family myth would be threatened. Thus, as the deaf counsellor who attempted to bring the deaf family member into the counselling relationship, I came to personify the threat. This situation is common if the child is young. Their presence is very powerful for the deaf counsellor who may experience a great deal of empathy with the child. However, because at this stage, many hearing parents have not yet learnt the skill of including their deaf child in communication which takes place, the child comes to take on the role of 'client-in-absence' as the parents discuss their feelings about him or her *as if he or she were not present*. With older deaf children and young people, listening and attending to the dynamics of this situation feels like watching a massacre from behind the bars of a cage. The parents are frequently resistant to breaking free from the safety of the collective shadow, whereas the child, like many children, is generally moving in the opposite direction, struggling to separate from the collective shadow and to find their identity and individualism. Young deaf children gesture freely and have very visual ways of behaving which does not diminish as they grow older, and the deaf counsellor's natural empathy with the child can feel at cross purposes with their need to establish trust with the parents within the counselling relationship. Thus, although the collective shadow is all around us and moving between us, it is internalised in parent, child and counsellor in very different ways. The hearing parents, the deaf child and the deaf counsellor have different personal agendas. In such circumstances it can be very difficult to be clear about who the client is and to work with the family as a whole unit.

A deaf client who is being subjected to such an attack nurtures the need within me as a counsellor to shun negative collusion and reinforcements and to see my identity as being of value in the hope that both parents and child will come to feel more positive. The compulsion to push this process is constantly battling with the need to protect myself against the disempowerment and impotence which demean my sense of self. I risk becoming the 'nurturer' because, in the child, I see my self mirrored, at least, the self I would have had for a lifetime without the influence of the collective shadow, and the fierce determination that I have on occasions to hang on to my 'pseudo-innocence' (Kopp, 1981). I can now identify what *is* for me, and so can the children in their unconscious, but they are somehow prevented from bringing this knowledge to conscious awareness within the kind of family dynamics described above. The mirroring between deaf counsellor and deaf client is often mutual and reinforced silently within the counselling relationship. In the parents, however, I struggle, in common with many counsellors threatened by 'failure', to see beyond the collective shadow, and to resist projecting the behaviours and attitudes which I learnt from my (hearing) parents as 'the norm' through transference:

> 'I'm getting really sick of myself not being able to get over this, but every time I hear "failure" coming from my client I am disempowered – I shrink away from him and put up my defences. I can see myself doing that while actively knowing that I should be working with what is happening. It goes back to echoes from my childhood which scream "failure" to me so loudly that I am still not able to rise above them.'

> (Mearns, 1990, p.94)

It *is* tempting in this situation to see the deaf child as the 'identified patient', the symptomatic family member who has been exploited into being the repository of the parents' problems, and it is easy, if dangerous, to collude with the child in seeing the parents as 'the enemy'. I have to know whether I am witnessing the child's shadow or my own, and that knowledge can be very elusive.

The particular set of hidden agendas I feel to be underlying most of my counselling relationships with hearing parents thus create an enormously complex set of transferences and countertransferences. All of us, whether parent or child, counsellor or client, have a different perception of the nature of the shadow and a different understanding of the status quo. Transferences and countertransferences may therefore be built around ego-defence operations designed to satisfy very different needs, and occurring at various levels of the unconscious. What is unconscious is often also invisible, especially to the clients themselves. Sometimes hearing parents like Sheila Reid talk about the stigma of hearing aids, poor speech or using sign language and it is these stigma that they perceive as the shadow which is inside the child. Thus, the child becomes objectified and not present in the counselling relationship. At the same time, they might look at me, the deaf counsellor, and see no obvious evidence of these readily observable stigma and they become confused. Placing me in the role of 'frustrator' or 'seer' (it is difficult to ascertain which), they question, silently, in their non-verbal language and otherwise, why their child cannot be like me (or at least their assumptions about who I am). Because in most of the cases I took on I was attempting to work with the parent–child unit, I frequently saw the projection of their disappointment (and sense of failure?) on to the child. On occasions when I have worked with families where there is a deaf teenager, this process becomes much more explicit. Some hearing parents, like Richard Wilson, have subjected me to a personal inquisition which goes well beyond tests of trust in their thirst for information and their desire to satisfy themselves that I am a worthy recipient of their feelings. I am asked whether I am married, with the emphasis on whether my partner is deaf or hearing; I am questioned about the details of my sex life, about whether I mix with hearing people all the time, how many friends I have, and whether my children are deaf or hearing. I am also asked for my advice on the relative merits of relationships with deaf and hearing people, and somehow my neutral responses to all these questions – for example, 'It is the people within the relationship which make or break the relationship' in response to the latter – are not acceptable. So the questioning continues and can, as we saw, become more urgent and intrusive. My way of dealing with this painful experience is to locate it firmly within the counselling relationship and ask myself if there is a yet more hidden shadow comprised of feelings about being different which are projected outwards and nurture what becomes a need for external stigma and tangible expression?

Equally, I have to be aware of what determines my reaction, as a counsellor, to their perception of difference. Is it that these perceptions mirror the internal horrors from which I wish to escape or is it attitude-based assumptions about the perceptions themselves? To self-disclose in a situation such as this feels like a conscious attempt at projection as a result of my boundaries being invaded. But failure to disclose presents a threat to my desire to be genuine. My uneasiness about this interaction is frequently picked up by the deaf family member, and, again, can be misinterpreted. The transferences and countertransferences occurring here can thus block growth, and be counterproductive to developing a cohesion in the deaf–hearing family unit.

Some parents are unquestioning, especially when it is their first meeting with a deaf adult. They may idealise me as a deaf person to such an extent that they cannot stay within the boundaries set at the start of the counselling relationship. Sandra Murphy went through a phase in our counselling where this was to the fore. She would phone me at difficult times, or, having arranged to meet with me in my advisory role, would, on arrival, attempt to draw me into my counselling role. Saying 'No!' was difficult because I knew that she had no-one else she could talk to and when I suggested that it might be better if she worked with a colleague on general matters of advice, she totally rejected the suggestion on the grounds that my colleague was hearing and could not possibly have the knowledge or the understanding of being deaf that could help her. If parents accepted the need to work with another person, it was sometimes the case that their meetings with the other person were littered with comments about me. Both situations proved threatening to my professional relationships with my hearing colleagues, because *they* were often left feeling de-skilled and bitter. But the reverse situation also happened. Sheila Reid, on discovering that I was not the deaf person she expected, refused to see me again, and I later discovered that she had made an appointment with a hearing colleague, perhaps because she could not cope with the cultural distance or what my particular way of being deaf represented for her.

Implications for Supervision

Clearly these processes have important implications for sensitive and aware supervision, but, as is the case with the vast majority of deaf counsellors, my 'supervisor' was hearing and also my line manager. At the time, it was all that was available to me, but I have to say that it was not an acceptable situation, for whatever their skills in management, my supervisor was not open to the difficulties arising from transcultural counselling where the *counsellor* is from an oppressed group, and experiences oppression from clients within the counselling relationship, and I, in any case, felt nervous of opening up emotionally to someone who was my line manager and, as my line manager, had certain expectations of me. As a result of this lack of openness, I felt increasingly alone and I spent a great deal of time working on my feelings through writing and self-exploration. The lack of availability of appropriate supervision is exacerbated by the tendency of some schools of counselling thought to believe that counsellors, if they adhere to the principles of that particular school of thought, should be able to work with any client. By implication, supervisors who take this view may not recognise issues such as conscious or unconscious counsellor oppression, and I would consequently feel unable to work with them, for these are live issues in transcultural work of this kind because they reverse our way of thinking about power within the counselling relationship. In monocultural settings, it is assumed by clients for many different reasons that the counsellor holds the power in the relationship, and the counsellor must work at equalising power. In the transcultural relationship, where the counsellor is from an oppressed group, the scales can be tipped in the opposite direction to the point where counselling can become a battleground of negative transference and countertransference. However strong I feel in my own identity and ability to work with my clients, there have been times when I have been reduced to tears by the cruelty of client transference, and the intensity of my feelings have been enhanced by the presence of my 'silent' deaf partners. The presence of an aware and empathic supervisor would have eased my sense of hurt so that it did not reach the point where it interfered with my self-perception and my subsequent ability to carry out the tasks of my many and varied roles:

> 'The fact that failure can cut so deeply is further justification for the importance which counselling in Britain attaches to *supervision*...an important criterion in selecting a supervisor is that the chosen person should be one with whom the counsellor feels sufficiently at ease to

explore even the most tortuous elements of self-doubt. For this reason, line managers make poor supervisors!'

(Mearns, 1990, pp.91–92)

The Ideal Situation – Lessons to be Learnt

The hardest lesson I have learnt from experiences such as the ones outlined above is that the circumstances I found myself in carried a high risk of circumstantial failure. Because there did not seem to be organisational frameworks or personal support structures in place which would have enabled me to meet the expectations of particular clients, I had little choice other than to accept that I could not work with this client group. Other deaf counsellors may have experienced the situation differently, but at the time these counselling relationships happened, it was difficult to identify others with these particular experiences. The trend since, as we shall see in Chapters 8 and 9,

---

BOX 7.2 DEAF COUNSELLORS WORKING WITH 'HEARING FAMILIES' – IMPORTANT CONSIDERATIONS

Priority to independent counselling services with counsellors who are free from other role demands and conflicts of interest.

Consideration of the development of peer counselling teams of deaf and hearing counsellors when working with the 'hearing family' unit.

Training for counsellors (both deaf and hearing) in transcultural ways of working, group work and deaf/hearing awareness.

Minimising negative or inaccurate 'deaf role model' interference through direct referrals to deaf counsellors with no pre-judgements made or voiced to prospective clients.

Developing increased awareness of the importance of removing bias in communication methodology from the sphere of counselling.

Organisational awareness of constructive ways of dealing with counsellor stress or 'burn-out'.

Organisational awareness of the additional pressures placed on deaf professionals in the counselling role, whether clients are deaf or hearing.

Facilitation of direct one-to-one work with either deaf children/young people or hearing parents to complement work with the family unit.

Widening training opportunities for counselling supervisors in transcultural issues.

Independent counsellor supervision, outside of organisational frameworks wherever possible.

has been towards confining deaf people to monocultural therapeutic alliances; thus we still have limited direct knowledge or information of transcultural dynamics where the counsellor is deaf. For myself, I was not experienced enough in the therapeutic use of 'failure' to be able to change the scenario from an individual standpoint, although I have successfully engaged such opportunities in work with hearing clients as opposed to 'hearing families'. It is the deafness angle assuming an unnatural significance within the counselling relationship which blocks growth, and I have found this is less likely to happen with individual hearing clients who have no prior connection with deaf people.

However, I am left with the feeling that there is another large client group whose *counselling* needs are neglected. This client group is as important for its own needs and how these can be met through counselling as it is for building positive and constructive relationships between deaf children and their families through counselling *at a time when it most matters*. If this valuable time is not used constructively, it is not too difficult to see how a frightened and confused 'hearing family' can become an abusing 'hearing family'. I have thought long and hard about how deaf people might work effectively with such client groups, for there is some value in the 'deaf role model' idea and its use in counselling even if it has become distorted by some organisational frameworks. Box 7.2 is a list of positive suggestions which make use of some of the hard lessons learned and may help in establishing an appropriate counselling service.

CHAPTER 8

Art-in-Therapy
The Role of Art-Communication and Picture-Art in Working with Abused Deaf Clients

Margaret Kennedy

In Chapter 5 we stressed the importance of facilitating full communication in the counselling context through the use of art and dramatherapy, particularly in situations where linguistic matching could not easily be achieved between counsellor and client. Here, Margaret Kennedy takes up this theme, suggesting that whilst art therapy is rightly the province of the trained art therapist, the skilled counsellor needs to develop the ability to engage with the deaf client in art-communication, which is viewed as an integral part of human nature and communication. She explores the relationship between art-communication, picture-art and sign language, with particular reference to her work with deaf clients who have been sexually abused in childhood.

In the work that I do with deaf people using sign language, I have come to see quite clearly the relationship between sign language and art. In using sign language, therapy has to be art in language since the pictures entwined in the iconic aspects of sign language and the heavy emphasis on visual linguistic structure constitutes an active art-communication. Here, in a most graphic way, language has become picture-art, and this is why art in therapy, through its ability to fulfil the human need and capacity for full expression of the self, appeals to deaf counsellors and clients so much. Indeed, the more I work with, and, on occasions, draw with deaf people, I for feel it is entirely appropriate to use drawing as a way of developing counsellor–client relationships, the more I feel that they have reached a pinnacle in the expression of self.

Iconic and Linguistic Expression

Full expression is both iconic and linguistic (Dubowski, 1990). In the early stages of child development, the iconic and linguistic modes of expression are separate. The early scribble accompanied by babbling in both deaf and hearing children run in parallel. At four to five years old the child begins the representational drawings and gives them a 'title'. Kellog (1970) calls these scribbles a vocabulary of marks and identifies twenty 'basic scribbles' includ-

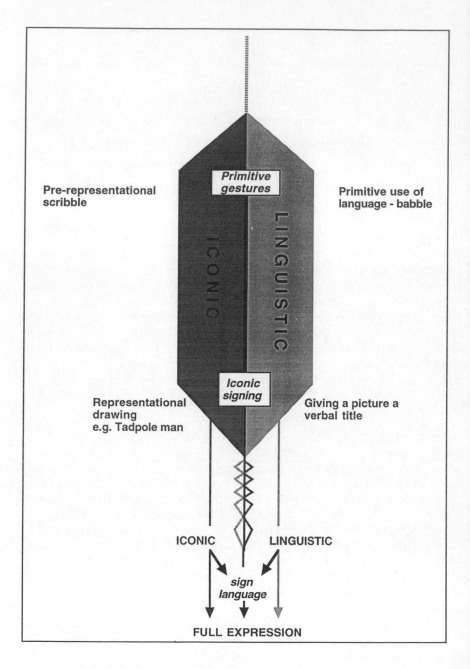

Figure 8.1 'Paths of Iconic and Linguistic Expression'

ing the dot, vertical lines, horizontal lines, roving open lines, single and multiple loop lines and imperfect circles. Eventually the developmental sequence culminates in the child being able to arrive at a particular configuration of marks commonly called 'tadpole-man' or stick figure. Matthews (1984) gives an additional understanding to the scribble in a notion of 'action representation'. For example the pencil running along the paper represents the passage of a motor car on a journey and this might be followed by a vigorous circular scribble corresponding to an imagined car crash. Figure 8.1, based on that of Dubowski (1990, pp.9–14), describes the parallel development of iconic and linguistic expression. I have tried to convey the difficulty of placing both iconic sign and sign language within this framework, because iconic signs are undoubtedly both an iconic means of expression (iconic line derivatives) which become integrated into full sign language *and* what might be called the linguistic equivalent of 'first words' in a hearing child. At a later stage, full sign language is the result of the marriage of iconic and linguistic, though the iconic line of development continues independently and the linguistic line may develop an off-shoot of spoken language or its written equivalent.

Using pictures, a clear relationship between the the modes of expression can be seen which can also be demonstrated when we ask a child engaged in drawing 'What is it?'. Here, the request is that the child translates the iconic mode of expression inherent in the picture to the linguistic by giving a title or other explanation. The hearing child may depict 'a tree' as shown in Figure 8.2a. When we ask 'What is it?', he says 'It's a tree'. A deaf child, on the other hand, may draw 'a tree' as shown in Figure 8.2b, and when asked the same question, will sign a response which is both linguistic ('It's a tree') and iconic, since the sign TREE is in itself iconic and conveys a great deal of information about the tree itself and the conditions which surround it, for example whether the branches are still or blowing in the wind, or whether the tree itself is being chopped down (Figure 8.2 c,d and e). This brings an exciting dimension to art-in-therapy.

However, in the same way that not all sign language is iconic, not all pictures are representational after the age of five years. Adults and children continue to use 'scribble' or 'pre-representational marks, within pictures. Abstract art is not meant to be representational, or resemble forms in the observed world outside of the artist's imagination. Iconic expression can develop independently and therefore be an alternative to linguistic development. In the absence of adequate linguistic development, the iconic line of development may offer another way of making sense and contributing order of an otherwise potentially chaotic adult world. This is a valuable insight for counsellors working with deaf clients, both children and adults, who are linguistically impoverished or who lack the range, depth and variety of vocabulary to describe their deepest thoughts and feelings, convey the full content of their world of meaning, or express and understand abstract concepts. It is particularly important where these clients have faced or are facing trauma in connection with sexual abuse, where the complexity of these thoughts and feelings can defy traditional description employing linguistic modes of expression. It must be remembered, however, that some sexually abused children *select* silence (Brown and Craft, 1989) or use simplistic language as a means of keeping secrets and because of being afraid to tell; they commonly perceive the usual verbal approaches to helping as threatening and emotionally loaded. Verbal communication may demand a skill level not always available to them, but they may feel able to express symbolically (Sgroi, 1982).

ART-IN-THERAPY WITH DEAF CHILDREN

Some art therapists have acknowledged the significance that art has for deaf children in therapy. For example, Arguile (in Case and Dalley, 1990, p. 206–7), describes his experience as an art therapist working with an aphasic[1] boy, who

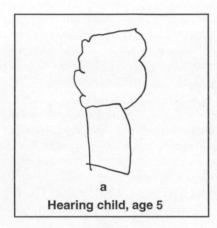

a
Hearing child, age 5

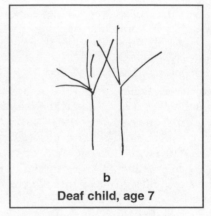

b
Deaf child, age 7

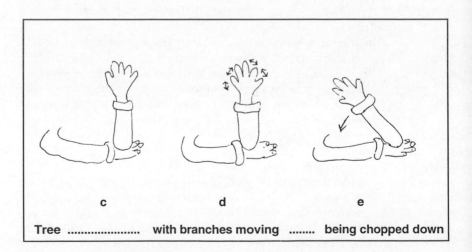

c   d   e

Tree .... with branches moving .... being chopped down

Figure 8.2 'The Development of Iconicity'

was initially diagnosed as deaf and forced to wear an 'aid' which he could not tolerate. He says:

'My concern was representing language in terms of visual art. My subject for this was Charles and the verbal and non-verbal language he spoke was the raw material I used to create the final drawn writings and photographic pieces.'

In his non-verbal expression Charles used the Paget-Gorman sign system which, Arguile stresses, is an aid for the acquisition of speech and language rather than a complete language in its own right such as BSL. Arguile photographed Charles signing and wrote on top of the photograph the concept being signed, thus creating Charles' 'drawn writings'. He also wrote down in poetic form Charles' signing. He continues (p. 207):

'As an artist, I find language of great import. By writing words we make speech visible, thus forming possible links between writing and visual art. Words then begin to work on two levels. They work in their own symbolised meaning but also in their acquired visual context on a non-verbal level as part of the drawing process and may function in their own right as images.'

In the same volume (Case and Dalley, 1990) Rabiger (p.35) refers to the significance that art has for deaf children:

'One severely deaf little boy soon revealed his high intelligence as he became more confident, and unusually, *painted* his name and figures up to ten... (I say unusually because most advances are habitually attained in graphic media rather than paint). It was in the art room that his intelligence was first noted.'

Much of my work with deaf young people and adults who have been sexually abused in childhood has attempted to integrate this knowledge in enhancing my particular style of counselling, some accounts of which now follow. In using art I find that I can be a more effective advocate of the 'inner child' (Kennedy, 1990), particularly in the areas of translating meaning and supporting my client's inner advocate and creativity and I feel that this enables me to offer warmth and care and to validate the experience more directly. But, because I use art in an interactive way when it is appropriate, I can also assist my clients in protesting against the perpetrators of their abuse in a more pro-active way which, I find, reinforces client feelings of support. With art as a tool, I can also overcome linguistic barriers within the therapeutic relationship.

FREEDOM, CHAOS AND CONTROL

Most clients come to therapy with the notion of 'gaining freedom', but that freedom in terms of everyday life should not be the freedom of chaos, nor the

---

1   Aphasia is an language disorder due to damage in the part of the brain concerned with the recognition and production of speech.

freedom gained from the perceived security from *over*-control. Deaf people have often become accustomed to a state of over-control, but it is a result of control which has been exercised by others, the accumulation of which results in deaf children and adults becoming passive, unable to take responsibility for themselves, perceiving themselves as powerless, and blaming events and forces outside of themselves for their situation (Luterman, 1987). Rotter (1966) would describe this as being characteristic of an external 'locus of control' (LOC). Abuse is an extreme form of control, and whereas the therapist must be careful of allocating blame, abuse is unacceptable behaviour, particularly against those who can be so easily taken advantage of or who are unable to 'tell'. The experience of abuse often provokes seemingly opposed and incompatible feeling-states, for example, fantasy and reality or disintegration or integration of conscious and unconscious thought, and art is one expression of these states. Though we may be able to observe a paradox of discipline (order) and freedom (chaos) in clients who have been abused, both states are accepted and allowed in the therapeutic setting.

I will now, within the above contexts, give some examples of how I have used art-in-therapy with three clients, whom I will call Anne, Sarah and Jenny, all of whom were sign language users and who were abused in childhood by 'significant others' in their lives.

EXPERIENCING ART-IN-THERAPY WITH CLIENTS

Anne composed several pictures which illustrate the perceived distinctions between chaos and order very well. If we compare pictures A and B with pictures C and D, we can see that the former two appear to fall within the chaos/anarchy range which permits disorder in the interest of emerging higher order or, as Arnheim (1954) says, allows some degree of ugliness. Pictures C and D on the other hand were created spontaneously outside the therapeutic milieu and do not show the same degree of chaos. The choice of colours, pictures and layout have all been controlled. I found myself wondering whether, in choosing to construct these collages so carefully, Anne was attempting to order her inner turmoil and to express or find meaning for this turmoil; but, at the same time, at home and alone, she may have felt too afraid to indulge in out-of-control chaotic artwork without someone being there to support her.

Another feature of Anne's pictures is her writing of words, which is also illustrated by Figure B. Furth says of words in pictures:

> 'the patient feels he or she may not have clearly conveyed the point or message of a drawing, so words add definition to the statement, and thus reduce the drawings chances of being misinterpreted. Of course we question what has been misinterpreted, and/or what presently is being misinterpreted in the patient's life. The whole issue of trust comes forth when words appear in drawings. It is also a question of how much the patient trusts non-verbal communication.'

(Furth, 1988, p. 74)

I also think that the client's level of desperation to have her life, world and feelings heard and understood is indicated. Further, if we look at picture C, we can see an example of what Rubin (1978) describes as regression and dissociation coming through. The Little Girl (regression) is shown effectively communicating feeling and dissociation is indicated by the phrase 'and disappear within seconds' – a mechanism used by Anne to cope during sexual abuse. There is a 'barrier' however between the little girl and the phrase which seems to suggest that the coping mechanism did not always work when she entered a dissociative state. It may simply have been wishful thinking or a memory of entrapment and a lack of ability to escape.

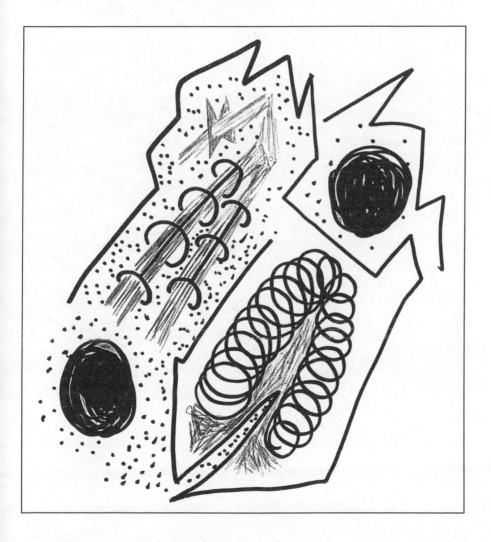

Figure 8.3a 'Anne – Chaos and Control'

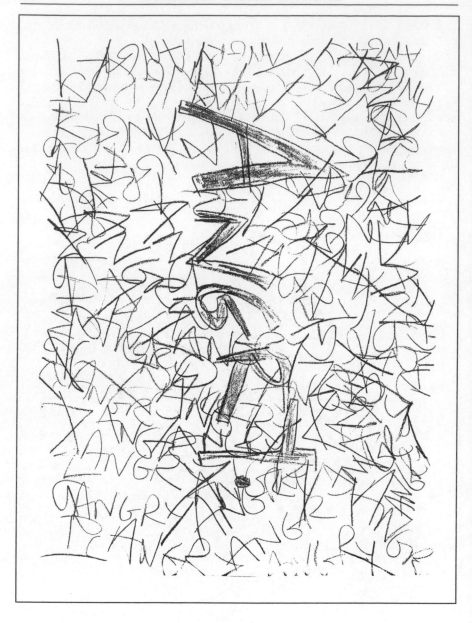

Figure 8.3b 'Anne – Chaos and Control'

Figure 8.3c 'Anne – Chaos and Control'

Figure 8.3d 'Anne – Chaos and Control'

We most often equate art with pictures, but for some, drawing a picture can be difficult. There may be negative reminders of school-days, or deaf clients in particular have been so used to being over-controlled that they cannot free themselves to draw and paint. However words or signs can in themselves be an art-form:

> 'Maybe you'll have to start with words, so draw words, tough words, tender words, ugly words, poetic words. Draw all the words you are feeling; sad, sadness, play, despair. Make the words big, little, plain, fancy and use different colours for different words; what colour is sex for you?, what colour is sad?'

(Rhyne, 1973, p. 105)

Anne, in picture E, did just this. Her confusion, vagueness and inner reality could not be conveyed only through pictorial means and so she used words very powerfully. Therapists can do this as well, particularly as it incorporates and develops the relationship between therapist and client through a more

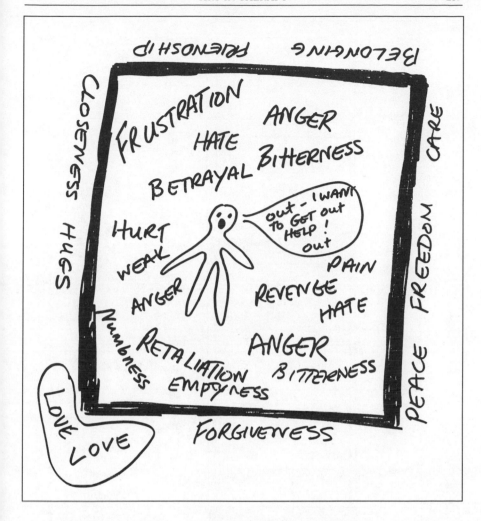

Figure 8.3e 'Anne – Chaos and Control'

interactive, two-way dialogue which is culturally meaningful to Deaf clients. This makes the art experience more reciprocal, and it becomes a very powerful tool of reinforcement and clarification. For example, another client, Jenny, signed to me WHY CONFUSED – WHY CONFUSED? Using Rubin's notion of art therapy as 'giving', 'showing' or 'telling', I myself later produced a word-picture with her. I put down all the many situations and factors that she was grappling with in her life, to give meaning to her confusion. She was able to see more clearly the roots of these situations and factors because she had been *shown* it and the amount she had to cope with. She could not grasp this through sign language, but did in the 'showing'. Showing can also be helpful in describing processes which are common in therapy. Sarah could not under-

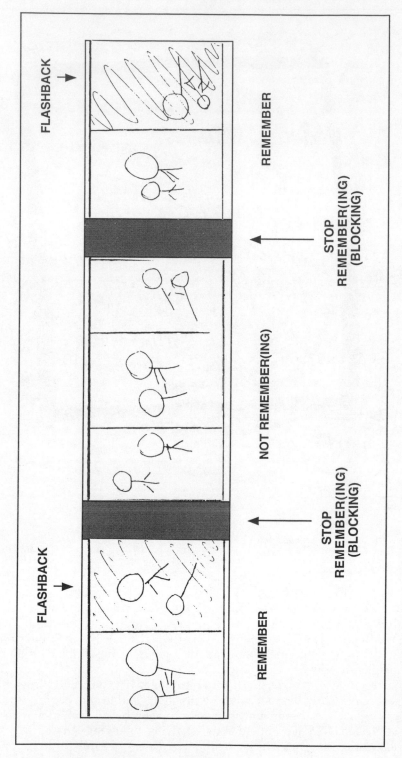

Figure 8.4 Jenny: 'Blocks and Flashbacks'

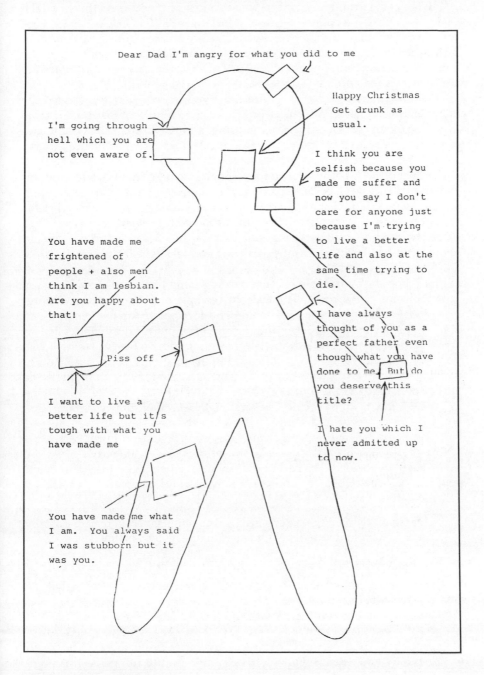

Figure 8.5 Jenny: 'Father'

stand how she could remember some things but not everything, which therapists might describe in terms of 'blocking' and 'flashbacks'. These concepts were proving difficult to explain, so I overcame our communication difficulties by drawing the following cartoon strip. Bars represent where she had stopped remembering (blocking) and the shaded areas are flashbacks or single events remembered suddenly.

Too often, when we are communicating verbally, we take for granted the fact that we are using the same word symbols to represent exactly the same idea. Too often, we thus miscommunicate, and get hopelessly caught in a semantic morass that hides our true meaning behind different usages (Rhyne, 1973).

Jenny stormed into my office for a session with 'all the boys in the Deaf club think I'm lesbian because I'm scared of them'. She was angry, upset, and close to tears. I felt, also, that somewhere she was angry with her father for the sexual abuse she endured from the age of 6 to 18 years and which had placed her in this position. I suggested that she 'tell' her father in this session about what had happened at the Deaf club and what she felt about it. I drew a life-size outline of her father and pinned it to the wall. I encouraged her to tell him, but she couldn't and became very scared because her 'father' was now with her in the room. This was an example of instances where representational art can become threatening and immediate for the client. It can reach feelings so much quicker and penetrate communication blocks like an arrow. Care, support and acknowledgement of Jenny's fearful feelings was imperative if she was not to be damaged in the process. So I encouraged her to tell me instead and I wrote what she said and asked her to pin it up on the outline of her father. She couldn't, so again, I did this for her – she needed me as a shield and as an advocate. I began to tell her father on her behalf. Tears began to flow freely and then she took up the task herself, writing and labelling her father with all her anger, frustration, fears and hurts.

Eventually, the tears stopped. As she left the session, calm but tired, she said 'I feel better now'. We had participated together, shared the anger and ventilation process together and eventually used an acceptable, non-threatening, creative way to do it:

> 'Art and art-making processes played an important and therapeutically beneficial role in the development of language *and interaction...*'

> (Arguile, in Case and Dalley, 1990, p.199, author's italics added)

However, even at the end, she could not say verbally to her 'father' what she was able to write or pin up.

A similar situation happened with Sarah when she came to a session very angry, but she couldn't name her feeling. With some explanation and encouragement, I gave her pen and paper and asked her to draw 'angry'. She began to sob quietly and viciously attack the paper. We could not get to this point solely through linguistic channels, but it was achieved by art. This exercise freed her and enabled her then to communicate her feelings more fully. She decided to represent the component parts of herself through symbols. Symbols are important in art and are sometimes repetitive, sometimes understood by the client and sometimes not. Sarah drew three distinct symbols, and explained them to me as she was drawing:

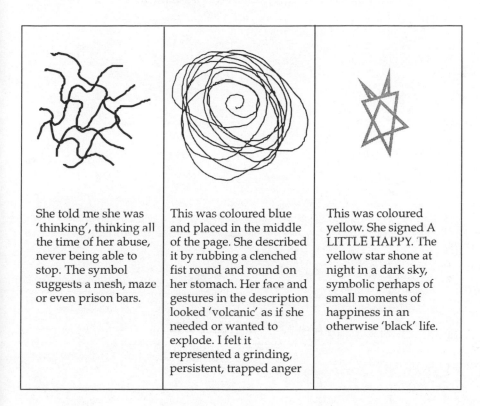

She told me she was 'thinking', thinking all the time of her abuse, never being able to stop. The symbol suggests a mesh, maze or even prison bars.	This was coloured blue and placed in the middle of the page. She described it by rubbing a clenched fist round and round on her stomach. Her face and gestures in the description looked 'volcanic' as if she needed or wanted to explode. I felt it represented a grinding, persistent, trapped anger	This was coloured yellow. She signed A LITTLE HAPPY. The yellow star shone at night in a dark sky, symbolic perhaps of small moments of happiness in an otherwise 'black' life.

Figure 8.6 'Sarah's Symbols'

Sarah and Jenny finally wanted to meet each other since neither had met another deaf survivor and were feeling isolated in their suffering, in part because of the lack of knowledge and understanding of abuse within the Deaf community. Sarah had been sexually abused by two men, her uncle and her cousin and Jenny by one man, her father. Sarah felt Jenny to be in the worse position since it was her father, whereas Jenny felt Sarah to be in the worse position since it was two men. Trying to explain in sign language that neither set of experiences was 'worse' than the other was difficult, so I drew the following diagram by way of explanation (see Figure 8.7).

They were both able to see that, at the end of the day, they were in a similar position; they were both betrayed, powerless and later angry, scared and lacking in confidence. Interestingly, in their description following the abuse they were struggling to describe the men in question and used the term 'wrong' as opposed to 'bad'. Words had become important and significant, if not always easily expressed.

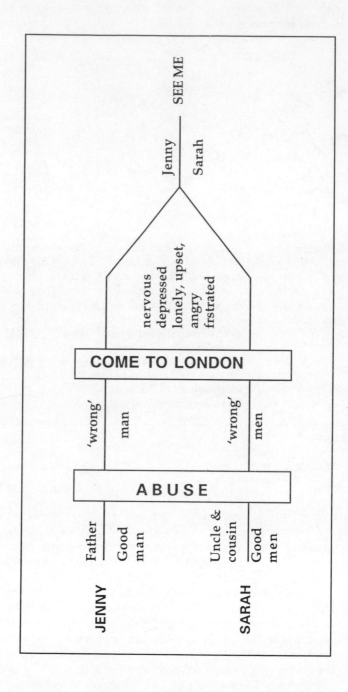

Figure 8.7 'Comparing experiences'

What we are sometimes in danger of doing as counsellors who are not trained art therapists is saying that we are unable to, or should not attempt to communicate visually. If we do this then I believe the value of our work with our clients will be diminished. I would stress that I recognise art therapy is a discipline and a profession in its own right, but this does not bar others from using art within their own frameworks. My understanding of art came through the use of language, particularly sign language, which has always allowed the fullness of expression I referred to at the beginning of this chapter. What I have always attempted to do is to find a complement to the verbal, analytical and more problem-centred approach to helping, to integrate more effectively the intellectual understanding and meaning with the feeling and the experience. Patricia Nowell Hall (1987) recalls her clients expressing how they felt the 'unfreezing or freeing nature of the activity...the beginning of letting down the defences, getting involved and experimenting', and this is the persistent feedback from my clients. Not only can they find expression for their deepest feelings, but also my attempts to represent their situations in different visual ways, supplement what can be a limited understanding through speech and language. Art-communication is like sign language, a natural skill of the deaf client. Art has 'happened' in my work simply because full communication with deaf people involves iconic expression. I could not operate without art-in-therapy and I believe that the deaf client epitomises the true meaning of communication. Sign language is both art and language, such that there can be no dichotomy between art and language. The Deaf sign language user or the non-speaking child (as opposed to the non-communicating child) conveys an abundance of meaning through iconic expression. Dubowski (1990) found that grasping an implement and directing it towards a picture surface was the start of making a statement about one's individuality — a statement that does not need words or language but which can express the most profound, sensitive and complex feelings about the human spirit.

CHAPTER 9

THE DEAF ALLIANCE

Sharon Ridgeway

'The skill of the psychotherapist is to learn the language of his or her patient, and, to help in creating a mutual language, a personal conversation.'

(Hobson, 1989)

The term 'Deaf' is vague. Comparisons between different degrees of deafness, differing types, groups and categories, serves little purpose other than to stereotype. In this chapter, the term Deaf refers to a state of being, and it therefore includes Deaf people who relate to or identify with other Deaf people in the community. In Chapter 1, it was made clear that the term Deaf has *cultural* connotations, and is used only in relation to those Deaf people whose common cultural and linguistic bond is BSL. The process of Deaf people's alignment and identification is influenced by many factors; educational setting and expectations; the age of onset of deafness; the degree of deafness, and the family and other external influences. But the cultural bond is rarely associated with physical or medical interpretations of deafness. Features such as the origin of deafness will not however be discussed because a pathological or medical perspective of deafness is not employed, nor, in the arena of counselling, is it appropriate for the vast majority of deaf or Deaf people. But other factors, such as family influences are inextricably linked to issues that run throughout this chapter, and must therefore be included in our discussion.

The knowledge that deaf people embrace a distinct sub-group who form a linguistic and cultural minority means that the Deaf therapeutic alliance must incorporate ways of working which parallel the anti-racist thought, awareness and practice at the heart of transcultural therapy. This is because Deaf people, like Black people share common cultural experiences and a common history of oppression. This oppression has taken the form of a widespread ban on the use of sign language and the active attempts to prevent Deaf people from marrying each other which are described in Harlan Lane's books *When the Mind Hears* (1984) and, more recently, *The Mask of Benevolence* (1992). The existence of historical oppression has encouraged the development of a unique and positive self-image and Deaf consciousness amongst deaf people, which gives the term 'Deaf community' a demographic, linguistic, political and social emphasis. This emphasis enables us to bypass the view that Deaf people are disabled by deafness, and reinforces the concept of Deaf identity; but in the context of therapy, it must not be assumed that the distinction between Deaf people and those who feel they are disabled by societal perceptions and expectations of deaf people is founded in judgement. On the contrary, because of the diversity of Britain's wider deaf community, and the therapist's ethics, it is important that therapists can remain non-judgemental in this area.

Practice in counselling and psychotherapy cannot be separated from our socio-political and economic climate and environment. Counselling has roots in the beliefs, values and preconceptions of our wider society, as we saw in the opening chapters of this book. Views of culturally different people are linked to the prevailing views of the dominant society, for example that Deaf people are disabled or 'dumb', and, within the therapeutic alliance, oppression is likely to be part of the Deaf client's frame of reference and dominance may be part of the therapist's frame of reference if they are not Deaf. In such a situation, the Deaf client may have to cope with the double assault of being treated as less than complete or perfect, as well as being reset and moulded to fit into the current cultural thinking and frame of reference of the non-Deaf therapist. In this chapter we will focus on the Deaf alliance, but it is inevitable that the features of this alliance will be compared with the dominant model of therapy, for, as we shall see, there are crucial differences between the two.

Many concepts have been developed within psychodynamic therapy and their uses have been incorporated into other frames of reference without changing the basic meanings of fundamental concepts. In the same way, psychodynamic theory can be applied to work with Deaf people using a similar approach. The ways in which psychodynamic work with Deaf people takes place requires a few underlying differences in approach. These differences can be narrowed down to processes which the Deaf therapist needs to attend to at the beginning of the alliance, or sometimes, before the alliance can commence, and those which are of on-going concern. The dividing line between these two areas is not always explicit, however, and the Deaf therapist needs to be alert to this.

PREPARATION

It is necessary to spend more time with the Deaf client in 'preparation', and the beginning of the therapeutic alliance can be enhanced and enriched by setting time aside for this. Preparation is further not only useful, but essential because it is important to have a clear understanding of the individual's conceptualisation of deafness – what it means for them. This understanding is one part of the preparation or groundwork which must be done when the Deaf client and therapist enter the therapeutic alliance. Initial suspicion and distrust might cloud the relationship in the same way that it can at the start of a hearing alliance, and this distrust may be difficult to remove without allowing time to enable the client to discuss issues that concern them, and which may be outside of their deafness. Preparation also helps to uncover issues which might not necessarily arise in the dynamic relationship.

In hearing terms, preparation may be equivalent to the therapist's early focus on the terms of the contract, and the way in which they set out the boundaries of the therapeutic alliance. But in the Deaf alliance, preparation has a deeper meaning, and may require more time. The need for preparation stems from the substantially different experiences of Deaf people which necessitate the therapist being more active and directive (Halgin and McEntee, 1986; McCrone, 1983; Quedenfeld and Farrelly, 1983; Harvey, 1989). Preparation means talking about the processes involved in the therapeutic alliance. It also enables the client to appreciate the professionalism, ethics and confidentiality to which therapists are bound, for these are relatively new concepts in the British Deaf community. Many Deaf people have a lack of confidence in these processes because they are unfamiliar and, sometimes, appear to work against Deaf cultural norms. Preparation is an attempt to resolve client feelings of mistrust or confusion.

For example, there is a certain openness within deaf culture, which is absent with hearing cultures and embraces the Deaf community worldwide:

> 'The Deaf community is somewhat comparable to a small town where everyone knows one another. Deaf women may meet acquaintances coming from or going to therapy. In fact, given the limited number of therapists who work with deaf people, this is likely to occur. Or deaf women may be observed at locations where it is known that certain events take place on particular evenings. Such information may then leak to other Deaf people and become a source of speculation or gossip among members of the Deaf community. If a woman's therapist is Deaf, or is involved to any degree in the deaf community, social contact is very likely to occur (whatever the therapist–client boundaries) because of the nature of the deaf community. In these instances, privacy for the therapist as well as confidentiality for the client may be problematic.'

> (Westerlund, 1990, p.106)

This openness may result in the presupposition by Deaf clients that boundaries are equally open within the therapeutic alliance, most especially when the therapist is Deaf. But, conversely, it may also mean that many potential clients are prevented from seeking a therapist when they are in need of help because, in the more anxious state created by their problem situations, they are more susceptible to the content and the nature of rumour and gossip, and will seek to avoid it in order that anxiety can be lessened (Anthony, 1992). One Deaf client had this to say:

> 'A lot of Deaf people know about each other so intimately that by going into a specific room, or even a specific centre, other Deaf people will assume they have problems. So there are many deaf people who are afraid to go to counsellors unless it was actually really anonymous. But for me, I would never go to a counsellor in a situation like that…because I would not want to broadcast the fact that I'm talking about my problems or my feelings, whatever.'

> (in Katz, 1993, p. 32)

The implications of this must be recognised by all therapists working with Deaf people, for they are cultural in their origin. Preparation must include time spent talking about what the client wishes to happen if they bump into their therapist outside of the alliance, and about the boundaries between therapy and friendship for example. I recognised the importance of careful preparation through my experiences with clients such as Jim, a Deaf man who was seen for brief psychodynamic counselling. He had a range of difficulties, which included issues concerning his own identity as a Deaf person. He had been educated in a mainstream setting and was fluent in BSL, which was his preferred means of communication. We bumped into each other quite by chance at a meeting. He greeted me in an affectionate manner and wanted to present the image that we were great pals, but I felt unable to respond in a similar way, though I was pleasant and polite. During our next session, he said that as far as he was concerned, I considered myself to be above him, that I was trying to keep a low profile and that he no longer wished to engage in the alliance. It ended there, perhaps because Jim's preparation had been incomplete.

On another occasion, a Deaf woman whom I had been seeing for some months terminated our relationship because she felt unable to cope with what she saw as my 'ignoring her', when we met at various social functions. This was despite the fact that we had discussed in preparation how she wanted us to greet each other and she had opted for just a brief 'Hello' as opposed to pretending we did not know each other, or being more friendly. When this was tested, it broke the alliance. This raises the question of cultural dimensions, where Deaf alliances may in fact have differences in terms of boundaries and aspects of what may be considered as professionalism may be viewed differently by Deaf and hearing cultures. The issue of professionalism is one that troubles a number of Deaf people. If a Deaf client were to see their therapist with a group of people, becoming drunk or behaving in an unconventional manner, it would be quite difficult for the client to remove this picture from their mind in therapy. This is an example of where preparation is needed for a number of issues which relate specifically to the Deaf community.

Some difficulties appear unavoidable, however. One Deaf client I saw for about one year was referred to therapy because she was having difficulty with a number of stressful situations and was developing negative ways of coping. When she arrived for her session, I would come out to meet her and we would enter the room together. On one occasion, as we left the room together, as was also my custom, she turned round to me in the corridor and announced that she had been raped when she was in her teens. The fact that she had said this out of the therapy carried implications for both of us and I felt that, as the session had ended, I could not respond. It was as if she had been talking lightly of the weather. When I mentioned it to her the following week, she had forgotten she had told me.

Deaf therapists are extremely likely to meet some of their deaf clients at Deaf centres, conferences and rally weekends; indeed the chance of doing so would certainly be much more likely than if both therapist and client were hearing. This presents boundary issues. The cases given above show the importance of using examples when conveying new concepts, such as the term 'boundaries', especially those which may seem alien to a Deaf person in the cultural sense. The therapist's use of boundaries may be seen as contrary to the openness of Deaf culture, or representative of 'the hearing way', for example, and interpreted in a negative light without sufficient explanation as to why boundaries are important *for therapy*. With respect to boundaries, for example, some therapist self-disclosure may be appropriate if more than an initial suspicion and mistrust is to be avoided.

The reason for such explanation is not that Deaf people need to have things explained to them more than a hearing person would, but that the current dominant way of thinking in psychodynamic work has developed entirely out of verbal associations and theories based on spoken and written languages. It is extremely important for the Deaf therapist to acknowledge and understand this if they are to avoid being seen as yet another persecutor.

The therapist's role needs to be made explicit and confined to the alliance, the nature of which also needs to be made clear. The importance of exploring the negative perceptions of the therapist and what they do must be emphasised and reinforced after preparation, because it remains likely that the neutrality of the therapist will be seen as an unfriendly and non-cultural feature of the usual given norms of the Deaf way. Within an alliance where both the client and the therapist are Deaf, they share common experiences as well as a common language, history and culture and it is likely that the dynamics of therapy will focus on being Deaf as a continuation of cultural necessity. A Deaf therapist could not reasonably be expected to withdraw from social affiliation with other Deaf people because of its cultural significance for membership of the Deaf community and the negative associations made by Deaf people about absences. Similarly, it is unreasonable to expect a Deaf therapist to wear their therapist's hat whenever they are in public. Deaf people can be more stereotyped in their attitudes towards how people behave and I have found that most clients I have spoken to in preparation feel that encountering the therapist as a real person in a chance encounter may affect their relationship with the therapist, especially if the therapist has let their guard drop. It is nevertheless quite easy to deny judgmental thoughts of this kind.

ON-GOING CONCERNS

There are other factors within a Deaf alliance (an alliance where both the therapist and the client are Deaf) that would be very different from a hearing alliance (a therapeutic alliance where both the therapist and the client are hearing), because there are differences between Deaf and hearing people in custom, family relations, the use of language, body language, humour and expression.

The Presenting Past

One of the major cultural differences between Deaf and hearing people lies in issues to do with relationships within the family. Often it is found that Deaf friends have a much greater role in the lives of deaf people than the usually hearing members of their own family, something which can be enhanced from a very early age by the network of Deaf schools, and is extended later in life through Deaf clubs and Deaf social activities. Since between 10 and 12 per cent of deaf children come from Deaf families, there will be a large percentage of deaf people who will not have formed the usual bonds of attachment with immediate family members. It has been estimated that 80 per cent of deaf people cannot communicate with their parents (Phoenix, 1988). Some authors have interpreted this widespread communication block as an example of emotional and psychological abuse or neglect (O'Hagan, 1992):

> 'Deaf children once had their thumbs tied together in the playground to discourage them from communicating through sign language, and to encourage them to lip-read (Watson, 1989). (This abuse) is likely to include or can lead to various forms and degrees of emotional and psychological abuse. Such abuse may be more damaging in its impact than that inflicted upon children without disabilities.'

(O'Hagan, 1992, p.51)

I have to say that my experiences of working with deaf clients supports this view. Such a large figure for those who may be at risk (for such abusive and damaging practices still exist through different kinds of psychological conditioning) indicates that we need to be acutely aware of the existence of damaged family dynamics and their influence on the therapeutic alliance, and open to this particular interpretation of abuse. Often, Deaf people will have negative feelings for their parents, associated with feelings of deprivation of language and communication. It is common for Deaf people to express resentment or disappointment towards their parents for not having learned to communicate with them or rejecting the possibility of a Deaf cultural identity. Conflicts, a basic concept in psychoanalytical theory, are often based on experiences in early childhood (McGrath, 1991); the Deaf therapist must remain constantly aware of how these experiences can present themselves through projection and transference.

Language and Communication

In the use of language in transcultural alliances, emotions may be over interpreted. For example, annoyance or irritation may be interpreted as anger by a therapist who is hearing. Equally, explicit descriptions of sexual activity have been known to cause some therapists to regard Deaf people and the Deaf community as uninhibited, perhaps because sexual sign language tends to be very graphic in its description of what actually happens in various sexual acts. Beside such graphic description, the phrase 'blow-job' or the word 'fellatio' seem innocuous, but the origin of the signs is perhaps more a reflection of Deaf people's need for concrete, direct expression, than an indication of uninhibitedness. Equally, the use of 'silences' carries different connotations within the Deaf therapeutic alliance. Within the hearing alliance, 'silence' can be prompted or closed by sound. Information is being conveyed within the alliance in consistent flow. If the therapist hears a sound or noise during a period of 'silence', she is brought immediately back into the alliance possibly from a 'reflecting' into a 'listening' mode without the client necessarily being aware of this.

Within Deaf culture, when two people are communicating, if one person transfers eye-contact on to something else, it would usually be because someone was visibly trying to attract their attention. Such 'interruptions' as they would be defined in a hearing community, are part of the norms and social repertoire of Deaf culture. The implications are that the therapist might be thought of as being bored or disinterested in the client once eye-contact is lost. Silences would be the only time when eye contact would be broken – Deaf people look away or down when they are thinking or reflecting. This can place a strain on the client, who then has to wave the therapist back into the communicating channel, and they may then not bother to communicate the reason for their need to break the silence. Conversely, the therapist, in an attempt to prevent this, may be distracted from the reflecting stance which they might naturally adopt during the silence by their need to maintain a listening stance so that they can be fully alert to the Deaf client's reentry into the communicative sphere. This may mean that the therapist has less time for reflection or thinking throughout the therapeutic process, and this can make the therapeutic process seem more pro-active or even directive. Within the Deaf alliance, deliberateness of communication is often a particular feature, more so than the 'unspoken' or otherwise intuitive features of silences.

Another factor that characterises Deaf alliances is that more non-verbal information is conveyed directly between the therapist and the client than is usually picked up within a hearing alliance. Confusion and anxiety, for example, are more immediately visible to the Deaf therapist without the need for advanced empathy, for facial expression and body language are part of Deaf people's normal social interaction and they are therefore 'tuned in' to non-verbal communication as a matter of course. The Deaf therapist can sometimes read with a great deal of accuracy where the client is experiencing feelings and what these feelings relate to before the client has given this information in a concrete way. It should be emphasised that we are not talking about the Deaf therapist making *assumptions* about the source of their client's feelings, but about the visio-spatial nature of sign language and the way in which it weaves a common Deaf consciousness between the Deaf therapist and their client, through the therapeutic process of empathy. Most therapists who are hearing can appreciate the power of non-verbal advanced empathy. Here, in the Deaf alliance, we have a situation where it is brought nearer to the surface of the dynamic process and is constantly integrated into the communicative infrastructure. For the therapist, this may create the difficulty that they feel in possession of 'privileged' information before it has actually been revealed by the client, and so they need to hold this information in order that their client's vulnerability or need to travel at a slower pace is not infringed. As in a hearing alliance, advanced empathy produces the risk of over-interpreting by the Deaf therapist, but because it is more concretely integrated in the Deaf alliance, the risk is higher. The Deaf therapist may therefore need to check with their client more often, which can throw some clients off-guard.

Conversely, a therapist who is hearing may 'give away' too much without being aware that they are doing so, and this might introduce conscious or unconscious feelings and responses from the client. A Deaf therapist would be more aware of non-verbal cues related to conflicts and unconscious feeling states being transferred from the client. Consequently, a higher level of empathy and genuineness has been attributed to Deaf therapists. This depth of empathy is unlikely to be achieved by a therapist who is hearing.

Identification and the 'Idealised' Therapist

Deaf therapists are still a rarity. It is often the case that Deaf clients entering a Deaf alliance for the first time are more likely to be facilitated in the process of identifying with the 'idealised' therapist, especially if they have had previous negative encounters with therapists who are hearing. Some studies have shown an improvement in therapy when this happens (Melnick, 1972). This has occurred where the client's degree of identification is associated with their subjective feelings of helplessness and weakness and their perception of the therapist as stronger. Identification with the therapist can often play a constructive role in the Deaf alliance. The client's perception in this kind of relationship would, however, often relate to the client's own feelings which are transferred on to the therapist, rather than any real traits of the Deaf therapist. In the countertransference, however, there is an increased risk of over identifying which is similar to the risk in other therapeutic alliances:

'The all-knowing omnipotent white therapist may undermine the expression of the patient's anger if the therapist appears too good and understanding of the effects of oppression.'

(Greene, 1985)

The Deaf therapist might also unconsciously try to provide too much support or reassurance, therefore preventing the client from confronting his inner feelings and conflicts. For example, if the therapist has experienced oppression directly at the hands of hearing people, and the Deaf client presents a problem situation which concerns oppression by hearing people, the therapist may convey their negative feelings about their own oppression which collude with those of their client. This negative reinforcement can deprive the client of both the means to explore how they might deal with oppression and whether their individual experience of oppression has other dimensions. If the client has idealised the therapist, they will be seen as an important and powerful person and the client will not, in such circumstances, be encouraged to consider that the therapist's experience of oppression *is theirs*, and does not necessarily parallel that of the client's. It is important for the Deaf therapist to be non-judgemental and to keep their own feelings and experiences carefully within their own frame of reference.

The role that being Deaf takes on for both client and therapist shapes how the client views being Deaf. Sometimes, in transference, Deaf clients may see the Deaf therapist as the Deaf parent they never had. In this transference relationship, the deafness becomes the reason why the therapist may be seen as 'good' or 'powerful'. Sometimes, the Deaf client sees the Deaf therapist as the role model – someone whose thoughts, feelings and actions are exemplary and to be followed. They are seen by the client to have managed better than the client has, so therefore they have to be right, whatever they say. In practice, the way in which this happens may be quite complex. One client I was working with changed her signing style in one session, and began to incorporate more English elements (moving from BSL to SSE) and started using hearing idiomatic expressions which are not part of Deaf culture nor a linguistic feature of BSL. It eventually materialised that in the transference, I was her hearing daughter with whom she felt inadequate and rejected because of her deafness, and whom she tried to impress by using more 'English' non-Deaf type expressions. It is possible in some circumstances that such a shift in linguistic emphasis can be misinterpreted, since it can be both a direct sign of disapproval of the therapist (they are too 'hearing inside', or are viewed as having an 'impairment' because they use SSE), or a sign that the Deaf client wants to impress the therapist (because they are seen as special or all-powerful) or, as in the above example, a transference of the presenting past. In the Deaf alliance, the therapist needs to be particularly alert for the nuances of the client's 'personal language' (Mearns and Thorne, 1988),[1] in addition to the content of what they sign.

There is another way in which the Deaf therapist can be viewed in a negative light within the Deaf alliance. They may be seen as not competent or unhelpful *because* they are Deaf (Melgoza, 1980). This possibly reflects the client's own anger, negative self-concept, or frustration with being Deaf. In this case, in the transference, the therapist is seen as in no way able to equal a hearing person's knowledge and experience and the client may remain critical and sceptical of the therapist. This has been found to be a feature of other Deaf alliances, for example, the Deaf teaching alliance (Corker, 1990c). Some Deaf therapists may attempt to minimise the impact of deafness in defence of what can be interpreted as a personal attack by the client, when it may be a projection of the client's low self-esteem which has been a result of the clients' having internalised the low expectations they have experienced from hearing people. Again, problems can be experienced in the countertransference if the therapist has been through negative experiences incurred in this way. How successfully the therapist can deal with this is related to her willingness to work through her own unconscious feelings in her own therapy or, occasionally, in supervision.

Enhancement of Experiencing

There are some features of psychodynamic therapy which are enhanced within the deaf alliance. Communication, as we have seen, is more explicit, with fewer 'nuances' which can be subject to interpretation. There is a strength of feeling in a Deaf alliance which probably does not exist to the same degree of intensity and expression within a hearing alliance. This intensity comes from the power of non-verbal expression and its contribution to empathy and genuineness, for the non-verbal is transparent, and a genuine therapist is transparent in their expression with their clients. Chapter 8 showed that in a

---

1   See Chapter 4.

transcultural alliance, the intensity can be misinterpreted or can be perceived to be overpowering. In a Deaf alliance, there can be an enormous sense of mutuality in the intensity, which enhances empathy, and again, has cultural origins:

> 'Of the Deaf and hearing signers who understood the play on sign, there was a definite qualitative difference in the laughter – a difference that broke along Deaf and hearing lines. The Deaf response was much more intense. The reason that humour is culturally specific for a group is more than just language; it is a matter of experience. It becomes clear that the one thing not held in common by the native hearing signers and the Deaf signers is the experience of being Deaf with all its cultural impli-cations. The experience of being a Deaf person in the hearing world is one that is fraught with daily communication frustration, in a way that is generally not part of a hearing person's life experience. Hearing signers, through professional or familial ties, are generally aware to one degree or another of the frustrations and injustices Deaf people face. However this awareness is usually on a more cognitive level, not on a deep, affective level.'

> (Rutherford, 1993, p.19)

The use of BSL metaphors, their ability to describe abstract events in poetic fashion, is one example. Though they are the subject of much debate, some would say disagreement, many therapists employ metaphor constructively in the therapeutic process (see Kopp, 1972; Hobson, 1985, for example). Hobson says of the effect of metaphor:

> 'As I listen to the conversation I hear echoes of a vast society of similar metaphors which speak of the traditions, the personal life, and the gloomy future of a society... These images and constellations of mean-ing are put side-by-side with (something which is apparently uncon-nected) and we *see* a meaning which emerges *between* them, and in which they are related.'

> (Hobson, 1985, p.53)

BSL metaphors can be compounded by facial expressions which convey the depth of feelings or reinforce what is being expressed. Rutherford continues:

> 'The deeper meaning is a crystallised reflection of a historical and sociological experience of the Deaf. It is a picture of lack of control, lack of self-determination, negation of identity, stifled development, blocked communication, external control characterised by benevolent paternalism and authoritarianism, and one of general conflict with the majority culture.'

> (Rutherford, 1993, p.21)

Built into the structure of BSL, reinforcers provide the emotive effects of figurative language in the same way that spoken language has defined metaphor. Metaphor use is rich within Deaf culture, and is a natural part of expression amongst Deaf people. The sign SUN, with varying degrees of brightness conveyed through the handshape, also conveys its power in the reinforcer. The speed at which the handshape forms into the sign SUN gives us an idea of its intensity and importance; furthermore, the *way* in which the sign is made conveys the sense of power involved in the emotions behind what is being said. A dramatic movement of the arm to burst into the sign SUN gives us an idea of the centrality that the theme has. Likewise, in poetry, the depths and degree of power and feeling behind the metaphor is actually revealed by how the reinforcer is provided. Hence BSL reinforcers become metaphors in themselves. Another example is in the use of role shifts.[2] In hearing alliances, the therapist might sometimes have to make use of role play situations as in the so-called 'empty chair' exercise, where the client is asked to change chairs and become another person, in order to enable expression of difficult feelings about that person through a kind of distancing. This kind of behaviour happens spontaneously within the Deaf alliance, and is much more immediate in its effect. Through being able to forge direct links with the expressive and emotive aspects of sign language, the Deaf therapist would more often be able to enter the client's state of being.

SUMMARY

There are important differences between a hearing alliance, a transcultural alliance and a Deaf alliance. Recognising these differences helps to reinforce equality between the therapist and a Deaf client. Taking an approach or a theoretical model and making Deaf people adapt to it does not indicate culturally sensitive counselling practice. Neither does adapting the theory to meet the perceived needs of Deaf people. Therapy has to be Deaf-centred, that is, it must come from a Deaf state of being at the point of entry into the alliance. The psychological tasks of Deaf people have to be understood in terms of the issues outlined in this chapter. The therapist needs to be sensitive as to how deafness makes an impact upon the therapeutic process, bearing in mind that the therapists's work will actually be a function of their own Deaf state of being. As well as requiring skills in sensitivity, a range of other communication skills needs also to be possessed by the therapist which allows them to interact with the deafness dimension. This can enable deafness to become a 'filter' for dynamic transactions to take place, using alternative means to reaching the same ends. All of these factors point to the absolute necessity for the counselling profession to take on board the need for fully trained Deaf therapists, trained from a Deaf centre. It is only when such a Deaf centre enters the therapeutic alliance that Deaf clients can feel the safety of a culturally contained environment where unrestrained communication on emotive *and* cognitive levels can be experienced. Only then can therapy occur.

---

2   'This is a general term which relates to the way in which sign language users take on different roles within a discourse. It may be indicated by body shift and eye gaze; once the signer has indicated a change of role, everything that is signed is produced as it it were from that person's perspective. Thus the role shift allows the signer to make use of what is sometimes called "direct address". Typically the signer also takes on key aspects of the other person's character, as portrayed in the discourse.' (British Deaf Association, 1993, p.162).

CHAPTER 10

ISSUES FOR DEAF PEOPLE
IN COUNSELLING TRAINING

Laraine Callow, Sharon Ridgeway and Mairian Corker

In this chapter, three deaf counsellors talk about their experiences as trainee counsellors. Both Laraine and Sharon trained or provided training through a 'discrete counselling course' – that is, a course for deaf or Deaf people only. Laraine's tutors were hearing, and access was generally provided by several sign language interpreters. Sharon trains Deaf people directly using BSL. Mairian, on the other hand, attended training aimed primarily at hearing people in a counselling training organisation with a positive attitude towards equal opportunities. She also used a sign language interpreter for access, but was fortunate in having the same interpreter throughout the duration of the course. The authors relate very different experiences of training, but there are some common threads which run throughout these accounts.

INTRODUCTION

We have very little concrete information about the availability of counselling training for deaf people in Britain. The only comprehensive research that has been carried out is an unpublished questionnaire survey of 63 organisations randomly selected from the BAC *Counselling and Psychotherapy Resources Directory* (Katz, 1993) which yielded a 68 per cent return rate (37 organisations). Of these, 21 provided training, though only nine had received applications from deaf people, five of which were institutionally based or voluntary sector services aimed at deaf people. Of the 37 completed responses, only 10 organisations had trained deaf people in the last ten years, but there is no indication of whether these people identified as culturally Deaf or disabled. However, as one-third of the organisations *were* aware of what a minicom was, only three of these being mainstream services, the survey suggests that there is limited awareness of the range and variety of deaf people. Perhaps one positive result of this survey was that 24 of the 37 responding organisations said that they would agree to the presence of an SLI to enable access for deaf people, but this represents only 35 per cent of the original sample and perhaps this can be taken as an indication that there is very limited availability of training lead by tutors who can communicate directly with deaf people. Important information missing from the survey is the status of BAC accredited training courses in relation to accessing deaf people, for this may give us some idea of the *quality* of training that is available to deaf people and the *attitudes* of recognised training organisations.

This survey did not contain a detailed analysis of the patterns of counselling methodology used by the responding organisations, though it pointed out that many organisations covered several methodological philosophies. The discrete services for deaf people were mainly psychodynamic in orientation. This begs a number of questions. If most training currently accessible to deaf people is based on one particular approach to counselling, the possibility for full and creative exploration of clients' problem situations may be limited as the counsellor searches within a single framework to find the skills to deal with a particular set of client feelings, and finds that the framework is lacking. Further, as methodological terminology often provides us with the language with which we can describe feelings, ways of behaving and counselling processes, there is an advantage to training which strikes a balance between providing us with this background knowledge and experiential work:

> 'Counsellors who have a poor theoretical understanding of their work are likely to lose their heads (and their hearts) when confronted by difficult clients or particularly complex dilemmas. Experiential learning which is unsupported by sound theoretical understanding is likely after a while to leave the trainee confused or incapable of describing and analysing the processes he or she is experiencing with clients.'

> (Dryden and Thorne, 1991, p.8)

Interestingly, however, these authors continue:

> 'Counselling does not take place in a vacuum and a training course needs to acknowledge this by drawing on relevant social science disciplines in order to illuminate the systems in which people live. Social, cultural, ethnic and political issues are but some of the ingredients of the kind of exploration which is required if justice is to be done to the study of the environment which in its different ways may profoundly affect the lives of clients.'

> (Dryden and Thorne, 1991, p.9)

We must remember that deaf people's access to information outside of training courses can be limited both in terms of access to a wide range of human experiences and to information concerning different approaches to counselling. It is also undoubtedly true that there are some aspects of the division between counselling culture and Deaf culture which are more likely to show themselves in situations where the approach to counselling which forms the basis of training is heavily rooted in spoken language. There are so many differences between spoken language and sign language, that the world of feelings can appear very confusing if the approach of the trainer is to take expression in one language and simply translate it into expression in the other. This is without the cultural confusions that can occur. Counsellors can also suffer from expertosis, and tend to be very defensive of their own patch. They may correspondingly withhold or distort information about alternative approaches which enable deaf trainees to make informed choices and decisions, without realising the implications that this might have for clients, in particular the deaf clients with whom most deaf counsellors are likely to work.

These are some of the issues which are explored in the following accounts. All the authors are deaf people who work in a number of different roles and are, to varying extents, subject to some of the difficulties described in Chapters 7 and 8 in respect of role models. They are also something of a rare breed because they are deaf people who have been through counselling training, and there will be certain expectations of them because of this, both from the Deaf community and from the counselling community. There is an element of their being 'guinea pigs' in a new 'experiment' which means that some of their experiences in training may not be shared by deaf people entering training courses now. These difficulties are in addition to the inherent difficulties of obtaining information about counsellor and client experiences, and the authors would all wish to stress that these are their own *subjective* thoughts and feelings about counselling training, and are not intended to be representative of the array of thoughts and feelings that other deaf people may have.

LARAINE (TRANSLATED FROM AN INTERVIEW IN SIGN LANGUAGE)

I trained on a discrete course aimed specifically at deaf people. Prior to taking this course myself, I had had some involvement in negotiating with and advising the training organisation in establishing the course, because deaf people were beginning to pinpoint the lack of appropriate counselling services generally. The course was a two year Certificate course in basic counselling skills and was heavily experiential. For many people, both deaf and hearing, training deaf people as counsellors tends to be an unknown area, and the course was possibly the first of its kind. It was inevitable that some of the course would focus on trying out different ways of working with deaf people because of this. The course tutors were hearing, either concentrating on delivering the course entirely through sign language interpreters or signing for themselves. There were varying levels of deaf awareness and being in touch with deaf issues. I find it difficult to say what the different styles of training meant for me. For example, I would describe myself as very working class with a middle class perspective and it may be that I would have expectations as a result of this which would affect how I related to the tutors, and to other course members. The same issues arise because I am deaf, and because I have particular preferences in the way in which I learn and absorb new material. It is inevitable also that the tutors would have expectations of the group, because this was a new venture. An involvement in deaf issues may lead to a higher level of involvement in the group, which, in turn, can increase the number of questions being asked by the tutor, and result in the feeling of being intruded on if it is carried too far too quickly whereas delivery through an interpreter can reduce the feeling of contact. These approaches will have different effects on different deaf people, though both are equally viable if it is possible to strike a balance between the two. I suppose I would call myself quite articulate, but I did not find it easy to contribute for a number of reasons, and would, at times, have felt more secure if the experiential group facilitation had been a little more sensitive, because I felt I needed help in drawing out my feelings. I felt comfortable with the experiential emphasis of the course because I could relate it to the way that I worked with deaf people, but I found the minimal academic structure of the course frustrating at times. What do I mean by structure in this context? I think it relates to themes – I would have liked clearer identification of counselling issues and approaches and a more structured approach to the information content of the course to supplement the more open-ended experiential structure that we had. This would have helped me with my learning, and perhaps would have enabled me to explore more unknown areas, and have given me some background to what we were doing.

There were also aspects of course delivery which needed improvement given that the participants were deaf. Perhaps because I am a trained teacher and I do so much training myself, I am aware of the difference between having a substantial knowledge and experience of counselling and being able to deliver this knowledge and experience to participants through training. It is the same for most subject areas. However, the two are not always simultaneous, one does not necessarily follow from the other, and this can affect learning. Sometimes I felt that more attention could have been paid to the use of visual presentation such as flip-charts, overhead projectors and video, which are important aids to deaf people's learning. I suspect that their absence was due to a lack of experience and awareness on the part of the tutors in working with deaf people, making the course a learning experience for the tutors as well as the participants. Another linked area was the explanation of the counselling process, in particular the references made to confidentiality which illustrate an important point. In the Deaf community, information is spread very quickly and directly because Deaf people are prepared to travel long distances in order to preserve friendships and the sense of community. At the start of the course we were told that confidentiality of material and feelings shared on the course was vital for trust to be established, but it later transpired that some course members perceived this to mean that the *course* was confidential – that is its existence should not be divulged. I do not know whether this was an interpreting error or whether it was because of the newness of the term 'confidentiality' in the Deaf community, but one effect it did have was to cause a breakdown in course publicity aimed at a new student intake! It is therefore vital that tutors and interpreters have a thorough understanding of how to convey important counselling concepts in a visual way which does not detract from their full meaning.

The training inexperience showed in other ways. In the experiential group, feelings would be expressed or issues would be raised which seemed important, but the tutor often did not pick them up. In the learning situation, deaf people are used to structured, tutor-led activity and if the tutor did not pick up these things, it was rare for the group to facilitate this. Thus the sense of movement within the group at times seemed very slow – too slow in fact. I would have liked more opportunity to express my own feelings and experiences, but this didn't seem to happen, in part because I was not able to thrust myself forward. The tutors tried hard not to make assumptions about deafness but somehow it was always there. They would sometimes jump in and say

'Oh that's because of deafness...' when the situation was a life experience common to many people whether they are deaf or not. There was a division between the tutors and the participants in this respect. I felt the tutors wanted more 'deaf problems and issues', whereas the participants tended to focus on life issues such as families and relationships which were not necessarily *related* to deafness although they may be *exacerbated* by being deaf. This distinction was not made and so there seemed to be some pressure on us to produce deaf problems; but the group resisted this. I do wonder whether this was because the group as a whole had a very strong deaf identity. They had been through all the difficult 'deaf problems' and were strong in themselves as deaf people. *Life* had more meaning than *deaf*. If we had been in a disabling environment, I suspect that deafness would have assumed greater importance. That being said, the group was very varied and encompassed different deaf perspectives, but I felt the diversity was not allowed to be. I did have expectations that there would be more talk about these deaf perspectives and I ended up by being quite amazed that this didn't happen.

We spent some time on identifying the 'good' counsellor and exploring how to get in touch with our own feelings. Some issues which I felt were quite important for us as deaf counsellors were skimmed over or only implicitly referred to. For example, an issue which did not come up was the deaf–disability divide, which was disappointing because there will be deaf clients who *see themselves* as disabled. I suppose this reflects the situation in the counselling world generally. For example, there is a Disability Sub-Committee within BAC which presumably includes deaf perspectives. But I have found that there are many areas where Deaf people and disabled people disagree and it therefore does not seem appropriate to put the two areas under one umbrella. But openness and sharing of feelings about issues such as these is important to deaf people from the 'access to information' perspective. The emphasis on the course was that if we were aware of racist or other discriminatory feelings in ourselves then we had a responsibility to refer clients on, but we did not explore experiential examples of this in any great depth. Linked to this, I feel that this produced the view that a hearing person who has never experienced oppression cannot empathise with a deaf person's experience, but they will be able to relate to *feelings* of anger, shame and so on. My personal view is that direct experience is important, and again, we missed opportunities to explore this.

Although I have some reservations, for example in the recognition that the predominant feeling I experienced throughout the course was anger, I feel I did gain a lot, and that I would now like to try a mainstream course to advance my training further. In particular it helped me to understand the difference between counselling and advice, to explore my strengths and weaknesses from a skills perspective, and to recognise the value of personal therapy, although this was not a requirement of the course (I feel it should be). The former was important because I came originally from a background where advisory activities were prominent, and the nature of my work now dictates that this is still the case. Deaf people did come to see me with problem situations which needed something more than advice, and I was uncertain of how I could help. The course honed my skills and clarified my thoughts and put a name to feelings in a way which enabled me to move away from simply problem solving. I learnt that if I could identify my own feelings, I was more able to empathise with the feelings of another and to recognise that 'problems' are really occasions when difficulties are experienced in explaining clearly what we need. Paradoxically, attempting to apply this understanding to my work with deaf clients has revealed strengths and weaknesses. Clients often talk about problems because of their life experiences, and I find it difficult to get them away from this particular approach. It feels as if it is difficult for deaf people to articulate their *feelings* and so they concentrate on their life stories and their problems. The course gave me the understanding that damaging behaviour patterns can only change if we are prepared to look inside ourselves, but it feels as if a deeper level of skill and a more conscientious approach to client education is needed before this can be achieved with deaf clients.

Much counselling that deaf people experience is given by the 'wrong' people, who have unresolved negative feelings about deafness or who have strong views on deaf communication and therefore tend to reinforce the deaf client's negative sense of themselves. Deaf people are given limited opportunity for open discussion and developing assertiveness skills, for example, at the time when it is most important. Because of the lack of appropriate counselling services and deaf counsellors, those of us who undertake counselling training have great demands placed upon us as it inevitably becomes known that we have been through training, despite the requirement of confidentiality. I have had my professional boundaries threatened on unexpected occasions; for example I have been asked to listen to 'problems' at conferences or meetings and have been told or have observed some shocking and difficult things at a time when it is difficult to give full attention to the 'clients' or to my own feelings.

SHARON (ABRIDGED FROM CHAPTER 9)

It is important to explore the issue of counselling training for Deaf people from the perspectives of both Deaf trainers and Deaf trainees. My recent experience has been as a provider of training through a Deaf-centred approach using BSL. Using this experience, it has been possible for me to identify that the practicalities of teaching counselling to Deaf people differ in some respects from those which arise in teaching hearing people. For example, if a course were to be run which aimed to train non-Deaf people in counselling approaches suitable for use with Deaf people, we might hope to see, at the very most, transcultural issues, in particular those relating to cultural minorities, and issues of linguistic matching integrated into the course structure at both theoretical and practical levels. In a Deaf-centred course, it is possible that the course will be underpinned by in-depth exploration of the concepts of role model, non-verbal communication, different deaf perspectives on communication, issues relating to minority group persecution, racism, the effects of ongoing systematic discrimination and culture and community, rather than these subjects being available as options which might be touched upon by participants. Most Deaf people are already directly familiar with these issues, but it is important to generate an understanding of how they come to be part of many Deaf alliances through counselling processes.

The teaching of counselling skills to non-Deaf people may begin with providing participants with an understanding of theory which eventually leads to opportunities to practice what has been taught, or the theoretical and practical content of the course run concurrently. A Deaf-centred approach, in my view, begins by identifying and practising core skills during the first stage of training because, as we saw in Chapter 9, many of the counselling concepts and counsellor ways of behaving are new to the Deaf community in Britain. It is also important to supplement Deaf participants' knowledge of issues which are likely to be of concern to the Deaf community but the details of which have yet to permeate the grass roots of the community for a variety of reasons. Examples are loss and bereavement, AIDS/HIV, relationships and partnerships, education and mental health. Using this dual approach means that tangible skills remain continuously exposed. The use of video as a learning tool is particularly effective because video reflects the first or pre-ferred language of Deaf people, whereas reading the available literature written by non-Deaf people usually reflects the hearing culture and their second language. Currently, due to the dearth of materials and resources in teaching counselling skills to Deaf people, Deaf-centred training does not enjoy the abundance of resources that are available to non-Deaf people.

Fundamental changes occur when learning takes place in a setting that is Deaf-centred. Being in a group with other Deaf people is, in itself, of thera-peutic value and benefit. It can generate an enormous sense of kinship and release of feelings. Deaf people become able, often for the first time, to work through issues relating to oppression which have been a residue of earlier learning. Feelings towards families and other external influences are allowed to materialise and are explored in both one-to-one and group settings. It is crucial that time can be taken to focus on these issues because of transference and countertransference processes at work within the Deaf alliance. If the focus is not there within training then transference issues might otherwise be borne out of collaborative factors which can then dominate or threaten the alliance. Learning in a potentially oppressive environment such as a main-stream course without any other Deaf participants can result in an internali-sation of non-Deaf values. It may then become difficult for the de-cultured participant to work with Deaf clients as effectively as a hearing colleague might with hearing clients, because the learning has not been Deaf-centred.

Although Deaf-centred training has many advantages for Deaf people wishing to become practising counsellors, and indeed, has elements which may be of both practical and theoretical value to any counsellor, there are some inherent difficulties. Training courses aimed specifically at Deaf people, to the exclusion of hearing people, run the risk of being devalued. Adding the word (Deaf) after a qualification gives hearing people and Deaf people the feeling that such a course cannot be equal to, or as good as a course aimed solely at hearing people. Certainly, disablist or patronising attitudes on the part of the counselling establishment contribute to such devaluation, possibly more so if the course is organised and taught by Deaf people themselves. This is sad, because these issues do not seem to arise in subjects taught in other minority languages such as Punjabi or Welsh, but it is probably linked to the prevalent view of sign language as a 'controversial or non-conformist' way of communicating. The implication, however, is that cultural features easily become submerged under the disability blanket in order that differences can be accounted for.

There are advantages and disadvantages on both sides for both trainers and trainees. A particularly important issue in mainstream courses and in courses aimed at Deaf people but taught by hearing tutors, is the use of a sign language interpreter. My view is that direct communication is always preferable than communicating through an interpreter. The reasons have been well documented within the literature in relation to transcultural approaches where similar issues have been found. Stansfield (1981) and Harvey (1989) have written extensively about the use of interpreters in therapy and have found that such use is best implemented, if at all, in group therapy. Psychodynamic group therapy has been useful for clients who have some Deaf and hearing identity confusion because of the mutual exchange and feedback that group work provides and the same would be true in Deaf-centred group activities within training. The SLI in one-to-one course work can affect transference factors for a number of reasons. An initial affinity between the interpreter (who is commonly hearing) and a hearing partner, for example, is unavoidable since both use the same language and, if the interpreter is providing voice-over, both are verbalising in the same language. This might be seen by the deaf partner as collusion. It would be difficult for the interpreter, however well trained and professional they are, not to enter into this, for it is *counselling* training which is relevant here. The 'power imbalance' complicates transference and the clarity of boundaries and roles, particularly when there is pressure on the interpreter to contribute to the awareness of the hearing partner or the course tutor of knowledge and understanding of deafness, the language of BSL, cultural norms and identity. The presence of an SLI commonly affects hearing people on integrated courses and often provokes focus on deaf issues from a hearing perspective. As this perspective is often oppressive, it can lead to the deaf participant feeling that the focus is too pronounced or all-consuming.

Other problems might involve confidentiality and the Deaf participant's view of its breach. Where the Deaf community is concerned, it is often the case that the interpreter will be known to the Deaf participant(s) as well as to other members of the Deaf community.The presence of the interpreter might sometimes be seen as a 'symbol' of deafness both by the interpreter themself and by the Deaf participant(s), and a 'symbol' of the Deaf community by the course tutor. The Deaf participant(s) may use the tutor to reinforce the fact that Deaf and hearing people are different, whereas the tutor may pose a conflict to the well-defined non-intrusive role of the interpreter where the task is to provide facilitation of communication and not to make voluntary contributions. Psychologically, the lack of identity or the neutrality of the interpreter can provide Deaf participants with an opportunity to exhibit certain types of defence mechanisms such as projection or displacement. The interpreter can also act as a catalyst for making unconscious feelings conscious in the same way that the Deaf therapist can, and this process in itself can be beneficial for training.

The research of Haley and Dowd (1988) and Roe and Roe (1991) has suggested that counsellors rated higher on social influence, counsellor effectiveness and empathy if they used sign language in alliances with Deaf people. Thus, in a course led by Deaf tutors, participants might feel more able to share deep-rooted feelings and views on being Deaf. There is also less pressure to internalise oppressive hearing values, the process of which can lead to a kind of emotional shut-down, and more opportunity to get in touch with and work through feelings. Discrete courses often raise the credibility and trustworthiness of the trainee counsellor in the eyes of Deaf clients since there is less likelihood of the counsellor internalising negative values. Deaf counsellors who have trained with hearing people might be seen as occasionally using the norms and values of a discriminatory and oppressive institution. Counselling itself, because of its relatively new entry as a concept into the Deaf community may be regarded with suspicion and therefore proving our credibility through experience may become more important than the actual display of a formal qualification.

MAIRIAN

I attended a mainstream course leading to a Diploma in counselling on successful completion after two years. My attendance on this particular course was not necessarily by choice, but there were elements of choice involved. At the time, there was a great reluctance on the part of counselling trainers to accept deaf people on courses as individuals, let alone when they were accompanied by an interpreter. This course would not necessarily have been my first choice because of course structure, size of participant groups (in the first year), the lack of a requirement that course participants were undergoing personal therapy, and the general approach used for selection of course participants (there were no obvious criteria at the time). All of these things felt important to me, but the attitude of the training organisation was more enlightened in respect of equal opportunities, and no questions were raised about the presence of the interpreter, so this seemed to convince me. There were no discrete courses available for deaf people in those days but I do not think their availability would have influenced the elements of choice in my decision. I have always felt that counselling is ultimately about expanding our knowledge and understanding of ourselves and others and I feel very strongly that that includes those people who we find difficult. My clients were both deaf and hearing and *both* tended to experience problem situations in relationships with the other. It would have been too easy for me to collude with deaf clients in their criticisms of hearing people by failing to face up to my own feelings about hearing people and making 'politically correct' decisions, but I don't feel that this would have helped my clients in the long run. Whereas, I acknowledge that I was experiencing particular difficulties in my counselling relationships with *hearing* clients (see Chapter 7) I am conscious both that I *wanted* to attend a mainstream course for a variety of reasons, some of them to do with what I wanted from the course, and some of them because I was frustrated and angry at the hearing dominance of society, including the counselling world, and that I was also quite scared at the prospect. I dare say that if I *had* been asked at selection why I wanted to train as a counsellor, I may have said that it was because I wanted to challenge the power bases of counselling and open up the counselling profession so that it became more representative of the client groups within society. I have a campaigning streak which, I have to say, conflicted with my more pressing inner needs to explore and share feelings deeply and honestly and to work more effectively with my client group. This conflict caused turmoil from the beginning, though most of it was inner turmoil. Having been in personal therapy for some time, I was no stranger to expressing feelings, and whilst I was aware of harbouring some very difficult and unpleasant feelings about the hearing world, I was as yet unable to deal with these feelings constructively. I felt that a mainstream course might help with this in allowing me both to explore and accept these feelings and enabling me to develop some structure to my work, particularly in the area of boundaries.

The course was divided up into two parts. The first year was equally split between an evening theory session and a morning skills session. We had different tutors for these sessions and they took place in different locations. We were required to keep a personal journal for both parts of the course and to complete a written assignment plus a skills assessment which was carried out by the peer group with supervision from the skills tutor. Passing all these was necessary for entry on to the second year of the course which led to the Diploma. The structure of the second year was different. We were required to work with clients outside of the course and to keep a record of sessions for submission at the end of the course. We were also required to have supervision, which proved difficult for me because I felt that I could only work with a deaf supervisor (see also Chapter 7). However, because I was in personal therapy, this requirement was waived. We had to keep personal journals reflecting on the practical work that we did together as a group and also to complete a written assignment and a detailed case study. Training in the second year was heavily experiential, consisting of counsellor role play, counsellee role play and experiential group work, both unguided here-and-now experiential work focusing on group dynamics and theme-based participant-led exploration of subjects such as child abuse. For the second year we divided into two groups of about ten people, each led by a different tutor, with the tutors swapping over for the facilitation of the experiential group work.

I have asked myself many times what the key issues were for me on this course. I feel, at the risk of leaving much important information out, there were three: the role of the interpreter, the need for information about life, and who I feel I became for the group. Overall, I found the course demanding and the degree of tutor supervision and facilitation too minimal. I was very stimulated by the content of the course, whether theoretical or practical, but there were too many times when I felt very alone and that I was not being listened to because contributions I made were often left in the air. I am aware that the lack of supervision in the second year was a factor in this, but although I formed several deep and lasting friendships amongst the course participants, I felt that I needed more support and guidance from an experienced counsellor in dealing with some of the issues that the course brought up for me. Because the tutors did not appear to see themselves in this supervisory role, and I had little opportunity for one-to-one contact with experienced practitioners, I never really felt a full sense of contact or connection with them. I think this made it difficult to trust, and there were isolated incidents which showed the tutors' lack of experience in working with deaf people. For example, on one occasion, a tutor asked my interpreter about something I was working on when I was out of the room and asked her to relay this information to me later. I was quite angry about this as I felt it was both abusing the interpreter's role and disrespectful of me. On several occasions the interpreter was asked direct questions by group members and despite her deferring to me for the answers, the groups were slow to learn her role or to accept that I was an individual in my own right.

In the first year, the theory group was too large, with quite a large number of people who were there for academic reasons only (they were not taking the skills course). I can remember walking in on my first evening and, on seeing the sea of faces (there must have been fifty people), almost walking out again. I was petrified, and if it hadn't been for the familiar face of my interpreter, I think I would have left. On an intellectual level, I could not see how learning could take place in a group that size, but with hindsight, I very much enjoyed learning about the multitude of different approaches to counselling – how they were related and how they differed, though I felt I was tackling this work alone. I had no sense of belonging and was experiencing many intense feelings which made me turn in on myself and withdraw from time to time. The theoretical learning process was encouraged by the tutor, who did not adopt any particular bias, and I felt that we were being given a genuine opportunity to go with the approach which felt right or integrate a variety of approaches. However, it was exhausting watching the interpreter for two hours continuously and, in her awareness of this, I think she tried to modify her way of working to make it more interesting for me to watch. My memory of watching is that I picked up much about process, atmospheres and feelings, but I did not get the information content of the course through interpretation. This is particularly true when the feelings were vague or difficult, as preoccupation with their visual expression deprived me of the energy to focus on information retrieval of other kinds. I was therefore heavily dependent on books to fill in the missing information, but I found that books did not always give me what I wanted or answer the questions I had. I will give an example of this below. In the end, I remember that it was the interpreter who unconsciously broke the deaf–hearing ice. The theory sessions also provided me with my first example – as it happened, a very amusing example of a Freudian slip in sign which, unfortunately, had a Jungian base. My interpreter accidentally finger-spelt the Jungian term ANIMA as ENEMA, and by the time the tutor realised what had happened, their were twenty-five course participants on my side of the room in uproarious suppressed laughter made worse by the fact that the tutor must have used that term in the region of sixty times throughout the session. I think that was the first time that I have ever seen an interpreter's professional veneer crack, as we were both forced to voluntarily leave the room for a few minutes until we calmed down. I never thought I would laugh so much on a *counselling course* but I think that many of the course participants realised that I had a sense of humour, which helped relationships to develop, through a balancing of the light-hearted and the deep.

Inevitably, the initial focus was on the interpreter and not on me. I noticed that people would watch her signing in fascination, with particular emphasis on how she would sign difficult concepts or lurid sexual terms. Indeed, so far as the latter were concerned, there was a visibly pregnant pause in the room as the group waited with baited breath for a visual transformation. In the practical sessions, my partners were always uneasy about working with me and this uneasiness showed itself in an uncertainty about where to look and a visible avoidance on the part of many people of working with me as a partner in pairs work. I often picked up resentment when they were 'lumbered with me'. Establishing eye-contact was difficult and disconcerting, but in the second year, this was off-set by my focus on the non-verbal within the 'role play' and the effect it seemed to have on drawing my 'client' out. I should explain that these sessions were not role play in the sense that real and immediate feelings were explored. They were intense and taxing and there was no sense of game-playing. This intensity rubbed off on the interpreter who, as the silent third party, became particularly involved in the non-verbal interplay of feelings. There was a point at which it was clear to me that something my 'client' was saying was touching on something deep *in the interpreter*, and I became confused as to whether what I was receiving from the interpreter was her feeling or my 'client's'. She was not aware that this was happening until I checked it out with her, but because we agreed that it was the unconscious working, there was little we could do to prevent it happening. However, we did change the way that we worked in that I asked the interpreter to sit just behind the 'client' so that she was out of the client's sight and also felt more physically distant from me. There were times on the course when the interpreter's level of empathy with me was acute, and this had the effect of distancing other course participants to the point where it became intrusive. I felt increasingly that this kind of work requires advanced skills of interpreters, particularly in how they deal with their feelings, and that it was an unacceptable situation for an interpreter to be in without sensitive supervision of their own. I do not mean interpreting supervision, but *counselling* supervision. It is a credit to my interpreter that she stayed for the whole two years of the course, and again, this had the advantage for the group in that it enabled trust to be more readily established than would have been possible if a variety of interpreters had been used. It gave *me* a constancy, even if it was through a third party.

As the interpreter's role became clearer, I felt that there was then more pressure on me to educate and inform the course on deaf issues. This was implicitly expressed on many occasions and sometimes explicitly expressed by course tutors. As a result, I felt at times that the focus was too deaf and intruded on my own learning needs and expectations as a person who happens to be deaf. For example, it was inevitable that much of the practical and experiential work was focused on verbal expression. The power of the non-verbal was alluded to many times but I felt it then became taken for granted rather than built into the course structure in a positive way. I found the verbal emphasis difficult and isolating because, on a feeling level, I could not gel with or relate easily to it. It felt at times that it was up to me to suggest alternative ways of doing things and there were times when my own inexperience became such a burden that I would have welcomed contributions from the more experienced among us. When we did work with body sculpts for example, it was agreed by all that it was a powerful experience, but the thread was lost until we picked it up again in the second year through brief experiential art work. Some of the non-verbal exercises that were tutor-devised were frightening for me because of their hearing emphasis. I can remember being asked to lie on the floor with my eyes shut and sense the proximity and body language of two course participants. I was so consumed by the fear of temporarily losing my vital sense that I was unable to look outside of my own body. I learnt in feedback that a blind woman on the same course found the silence of this exercise disorientating.

I gave as much as I felt able in the way of information without accepting the responsibility for the burden. However my own need to expand my direct experience and for information was not always satisfied and sometimes backfired on me. Because I am cut off from full or even partial use of so many channels of information in everyday life, I find that I compensate by making as much use as I can of those direct opportunities I *do* have. Books, as I said earlier, do not contain all the answers. In the second year of the course, there were two Black people in my experiential group. I found myself increasingly wanting to understand whether their experience of oppression was connected to mine within the group, and I decided to risk asking a direct question only to be accused of being racist by one of them. This was a very difficult experience to deal with, and seemed to enhance my feeling of being in the role of 'victim'. I was, on this occasion, rescued by another group member, but this was interpreted as a further attack which led to a prolonged and loaded silence. The following week, one of the Black people did not come and we learnt that he had withdrawn from the course. Whatever the reasons for his withdrawal, it seemed too much of a coincidence, and this proved to be a test of whether I could acknowledge their 'stuff' as theirs. Whereas I was clear from the start about what I wanted from the course, I quickly became muddled by other participants' thoughts and feelings as I came to the realisation that I had very fragile personal boundaries. Indeed this was a key learning discovery for me. The result of this encounter was that afterwards everything seemed so incredibly *intense*, and all the difficult feelings I was struggling with burst to the surface. When I finally cried, it felt as if every pore in my body was crying, and this left me completely burnt out. I learnt later that others were crying also, and there was something about that experience that precipitated a fragile union within the group, and clarified who I was for the group. Many conflicting words came out – anger, persecution, courage, openness, jealousy, pioneer, leader, risk-taker, powerlessness, sensitivity, and, for me, humility because I had truly believed that the group's experience of me was a wholly negative one when there was an array of feelings which had been hidden for a long time, perhaps even throughout history. The reason that I had never discovered the truth was that I had never been able to ask in a place of safety, and so I had become stuck in my own 'stuff'. I learnt the value of being genuine and of owning my feelings as they arose rather than putting them off for the 'right' time or ignoring them.

BOX 10.1 EQUALISING THE COUNSELLING TRAINING CURRICULUM

Emphasis on experientially and culturally relevant learning and its implications for personal growth and change.

Emphasis on experientially and culturally relevant learning and its implications for the information content of training.

Awareness of different deaf perspectives rather than undue focus on deafness and the facilitation of the expression of deaf experiences and feelings.

Preparedness to look at difficult issues such as oppression from different perspectives.

Visual teaching approaches making full use of visual resources such as flip charts, overhead projectors and subtitled video.

Clearer definition of content and delivery and the distinctions and links between the two.

Pro-active development of non-verbal counselling skills and their positive and explicit integration in both theory and practice throughout training.

More balance between structured theme-based learning and experiential work.

Increased time allocation for more direct self-exploration, attention to the concept of self as role model and boundary issues.

Development and standardisation of signed and other visual representation of counselling terminology and the language of feelings, so that accurate meaning can be conveyed directly or through interpreters.

Redefinition of the role and training requirements of interpreters in counselling settings.

Sensitive group facilitation (especially in mixed deaf–hearing groups) and positive opportunitites for one-to-one supervision.

Direct experiencing of different world views, perceptions and feelings as opposed to theoretical understanding, and opportunities to explore these.

Although the course was a very angry, powerful and exhausting experience, I do not regret having made the decision to enrol on a mainstream counselling course as a result of what I, in the end, learnt about deaf–hearing interaction.

Correspondingly, I would now welcome the opportunity to take part in a Deaf group. Counselling courses facilitate an atmosphere where sharing is possible in a way which cannot easily be achieved in other kinds of encounters with hearing people. Feelings run deeper and are more sustainable within this environment. I don't have any answers about dealing with the aloneness of the deaf person in this situation or the communication divide, but these answers will never be found unless diametrically opposed experiences are brought into the open and explored. I have asked myself if I would have made any changes other than those relating to content of the course. On an experiential level, and in terms of the opportunities for both learning and personal growth, the answer is no.

COMMON THREADS

The experiences described above are obviously very different in emphasis, part of which stems from the different deaf identities of the authors. There are very strong veins of anger which are expressed by all, explicitly or implicitly, but it is also clear that all the authors recognise the value of counselling training and how it contributes to both personal and professional growth. Clearly, there is a need for more training opportunities, both discrete and mainstream, which do not reduce the deaf experience to second class status. These accounts are most enlightening where they make suggestions as to how counselling training for deaf people should be structured and why. It is in this arena that the common threads may perhaps be used to outline the features of a curriculum which is responsive to deaf people's needs and expectations of counselling training (see Box 10.1), and which form an appropriate entry point to meeting *The Deaf Challenge*.

Endings and New Beginnings – Meeting The Deaf Challenge

I remember not so very long ago attending a counselling conference, where I became engrossed in yet another attempt to pose *The Deaf Challenge*. It was a difficult few days, at the end of which a member of my 'support group' suggested that I might like to think a little more about counselling and a little less about campaigning. As this counsellor's meaning hung in the air waiting to be grasped, the scene was set yet again for the very first conference I attended as a deaf professional many years ago. I sat in the front row, as I was accustomed to doing, watching a string of eminent hearing professionals, including a well-known psychotherapist, presenting their views on the 'problem' of deafness. Although I had throughout my life experienced many episodes where I felt oppressed, I had not yet put a name to these feelings because I had not been given the opportunity to share with other deaf people or to realise that these feelings flow easily when deaf people come together. At some stage during this conference, I started to feel very angry at the tone of the presentations and the laughter which they evoked, which was at the expense of deaf people. I don't suppose my eminent colleagues realised that there was a deaf person in the audience because in the old days sign language interpreters were nowhere to be seen outside of the Deaf clubs, residential hostels and institutions. As a new recruit to this particular profession, I rose with trembling knees to ask a question of the panel at the end of the conference, which began with 'I am deaf and...' The shock was tangible. After a frenzied shuffling of papers, one panel member was reluctantly selected to answer my question. He began with 'I suspect *your* problem is...' and proceeded to put forward a professional diagnosis of what he perceived *my* problem to be, much to the amusement of his colleagues. He did not answer my question, which of course was not about me but about deaf people, nor did he give any signal that he had listened to the question. He used the opportunity to turn the tables on *me*, because my question threatened to destroy the framework of what he had said. That is why I began campaigning sixteen years ago.

Coming back to the here and now, I felt the old anger returning, the old despair that the archetypal blocks to listening are still there. Many responses entered my head and many feelings churned inside me. The questions included 'Is counselling not about *listening* and *attending*?', 'Is my role as counsellor not in part to *protest* at what is done to my clients?', 'As counsellor, am I not in the business of *nurturing self-esteem* in my clients and believing that this is what they want?' and 'Is counselling somehow separated from *education*?' All of these activities are part of the campaigning that many deaf people become involved in. For me, the campaign has become *The Deaf Challenge*, because my campaign is a human one, about the right of every human being, deaf or hearing, disabled or not, Black or white, gay or straight, man or woman, old or young, to be understood:

> 'One lesson that all this teaches us, is that we do not exist for ourselves alone…and since we are thus one organism, we have to learn from our dear friend's death as well as her life. We must look out for one another, for those who are hurting, tired or stressed from the load. We must lift ourselves from the pettiness of gossip and jealousies, towards the larger picture of our people.'

(Ladd, 1993, p.7)[1]

Meeting *The Deaf Challenge* requires a human response. It is not about finding a cure for deafness but about finding deaf people's soul, allowing deaf people to be strong and secure in themselves. If this book has facilitated the arrival of our boats on the Island of Growth, its goal has been achieved. But the real work has yet to be done. Therapy that constantly plays or builds on a person's *perceived* weakness, disadvantage or disability cannot possibly be called therapy. I have tried to focus on deaf people's uniqueness – their abilities, strengths and skills which can often only be discovered after the complacency of hearingness is challenged and when we accept that as human beings, deaf people encounter problem situations like everyone else, which are not necessarily of their own making. I have suggested that the counsellor's task is to meet this challenge with the core values of the counsellor's trade, rather than to colonise the minds of deaf people with hearing culture, norms and values and narrow definitions of these core values. Counselling is a powerful tool for achieving both of these ends, and like most tools, it can be used to build a house of strength and integrity or a cardboard cut-out which wilts and cracks with time.

To return to my personal odyssey, the point at which we began our journey, I cannot see why being hearing should be any better than being deaf, though I can see why it might be different. The only problem I have with this partnership is to do with the crossed wires and miscommunications which result from my attempts to be deaf coming into conflict with others' stereotyped images of what being deaf means. Otherwise, individual deaf people might be allowed to value themselves *as they are*, sustained by the notion that one day people in general will wake up and see what they are doing to each other with the rock logic of their 'I am right and you are wrong' doctrines which undoubtedly provide a shelter against disenchantment. For myself, I can say that like most people, all I ever wanted was to be accepted for who I am, and not for others' perceptions of me. As they say, 'beauty is in the eye of

---

1   From a tribute to Dorothy Miles, Deaf leader and human being, recently deceased.

the beholder'. If I were left in peace to view myself objectively and to build upon a strong sense of self, if I surrounded myself with people who accepted me for who I am, I dare say that I would begin to develop and hold on to a clear image of 'deaf is beautiful'. This is not the same as being Deaf, but it is not incompatible with it.

I believe that every human being harbours this desire to have a positive self-image and that they have the resources with which they can achieve this. *Real* caring sustains and promotes this. When the prevailing wind is acting as a negative force, it is difficult to find the strength of will to stand up to it especially with the promise of the sun on the horizon, and the pull of the anchor embedded in the rocks below. As we have seen, one of the difficulties of bringing counselling and deaf people together is the tendency to confuse the kind of growth which can be nurtured by that sun with the sustenance which can be provided by the firmness of the anchor. However, because reaching a healthy state involves a journey that is strewn with obstacles, it does not follow that I wish to increase my chances of achieving it by embracing the 'cure' that hearingness foists upon me. There are two very simple reasons for this. The first is that I would have to unlearn my deaf way and start my life all over again. This would be difficult, because deafness is part of me and I have lived in partnership with it for a long time. The second is that I have opened my eyes to the world around me, and I do not live in the state of communal innocence. I am aware of the beast within, because I have learnt to look at it in the face.

But is the beast within or without? Is it my beast or a strand which runs throughout humanity, granting an uneasy sense of commonality? Sometimes it is so hard to distinguish that it is barely tangible – at times, like Rachel's cobweb it traps me in its gossamer hold as I await, fearful, the presence of its unknown maker. But why do I have a sense of the threads reaching outwards, stretching towards another unknown? What is this power that I have which is powerless to prevent the web of intrigue spreading further, powerless to restrain the tentacles of mystery as they weave my history around future generations? I call this power a beast, but is there beauty within the beast, a blessing in disguise? The web is in those early misty mornings of awareness, a shimmering gold-drenched wheel within a wheel of exploding droplets, a pattern of apparent chaos coming from a perfect order of opposites. Even as I am confused and afraid, I can find a poetry in the motion, a harmony if not a melody, a new dimension to my existence.

Though my feelings can be angry, they can also be my strength. Though they can be prejudiced, they can be the courage to transform to pride. Though the beast can lurk within the darkest depths of mire, it can become a blinding moment of clarity and an energy that in its potential destructiveness, builds bridges and monoliths. It is the dream of transformation that needs the reality of partnership, a meeting of equals, strength where there is vulnerability, calm where there is turbulence, safety where there is uncertainty, respect where there is self-denigration and wings where there are obstacles. It is the dream of relating, a valued meeting of the four, two makers and two webs, the birth of something new, the transition from one state to another through sharing. I hope that we may yet see the day when deaf counsellors are co-facilitating integrated groups with hearing counsellors as the profession becomes more pro-active in its recognition of the power of the non-verbal as it weaves its way through human relationships, and that Deaf people may spread their culture within the profession, for culture is both the mechanism and the organism of adaptation and adjustment in hostile or strange environments. That must be the beginning of the end of deaf people's oppression, and the start of true understanding.

'I was out for a walk and noticed a young couple a few steps ahead, both tall; they had a little boy with them, about two years old, who was running alongside and whining. (We are accustomed to seeing such situations from the adult point of view, but here I want to describe it as it was experienced by the child). The two had just bought themselves ice-cream bars on sticks from the kiosk and were licking them with enjoyment. The little boy wanted one too. His mother said affection- ately, "Look, you can have a bite of mine, a whole one is too cold for you." The child did not want just one bite but held out his hand for the whole ice, which his mother took out of his reach again. He cried in despair, and soon, exactly the same thing was repeated with his father: "There you are, my pet", said his father affectionately, "you can have a bite of mine". "No, no" cried the child and ran ahead again, trying to distract himself. Soon he came back again and gazed enviously and

Figure E.1 'New Beginnings'

sadly up at the two grown ups who were enjoying their ice creams contentedly and at one. Time and time again he held out his little hand for the whole ice-cream bar, but the adult hand with its treasure was withdrawn again.

The more the child cried the more it amused his parents. It made them laugh a lot and they hoped to humour him along with their laughter, too: "Look, it isn't so important, what a fuss you are making." Once the child sat down on the ground and began to throw little stones over his shoulder in his mother's direction, but then he suddenly got up again and looked around anxiously, making sure that his parents were still there. When his father had completely finished his ice-cream, he gave the stick to the child and walked on. The little boy licked the bit of wood expectantly, looked at it, threw it away, wanted to pick it up again but did not do so, and a deep sob of loneliness and disappointment shook his small body. Then he trotted obediently after his parents.'

(Miller, 1988, p.86–87)

Imagine that the little boy is the deaf client, the parents are the counselling profession, and the ice-cream is the promise of growth. That is, in the end, the message conveyed by *The Deaf Challenge*. It is from this message that we can forge new beginnings.

BIBLIOGRAPHY

Ackerman, N.W. (1966) *Treating the Troubled Family*. London: Basic Books.

Alliance of Deaf Service Users and Providers (ADSUP) (1993) *Partners at Work: Report from the vonference held on 6th February in Nuneaton*.

Anderson, G.B. and Rosten, E. (1985) In G.B. Anderson and D.Watson (eds) *Counselling Deaf People: Research and Practice*. Little Rock, Arkansas: Arkansas Rehabilitation Research and Training Centre on Deafness and Hearing Impairment.

Andrews, E. (1992) Issues for Teachers of the Deaf Working with the Families of Young Hearing Impaired Children. Paper presented to the Annual Conference of The British Association of Teachers of the Deaf, London.

Anon. (1993) An open letter to the powers that be. *Disability, Handicap and Society 8*, 3, 317–329.

Anthony, S. (1992) The influence of personal characteristics on rumor knowledge and transmission among the deaf. *American Annals of the Deaf 137*, 1, 44–47.

Aramburo, A.J. (1989) Sociolinguistic Aspects of the Black Deaf Community. In C. Lucas *The Sociolinguistics of the Deaf Community*. London: Academic Press Ltd.

d'Ardenne, P. and Mahtani, A. (1989) *Transcultural Counselling In Action*. London: Sage Publications.

Argyle, M. (1975) *Bodily Communication*. London: Methuen.

Arnheim, R. (1954) *Art and Visual Perception*. Berkley: University of California Press.

Arnold, P. (1990) The Trouble with Time. *Deafness and Development 1*, 1, 8–9.

Asher, S., Parkhurst, J., Hymel, S. and Williams, G. (1990) Peer rejection and loneliness in childhood. In S. Asher and J. Coie (eds) *Peer Rejection In Childhood*. New York: Cambridge University Press.

Baker, C. and Cokeley, D. (1980) *American Sign Language: A Teacher's Resource Text on Grammar and Culture 1*. Maryland: T.J. Publishers Inc.

Bandura, A. (1986) *Social Foundations of Thought and Action: A Social-Cognitive Theory*. Englewood Cliffs, NJ: Prentice-Hall.

Banton, M. (1965) *Roles: An Introduction to the Study of Social Relations*. London: Tavistock.

Barrett, M.E. (1986) Self-image and social adjustment change in deaf adolescents participating in a social living class. *Journal of Group Psychotherapy, Psychodrama and Sociometry 39*, 1, 3–11.

Basso, K. (1979) *Portraits of 'The Whiteman'*. New York: Cambridge University Press.

Berman, L. (1993) *Beyond the Smile: The Therapeutic Use of the Photograph*. London: Routledge.

Bishop, J., Gregory, S. and Sheldon, L. (1991) School and Beyond. In G. Taylor and J. Bishop (eds) *Being Deaf – The Experience of Deafness*. London: Pinter Publishers/Open University.

Bozarth, J. and Temaner Bradley, B. (1986) *The Core Values and Theory of the Person-Centred Counsellor*. Paper prepared for the first annual meeting of the Association for the Development of the Person-Centred Approach, Chicago.

Brechin, A., Liddiard, P. and Swain, J. (1981) (eds) *Handicap in a Social World*. Sevenoaks: Hodder and Stoughton.

British Association for Counselling (BAC) (1984) *Code of Ethics and Practice for Counsellors*. Rugby: BAC.

British Association for Counselling (BAC) (1989) *Code of Ethics and Practice for Counselling Skills*. Rugby: BAC.

British Association for Counselling (BAC) (1990) *Code of Ethics and Practice for Counsellors*, (update). Rugby: BAC.

British Association of Teachers of the Deaf/National Deaf Children's Society (1986) *National Survey of Hearing-Impaired Children and Young People in Education*.

British Deaf Association (1992) *A Dictionary of British Sign Language/English*. London: Faber and Faber.

Bronfenbrenner, U. (1977) Toward an Experimental Ecology of Human Development. *American Psychologist 32*, 513–531.

Brown, H. and Craft, A. (1989) *Thinking the Unthinkable: Papers on Sexual Abuse and People with Learning Difficulties*. London: Family Planning Association.

Bugental, J.F.T. (1978) *Psychotherapy and Process: The Fundamentals of an Existential – Humanistic Approach*. Reading, Mass: Addison-Wesley.

Burgess, A. (1992) *A Mouthful of Air – Language and Languages, Especially English*. London: Hutchinson.

Byng-Hall, J. (1973) Family myths used as a defence in conjoint family therapy. *British Journal of Medical Psychology 46*, 3.

Callow, L. (1991) Counselling deaf people. *Deafness 7*, 2, 4–7.

Case, C. and Dalley, T. (1990) *Working with Children in Art Therapy*. London: Travistock.

Casement, P. (1985) *On Learning from the Patient*. London: Tavistock.

Cattanach, A. (1992) *Play Therapy with Abused Children*. London: Jessica Kingsley Publishers.

Cayton, H. (1988) Does the Education of Deaf Children have an Aim? In I.G. Taylor (ed) *The Education of the Deaf – Current Perspectives*. London: Croom Helm.

Chaplin, J. (1988) *Feminist Counselling in Action*. London: Sage Publications.

Clarkson, P. (1989) *Gestalt Counselling in Action*. London: Sage Publications.

Clarkson, P. (1990) A Multiplicity of Psychotherapeutic Relationships. *British Journal of Psychotherapy, 7* (2), 148–63.

Cohene, S. and Cohene, L.S. (1989) Art therapy and writing with deaf children. *Journal of Independent Social work 4*, 2, 21–46.

Cooper, C. (1984) Psychodynamic Therapy: The Kleinian Approach. In W. Dryden (ed) Individual Therapy in Britain.

Corker, M.E.M. (1989) Systems Theory, Communication Strategies and Personal Languages. Unpublished Paper for the Centre for Advancement of Counselling, London.

Corker, M. (1990a) *Deaf Perspectives on Psychology, Language and Communication – Part 1, Experience*. Coventry: NATED/SKILL.

Corker, M.E.M. (1990b) *Deaf Perspectives on Psychology, Language and Communication – Part 3, Psycholinguistics*. Coventry: NATED/SKILL.

Corker, M.E.M. (1990c) *Deaf Perspectives on Psychology, Language and Communication –
Part 5, Intervention.* Coventry: NATED/SKILL.

Corker, M.E.M. (1990d) *Deaf Perspectives on Psychology, Language and Communication, 6:
Systems.* Coventry: NATED/SKILL.

Corker, M.E.M. (1992a) Keeping counsel: parent counselling – mending families
broken by disability. *Talking Sense 38*, 1, 17–20.

Corker, M.E.M. (1992b) Models of Deafness. In *Roles and Relationships: Perspectives on
Practice in Health and Welfare.* Open University Course K663, Workbook 3, pp.21–31.

Corker, M.E.M. (1993a) Integration and deaf people: The policy and power of
enabling environments. In J. Swain *et al. Disabling Barriers – Enabling Environments.*

Corker, M.E.M. (1993b) *Counselling and Emotional Support of Deaf Young People.*
Distance learning module for M.Ed Distance Learning Programme for Teachers of
the Deaf: Manchester University Department of Audiology, Education of the Deaf
and Speech Pathology.

Crammatte, A. (1983) Comments, questions and answers – three is a crowd. *American
Annals of the Deaf 128*, 371–373.

Dalley, T., Case. C., Schaverien, J., Weir, F., Halliday, D., Nowell-Hall, P., Waller, D.
(1987) *Images of Art Therapy: New Developments in Theory and Practice.* London:
Tavistock.

Danek, M.M., Seay, P.C. and Collier, M.L. (1989) Supported employment and deaf
people: Current practices and emerging issues. *Journal of Applied Rehabilitation
Counselling 20*, 3, 34–43.

David, M. and Trehub, S.E. (1989) Perspectives on Deafened Adults. *American Annals
of the Deaf 134*, 3, 200–204.

de Bono, E. (1991) *I Am Right and You are Wrong.* London: Penguin Books.

de Caro, P.M. and Foster, S.B. (1992) Interaction between deaf and hearing students in
postsecondary educational settings. In S.B. Foster and G.G. Walter (eds) *Deaf
students in postsecondary education.* London: Routledge.

Denmark, J.C. (1966) Mental Illness and Early Profound Deafness. *British Journal of
Medical Psychology 39*, 117–123.

Denmark, J.C. and Eldridge, R.W. (1969) Psychiatric services for the Deaf. *Lancet,*
August, 259–262.

Denmark, J.C., Rodda, M., Abel, R.A., Slelton, U., Eldridge, R.W., Warren, F. and
Gordon, A. (1979) *A Word in Deaf Ears.* London: RNID.

Denmark, J.C. and Warren, F. (1972) A Psychiatric Unit for the Deaf. *British Journal of
Psychiatry 120*, 423–428.

Dixon, R. (1993) Access to training for student counsellors who are deaf – an
exploration of the issues. Unpublished MSc dissertation for Stuart College,
Roehampton Institute.

Dominelli, L. (1988) *Anti-Racist Social Work.* London: McMillan Education.

Douglas-Cowie (1990) Acquired Deafness and communication. *Deafness 6*, 2, pp.8–11.

Downie, R.S. (1971) *Roles and Values: An Introduction to Social Ethics.* London: Methuen.

Driscoll, R. (1984) *Pragmatic Psychotherapy.* New York: Van Nostrand Reinhold.

Dryden, W. (1984) (ed) *Individual Therapy in Britain.* London: Harper and Row Ltd.

Dryden, W. (1986) Language and Meaning in RET. *Journal of Rational–Emotive Therapy
4*, 131–142.

Dryden, W., Charles-Edward, D. and Woolfe, R. (1993) *Handbook of Counselling in Britain*. London: Routledge.

Dryden, W. and Thorne, B. (1991) (eds) *Training and Supervision for Counselling in Action*. London: Sage Publications.

Dryden, W. and Feltham, C. (1992) *Brief Counselling*. Buckingham: Open University Press.

Dubowski, J. (1990) Art Versus Language – (separate) Development During Childhood. In C. Case and T. Dalley (eds).

Edwards, A.D. (1980) Patterns of Power and Authority in Classroom Talk. In P.Woods (ed) *Teacher Strategies: Explorations in the Sociology of the School*. London: Croom Helm.

Egan, G. (1990) *The Skilled Helper*, fourth edition. Pacific Grove, CA: Brooks Cole.

Eldredge, N. and Carrigan, J. (1992) Where do my kindred dwell?... Using art and storytelling to understand the transition of young indian men who are deaf. *The Arts in Psychotherapy 19*, 29–38.

Ellis, A. (1984) Must most psychotherapists remain as incompetent as they are now? In J. Harriman (ed) *Does Psychotherapy really help people?* Springfield, Ill: Charles C. Thomas.

Erikson, E. (1950) *Childhood and Society*. New York: Norton.

Erikson, E. (1968) *Identity: Youth and Crisis*. London: Faber.

Feilden, T. (1990) Art therapy as part of the world of dyslexic children. In M. Liebman (ed) *Art Therapy in Practice*.

Finkelstein, V. (1980) *Attitudes and Disabled People: Issues for Discussion*. New York: World Rehabilitation Fund.

Finkelstein, V. (1990) 'We' Are Not Disabled,'You' Are. In S. Gregory and G.M. Hartley (eds) *Constructing Deafness*. London: Pinter Publishers Ltd in association with The Open University.

Finkelstein, V. (1993) The commonality of disability. In J. Swain *et al. Disabling Barriers - Enabling Environments*.

Fong, M.L. and Cox, B.G. (1983) Trust as an underlying dynamic in the counselling process: How clients test trust. In W. Dryden (ed) *Key Issues for Counselling in Action*.

Foster, S.B. and Walter, G.G. (1992) *Deaf Students in Postsecondary Education*. New York: Routledge.

Foucault, M. (1986) An Interview with Michel Foucault. In Charles Ruas (tr) *Death and the Labyrinth: The World of Michel Foucault*. London: Athlone Press.

Furnham, A. and Bochner, S. (1986) *Culture Shock: Psychological Reactions to Unfamiliar Environments*. London: Methuen.

Furth, G.M. (1988) *The Secret World of Drawings – Healing Through Art*. Boston: Sigo Press.

Gibb, J.R. (1968) The counselor as a role-free person. In C.A. Parker (ed) *Counseling Theories and Counselor Education*. Boston: Houghton Mifflin.

Gibb, J.R. (1978) *Trust: A New View of Personal and Organisational Development*. Los Angleles: The Guild of Tutors Press.

Glickman, N. (1986) Cultural identity, deafness and mental health. *Journal of Rehabilitation of the Deaf 20*, 1–10.

Gomm, R. and Woolfe, R. (1992) Relationships. In Course K663. *Roles and Relationships – Perspectives on Practice in Health and Welfare, Workbook 2, Focusing on Roles and Relationships*. Milton Keynes: The Open University.

Gough, D.L. (1990) Rational-Emotive Therapy: A Cognitive-Behavioural Approach to working with Hearing Impaired Clients. *Journal of the American Deafness and Rehabilitation Association 23*, 4, 96–104.

Greene, B.A. (1985) Considerations in the treatment of black patients by white therapists. *British Journal of Psychotherapy 22*, 2.

Greene, L. (1976) *Relating – An Astrological Guide to Living with Others*. Northampton: The Aquarian Press.

Gregory, S. (1993) The language and culture of deaf people: Implications for education. *Deafness 9*, 3, 4–11.

Gregory, S. and Bishop, J. (1989) The Integration of Deaf Children into Ordinary Schools – A Research Report. *Journal of the British Association of Teachers of the Deaf 13*, 1, 1–6.

Haase, R.F. and Tepper, D.T. (1972) Nonverbal components of empathic communication. *Journal of Counselling Psychology 19*, 417–24.

Haley, T.J. and Dowd, E.T. (1988) Responses of deaf adolescents to differences in counsellor method of communication and disability status. *Journal of Counselling Psychology 35*, 3, 258–262.

Halgin, R.P. and McEntee, D.J. (1986) PsychOtherapy with hearing impaired clients. *Professional Psychology: Research and Practice 17*, 5, 466–472.

Handy, C.B. (1976) *Understanding Organisations*. Harmondsworth: Penguin.

Harre, R. (1980) *Social Being*. Totowa, NJ: Adams, Littlefield.

Harvey, M.A. (1989) *Psychotherapy with Deaf and Hard of Hearing Persons – A Systemic Model*. London: Lawrence Erlbaum Associates.

Havighurst, R. (1972) *Developmental Tasks and Education* Third edition. New York: David McKay.

Henley, A. (1979) *Asian Patients in Hospitals and at Home*. London: King Edward's Hospital Fund.

Henley, D. (1987) An art therapy program fro hearing-impaired children with special needs. *American Journal of Art Therapy 25*, 3, 81–89.

Hobson, R.E. (1989) *Forms of Feeling – The Heart of Psychotherapy*. London: Tavistock Publications Ltd.

Holcomb, T. and Coryell, J. (1992) Student Development. In S.B. Foster and G.G. Walter. *Deaf Students in Postsecondary Education*.

Honess, T. (1992) The Development of Self. In J. Coleman (ed) *The School Years: Current Issues in the Socialisation of Young People*, second edition. London: Routledge.

Hore, I.D. (1983) Can Managers Counsel? *Counselling 47*, March.

Horovitz, D. and Ellen, G. (1991) Family art therapy within a deaf system. *Arts in Psychotherapy 18*, 3, 251–261.

Houston, G. (1990) *The Red Book of Groups*. London: The Rochester Foundation.

Jacobs, M. (1988) *Psychodynamic Counselling in Action*. London: Sage Publications.

Jeffers, J. and Barley, M. (1975) *Speechreading (Lipreading)*. Springfield, Ill: Charles C. Thomas.

Jennings, S. (1992) *Dramatherapy with families, Groups and Individuals*. London: Jessica Kingsley Publishers.

Jennings, S. and Minde, A. (1993) *Art Therapy and Dramatherapy – Masks of the Soul*. London: Jessica Kingsley Publishers.

Jepson, J. (1991) Some aspects of the deaf experience in India. *Sign Language Studies 73*, Winter, 453–459.

Jones, L., Kyle, J.G. and Wood, P.L. (1987) *Words Apart – Losing your hearing as an adult*. London: Tavistock.

Jones, L. and Pullen, G. (1992) Cultural Differences: Deaf and Hearing researchers working together. *Disability, Handicap and Society 7*, 2, 189–196.

Jordan, W. (1970) *Client-Worker Transactions*. London: Routledge and Kegan Paul.

Jung, C.G. (1959) *Aion*. London: Routledge and Kegan Paul.

Jung, C.G. (1969) *The Psychology of the Transference*. London: Ark Paperbacks.

Jung, C.G. (1971) *Psychological Types In The Collected Works of C.G.Jung 6*. London: Routledge and Kegan Paul.

Kannapell, B. (1974) Bilingualism: A new direction in the education of the deaf. *The Deaf American 26*, 9–15.

Karuza *et.al.* (1982) Attribution of Responsibility by Helpers and Recipients. In T.A. Wills (ed) *Basic Processes in Helping Relationships*. New York: Academic Press.

Katz, J. (1993) Counselling Deaf People: Issues for Deaf People, Counsellors and Trainers – Towards an Informed Perspective. Unpublished BA Dissertation, University of East London.

Kellog, R. (1970) *Analysing Children's Art*. California: National Press Books.

Kempe, R.S. and Kempe, C. (1978) *Child Abuse*. London: Fontana.

Kennedy, M. (1988) The Abuse of Deaf Children. *Child Abuse and Neglect 13*, 5, 3–6.

Kennedy, M. (1990) Childhood Sexual Assault – Part 2. *Deafness 3*, 6, 6–8.

Kopp, S. B. (1971) *Metaphors from a Psychotherapist Guru*. Palo Alto, CA: Science and Behaviour Books.

Kopp, S.B. (1972) *If You Meet The Buddha on the Road, Kill Him*! London: Sheldon Press.

Kopp, S.B. (1977) *Back to One*. Palo Alto, CA: Science and Behaviour Books.

Kopp, S.B. (1981) *An End to Innocence – Facing Life Without Illusions*. London: Bantam Books.

Kuczaj, E. (1990) Art therapy with people with learning difficulties. In M. Liebman (ed) *Art Therapy in Practice*.

Kyle, J.G., Jones, L.G. and Wood, P.C. (1985) Adjustment to acquired hearing loss: A working model. In H. Orlans (ed) *Adjustment to Adult Hearing Loss*. San Diego, CA: College-Hill Press.

Kyle, J.G. and Pullen, G. (1988) Cultures in contact: Deaf and hearing people. *Disability, Handicap and Society 3*, 1, 49–61.

Ladd, P. (1993) Going where the wind don't blow so strange. *British Deaf News*, April, 7.

Laing, R.D. (1970) *Knots*. London: Penguin Books.

Landell, T. (1991) from *Signs of Change: Politics and the Deaf community*, video from the Open University Course Issues in Deafness. Milton Keynes: The Open University.

Lane, H. (1984) *When The Mind Hears*. New York: Random House.

Lane, H. (1985) On Language, Power and the Deaf. In R. Lee (ed) *Deaf Liberation*. London: National Union of the Deaf.

Lane, H. (1988) Is There a Psychology of the Deaf? In S. Gregory and G. Hartley (eds) *Constructing Deafness*. London: Pinter Publishers/Open University.

Lane, H. (1992) *The Mask of Benevolence*. New York: Alfred A. Knopf.

Lang, H.G. and Meath-Lang, B. (1992) The deaf learner. In Susan B. Foster and Gerard G. Walter. *Deaf Students in Postsecondary Education*. London: Routledge.

Leibman, M. (1990) *Art Therapy in Practice*. London: Jessica Kingsley Publishers.

Leith, D. (1983) *A Social History of English*. London: Routledge and Kegan Paul.

Levine, E.S. (1981) *The Ecology of Early Deafness*. New York: Columbia University Press.

Lorion, R.P. and Parron, D.L. (1985) Countering the Countertransference: A Strategy for Treating the Untreatable. In P. Pedersen (ed) *Handbook of Crosscultural Counselling and therapy*. Westport: Greenwood Press.

Luterman, D. (1987) *Deafness in the Family*. Boston: Little Brown and Co.

Matthews, J. (1984) Children drawing: Are young children really scribbling. *Early Child Development and Care 18*.

McCrone, W.P. (1983) Reality therapy with deaf rehabilitation clients. *Journal of Rehabilitation of the Deaf 17*, 2, 13–15.

McGrath, G. (1991) *An Introduction to Psychotherapy*. Manchester: Manchester Royal Infirmary.

McKnight, J. (1981) Professionalised service and disabling help. In Brechin, Liddiard and Swain (eds) *Handicap in a Social World*.

McLeod, J. (1990) The client's experience of counselling and psychotherapy: A review of the research literature. In D. Mearns and W. Dryden (eds) *Experiences of Counselling in Action*.

Mahan, T. (1993) The courage to dream and perceived limits on development: The counsellor's quandary. *Counselling 4*, 3, 207–214.

Maslow, A. (1943) *Motivation and Personality*. New York: Harper and Row.

Massen, J. (1989) *Against Therapy*. London: Fontana.

Mayer, J. and Timms, N. (1970) *The Client Speaks: Working-Class Impressions of Casework*. London: Routledge and Kegan Paul.

Mayeroff, M. (1971) *On Caring*. New York: Perennial Library (Harper and Row).

Mayor, B.M. (1987) Language, Power and Control – Introduction. In B.M. Mayor and A.K. Pugh (eds) *Language, Communication and Education*. London: Croom Helm/The Open University.

Mead, G.H. (1934) *Mind, Self and Society*. Chicago: University of Chicago Press.

Mearns, D. (1990) The counsellor's experience of failure. In D. Mearns and W. Dryden (eds) *Experiences of Counselling in Action*.

Mearns, D. and Dryden, W. (1990) (eds) *Experiences of Counselling in Action*. London: Sage Publications.

Mearns, D. and Thorne, B. (1988) *Person-Centred Counselling In Action*. London: Sage Publications.

Mehrabian, A. and Reed, H. (1969) Factors influencing judgements of psychopathology. *Psychological Reports 24*, 323–330.

Melgoza, B. (1980) Transferential aspects in therapy: The therapist with a physical impairment. *The Clinical Psychologist 33*, 11–12.

Melnick, B. (1972) Patient–therapist identification in relation to both patient and therapist variables and therapy outcome. *Journal of Consulting and Clinical psychology 38*, 1, 97–104.

Miller, A. (1987a) *For Your Own Good*. London: Virago Press.

Miller, A. (1987b) *The Drama of Being a Child*. London: Virago Press.

Miller, M.S. and Moores, D.F. (1990) Principles of Group Counselling and their
    Application for Deaf Clients. *Journal of the American Deafness and Rehabilitation
    Association 23*, 4, 82–86.
Milner, J. and Blyth, E. (1988) *Coping with Child Sexual Abuse: A Guide for Teachers*.
    London: Longman Group UK Ltd (now out of print).
Mitchell, G. (1989) Empowerment and Opportunity. *Social Work Today*, 16 March, p.14.
Mitchell, J. (1986) *The Selected Melanie Klein*. London: Penguin Books.
Nelson-Jones, R. (1982) *The Theory and Practice of Counselling Psychology*. London:
    Cassell.
Nelson-Jones, R. (1988) *Practical Counselling and Helping Skills*. Second edition.
    London: Cassell.
Nickerson, W., Zannetou, I. and Sutton, J. (1986) *Succeeding with the Deaf Student in
    College*. York: Longman/FEU.
Nowell-Hall, P. (1987) Art Therapy: A way of healing the split. In T. Dalley *et.al*. (1987)
    op/cit.
O'Hagan, S. (1992) *Emotional and Psychological Abuse of Children*. Buckingham: Open
    University Press.
Oliver, M. (1978) Disability, adjustment and family life – some theoretical
    considerations. In A. Brechin, P. Liddiard and J. Swain (eds) *Handicap in the Social
    World*.
Padden, C. (1989) The deaf community and the culture of deaf people. In S. Wilcox
    (ed) *American Deaf Culture*. Silver Spring MD: Linstok Press.
Padden, C. and Humphries, T. (1988) *Deaf in America – Voices from a Culture*.
    Cambridge, Mass: Harvard University Press.
Patterson, C.H. (1986) *Theories of Counselling and Psychotherapy* (fourth Edition). New
    York: Harper and Row Ltd.
Phoenix, S. (1988) Food for Thought. *TALK*. Spring issue.
Pilger, J. (1992) *Distant Voices*. London: Vintage.
Poizner, H., Klima, E.S. and Bellugi, U. (1987) *What the Hands Reveal about the Brain*.
    Cambridge, Mass: MIT Press.
Powers, S. (1990) A survey of Secondary Units for Hearing Impaired Children – Part 1.
    Journal of the British Association of Teachers of the Deaf 14, 3, 69–79.
Quendenfeld, C. and Farrelly, F. (1983) Provocative therapy with the hearing impaired
    client. *Journal of Rehabilitation of the Deaf 17*, 2, 1–12.
Ramsdell, D.A. (1978) The psychology of the hard-of-hearing and deafened adult. In
    H. Davis and S.R. Silverman (eds) *Hearing and Deafness*. Fourth Edition. New York:
    Holt, Rinehart and Winston.
Rawlings, B.A., Karchmer, M.A., DeCaro, J.J. and Eggleston-Dodd (1986) *A guide to
    college/career programs for deaf students*. Washington, DC: Gallaudet College and
    Rochester, NY: Rochester Institute of Technology.
Redfern, P. (1992) Counselling Deaf Adolescents. Address given to The British
    Association of Teachers of the Deaf Conference, November.
Reiser, R. and Mason, M. (1992) *Disability Equality in the Classroom – A Human Rights
    Issue*. London: Disability Equality in Education.
Reynolds, J. (1992) Roles. In *Course K663 Roles and Relationships – Perspectives on
    Practice in Health and Welfare, Workbook 2: Focusing on Roles and Relationships*. Milton
    Keynes: The Open University.

Rhyne, J. (1973) *The Gestalt Art Experience – Creative Process and Expressive Therapy.* Monterey, CA: Brooks-Cole.

Robinson, L. and Falconer, L. (1982) Teacher will you listen? *The BC Teacher,* November/December issue.

Rodda, M. and Grove, C. (1987) *Language, Cognition and Deafness.* London: Lawrence Erlbaum Associates.

Roe, D.L. and Roe, C.E. (1991) The third party: Using interpreters for the deaf in counselling situations. *Journal of Mental Health Counselling 13,* 1, 91–105.

Rogers, B. (1993) Counselling: The Heart of the Institution. *Counselling Journal of the British Association for Counselling 4,* 1, 36–39.

Rogers, C.R. (1951) *Client-Centred Therapy – Its Current Practice, Implications and Theory.* Boston: Houghton Mifflin.

Rogers, C.R. (1957) The necessary and sufficient conditions of therapeutic personality change. *Journal of Consulting Psychology 21,* 95–103.

Rogers, C.R. (1967) (ed) *The Therapeutic Relationship and its Impact.* Madison: University of Wisconsin Press.

Rogers, C.R. (1977) *Carl Rogers on Personal Power.* New York: Delacorte.

Rogers, C. (1983) *Freedom to Learn for the 80s.* New York: Merrill.

Rotter, J.B. (1966) Generalised expectancies for internal versus external control of reinforcement. *Psychological Monographs 80,* (1, 609).

Rowan, J. (1976) *The Power of the Group.* London: Davis-Poynter.

Royal Association in Aid of Deaf People (1991) *A Change in Approach: A Report on the Experience of Deaf People from Black and Ethnic Minorities.* London: RAD

Ruane, T. (1993) Thirty years of Deaf theatre. *British Deaf News,* June, 8–9.

Rubin, J.A. (1978) *Child Art Therapy –Understanding and Helping Children Grow Through Art.* New York: Van Nostrand Reinhold.

Ruddock, R. (1969) *Roles and Relationships.* London: Routledge and Kegan Paul.

Rutherford, S. (1993) *A Study of American Deaf Folklore.* Burtonsville, MD: Linstok Press.

Sacks, O. (1989) *Seeing Voices.* London: Picador.

Satir, V. (1988) *The New Peoplemaking.* Mountain View, CA: Science and Behaviour Books.

Saur, R.E. (1992) Resources for deaf students in the mainstreamed classroom. In S.B. Foster and G.G. Walter. *Deaf Studies in Postsecondary Education.*

Saxton, M. and Howe, F. (1987) *With Wings: An Anthology of literature by Women with Disabilities.* London: Virago.

Schiff, J.L. (1975) *Cathexis Reader: Transactional Analysis Treatment of Psychosis.* New York: Harper and Row.

Schlesinger, H.S. (1985) The Psychology of Hearing Loss. In H. Orlans (ed) *Adjustment to adult hearing loss.* San Diego, CA: College-Hill Press.

Scollon, R. (1985) The machine stops: Silence in the metaphor of malfunction. In. D. Tannen and M. Saville-Troike. *Perspective on Silence.*

Segal, J. (1993) Counselling People with Disabilities/ Chronic Illnesses. In W. Dryden, D. Charles-Edwards and R Woolfe *Handbook of Counselling in Britain.* London: Routledge.

Seligman, M.E.P. (1975) *Helplessness: On Depression, Development and Death.* San Francisco: W.H. Freeman.

Sgroi, S.M. (1982) *Handbook of Clinical Intervention in Child Sexual Abuse*. Massachusett: Lexington Books.

Shackman, J. (1985) *A Handbook of Working with, Employing and Training Interpreters*. Cambridge: National Extension College.

Shapiro, J.G., Foster, C.P. and Powell, T. (1968) Facial and Bodily Cues of genuineness, empathy and warmth. *Journal of Clinical Psychology 24*, 233–6.

Simons, A.D., Lustman, P.J., Wetzel, R.D. and Murphy, G.E. (1985) Predicting response to cognitive therapy of depression: The role of learned resourcefulness. *Cognitive therapy and research 9*, 1, 79–89.

Sloman, L., Perry, A. and Frankenburg, F.R. (1987) Family therapy with deaf member families. *American Journal of Family Therapy 15*, 3, 242–252.

Smith, E.M.J. (1985) Ethnic minorities: Life stress, social support and mental health issues. *The Counselling Psychologist 13*, 4, 537–79.

Southgate, J. and White, K. (1989) Alienism – the underlying root of oppression. *Journal of the Institute for Self-Analysis 3*, 1, 35–38.

Stansfield, M. (1981) Psychological issues in mental health interpreting. *RID Interpreting Journal 1*, 18–31.

Stansfield, M. (1987) Therapisy and Interpreter: A Working Relationship. Paper presented at the Mental Health and Interpreting Conference, Annapolis, MD, February.

Steinberg, A. (1991) Issues in providing mental health services to hearing impaired persons. *Hospital and Community Psychiatry 42*, 4, 380–389.

Stiefel, D. (1991) *The Madness of Usher's*. Texas: The Business of Living Publications.

Stone, D. (1985) *The Disabled State*. Basingstoke: McMillan.

Storr, A. (1983) *Jung: Selected Writings*. London: Fontana.

Strauss, A. (1977) *Mirrors and Masks: The Search for Identity*. London: Martin Robertson.

Strensrud, R. and Strensrud, K. (1981) Counselling may be Hazardous to your health: How we teach people to be powerless. *Personnel and Guidance Journal 59*, 300–304.

Strong, M. and Day-Drummer, C. (1990) Peer counselling programs for hearing impaired persons. *Journal of the American Deafness and Rehabilitation Association 23*, 4, 88–95.

Stuart, O. W. (1992) Race and Disability: Just a double oppression? *Disability, Handicap and Society 7*, 2, 177–189.

Sullivan, P.M. and Scanlan, J.M. (1990) Psychotherapy with handicapped sexually abused children. *Developmental Disabilities Bulletin 18*, 2, 21–34.

Sussman, A. (1988) Approaches to Counselling and Psychotherapy Revisited. In D. Watson, G. Lon, M. Taff-Watson and M. Harvey (eds) *Two Decades of Excellence: A Foundation for the Future*. Little Rock, Arizona: American Deafness and Rehabilitation Association.

Sutcliffe, T.H. (1990) *The Challenge of Deafness*. Taunton: Desktop Printing and Publishing Services.

Swain, J., Finkelstein, V., French, S. and Oliver, M. (eds) *Disabling Barriers – Enabling Environments*. London: Sage Publications in association with The Open University.

Tannen, D. and Saville-Troike, M. (1985) (eds) *Perspectives on Silence*. Norwood, NJ: Ablex Publishing Corporation.

Tesni, S. (1991) The Counselling Requirements and Needs of Hearing Impaired Students. Unpublished dissertation for University Diploma in Counselling Studies, Gwent College of Higher Education.

Thomas, T. and Sillen, S. (1972) *Racism and Psychiatry*. Secaucus: The Citadel Press.

Tomlinson, S. (1982) *The Sociology of Special Education*. London: Routledge and Kegan Paul.

Treichler, P.A. *et al.* (1984) Problems and problems: Power relations in a medical encounter. In C. Kramarae, M. Schulz and W.M. O'Barr (eds) *Language and Power*. New York: Sage.

Truax, C.B. and Carkhuff, R.R. (1967) *Towards Effective Counselling and Psychotherapy: Training and Practice*. Chicago: Aldine.

Turner, A. (1991) The Vital Distinction. *Soundbarrier*, October, 14–15.

Urban, E. (1990) The eye of the beholder: Work with a ten year old deaf girl. *Journal of Child Psychotherapy 16*, 2, 63–81.

van Deurzen-Smith, E. (1984) Existential Therapy. In W. Dryden (ed) *Individual Therapy in Britain*.

Veasey, D. (1993) Counselling for development through personal and social education (PSE): Values, quality and accountabilty, with special reference to sex education. *Counselling 4*, 2, 106–108.

Walker, M. (1992) *Surviving Secrets*. Buckingham: Open University Press.

Walmsley, J, Reynolds, J, Shakespeare, P. and Woolfe, R. (1993) *Health Welfare and Practice: Reflecting on Roles and Relationships*. London: Sage Publications in association with The Open University.

Ward, D. and Mullender, A. (1993) Empowerment and oppression: An indissoluble pairing for contemporary social work. In J. Walmsley, J. Reynolds, P. Shakespeare and R. Woolfe (eds) *Health Welfare and Practice: Reflecting on Roles and Relationships*.

Watson, G. (1989) The abuse of disabled children and young persons. In W.S. Rogers, D. Hevey and E. Ash (eds) *Child Abuse and Neglect*. London: Batsford.

Westerlund, E. (1990) Thinking about incest, deafness and counselling. *Journal of the American Deafness and Rehabilitation Association 23*, 3, 105–107.

Wilkie, E. (1990) Who's the cripple, Mr Airline? In E. Wilkie and J. Gunn. *A Pocket Full of Dynamite*. London: Hodder and Stoughton.

Williams, J. (1993) What is a profession? Experience versus expertise. In J. Walmsley, J. Reynolds, P. Shakespeare and R. Woolfe (eds) *Health Welfare and Practice: Reflecting on Roles and Relationships*.

Winnicott, D. W. (1986) Fear of breakdown. In G. Kohon (ed) *British School of Psychoanalysis: The Independent Tradition*. London: Free Association Books.

Wittgenstein, L. (1967) *Philosophische Untersuchungen* Oxford: Basil Blackwell.

Wood, S. (1988) Parents: Whose Partners? In Len Barton (ed) *The Politics of Special Educational Needs*. London: Falmer Press.

Woolley, M. (1987) Acquired Hearing loss, Acquired Oppression. In J.G. Kyle (ed) *Adjustment to Acquired Hearing Loss*. Bristol: Centre for Deaf Studies.

Wright, D. (1990) *Deafness*. London: Faber and Faber.

Wynne, L. (1965) Some indications and contra-indications for exploratory family therapy. In I. Boszormenyi-Nagy and J. Framo (eds) *Intensive Family Therapy*. London: Harper and Row.

THE CONTRIBUTORS

Laraine Callow is the Director of Deafworks, a national organisation based in London providing consultancy, education, training, projects and events related to deaf people. She is a former teacher of deaf children and acting Head of Service for deaf children. She writes the 'Agony Aunt' column for *See Hear!*, the monthly magazine of the Royal National Institute for Deaf People (RNID), and provides pre-counselling sessions and career counselling for deaf people. Laraine is deaf from a hearing family.

Margaret Kennedy founded and is now the National Co-ordinator of the 'Keep Deaf Children Safe' Child Abuse Project which is funded and supported by The National Deaf Children's Society. She recently co-edited the ABCD Training and Resource Pack (The Abuse of Children who are Disabled), and represents disability issues on the British Association for the Study and Prevention of Child Abuse (BASPCAN) National Executive, Margaret is a State Enrolled Nurse and qualified social worker. For the last seven years, she has worked exclusively within the deaf community, more especially with deaf teenagers and young adults within a psycho-social rehabilitation framework. She is deaf.

Jane McIntosh is an experienced counsellor using the person-centred approach. She has a counselling Diploma from South West London College and a Certificate in Person-Centred Art Therapy. Formerly a senior teacher of pastoral care and counselling and counsellor in private practice, she now works at an inner city Further Education College as a student counsellor and in Adult Continuing Education as a trainer in counselling skills and person-centred art therapy.

Paul Redfern is a self-employed trainer and writer, running his own company, Face to Face. He is the Editor of *Deafview*, the television magazine for deaf people produced by Teletext UK in association with the RNID, and a co-presenter of the weekly television programme for Deaf people on Channel 4, *Sign On!* Paul is a qualified social worker and acted as an advisor to The Westminster Pastoral Foundation in setting up their counselling training for deaf people. He is Deaf with hearing parents.

Sharon Ridgeway is Research Psychologist and Counsellor presently working at the The National Centre for Mental Health and Deafness at Prestwich Hospital in Greater Manchester. She uses psychodynamic approaches to counselling and is involved in the provision of specialist counselling training for Deaf people at the Department of Counselling and Psychology at the University of Manchester. Sharon is Deaf herself and comes from a Deaf family. She has British Sign Language (BSL) as her native language.

Subject Index